ADVANCE PRAISE FOR

Speaking to Reconciliation

"*Speaking to Reconciliation* is a masterful collection of speeches that examines not only the need to seek forgiveness and reconciliation but also the public practice of apologizing. Drawing on the Christian, Jewish, Islamic, and Buddhist religious traditions, Professor Hatch has assembled a wide-ranging book that includes such luminaries as Abraham Lincoln, Martin Luther King, Jr., Elie Wiesel, Desmond Tutu, Barack Obama, and U.S. Representative Tony Hall, the first member of Congress to call for a formal apology for American slavery. Situating these readings within the context of his own scholarly work on race and reconciliation, Hatch provides both a theoretical rationale and powerful practical examples of how reconciliation might begin. This is a must-read book for all scholars of rhetoric and race."

—Martin J. Medhurst, Distinguished Professor of Rhetoric and Communication, Baylor University

"This is a significant contribution to the study and practice of reconciliation that should be read by all students and scholars within and beyond the discipline of communication who hope to create a just and equitable world through the resources of symbolic and spiritual engagement and interaction. *Speaking to Reconciliation: Voices of Faith Addressing Racial and Cultural Divides* amplifies and expands John Hatch's important theoretical work on reconciliation through the words of speakers across cultures who have grappled with the dangers and opportunities of addressing the injustices that have shaped our shared history. In this important and timely contribution to rhetorical education and pedagogy, Hatch has woven together diverse voices of people of conscience into a tapestry of hope, faith, and courage. The book combines the rational resources of practical reasoning with the powerful impulses of spiritual faith to provide a blueprint for traversing the difficult terrains of reconciliation. Through his own critical and theoretical insights and the voices of the speakers whose words and deed he documents, Hatch reminds us of the interrelatedness and mutuality envisioned by Dr. Martin Luther King, Jr., that we are 'tied in a single garment of destiny,' and that through rhetorical and spiritual coherence, 'society's wounds are stitched up, and divided peoples are somewhat woven together into a social fabric of interdependent wholeness.'"

—Mark L. McPhail, Senior Research Fellow, Office of the Vice President for Diversity, Equity, and Multicultural Affairs, Indiana University

"John Hatch is a leading scholar of rhetoric and reconciliation. *Speaking to Reconciliation: Voices of Faith Addressing Racial and Cultural Divides*, is an elegant and accessible overview of strikingly courageous speeches that have drawn from the wellsprings of religious faith to promote reconciliation. Dr. Hatch's book is an ideal selection for students and scholars seeking explanatory introductions, historical contextualizations, and analytic insights on reconciliation as a rhetorical process expressed in public address."

—David A. Frank, Professor of Rhetoric, University of Oregon

"Hatch's heartfelt commitment to and insight on reconciliation shapes this collection of historical and contemporary public address into a tool for truth and justice. Cognizant of the religious roots of the rhetoric, this book proclaims the good news that the understanding and action required for reconciliation yield healing, empowerment, and community. Feast on this book for true soul food and strength for the work of battling injustice."
—Annalee Ward, Director, Wendt Character Initiative, University of Dubuque

"The importance of reconciliation in our world today cannot be overstated, yet the concept is frequently presented in confusing or vague terms. Not so in *Speaking to Reconciliation*. The speeches in this book, together with John B. Hatch's insightful comments about them, bring reconciliation's meanings in particular situations into sharp focus. What is more, Hatch's commentary illuminates how the speeches—drawn from different contexts and diverse faith traditions—speak to one another in significant ways. Students and practitioners of reconciliation stand to benefit greatly from the rich, and even transformative, conversations in this book."
—James E. Beitler, Associate Professor of English, Wheaton University

"*Speaking to Reconciliation* provides a thoughtful, unique and in-depth analysis of speeches. The tragic-comic rhetorical framework Hatch uses for the speech analysis elucidates themes and meaning that might otherwise be missed. This approach to rhetorical analysis is very much needed and will enable faculty and students to engage in meaningful discussions about reconciliation, a theme and practice that is needed in current political and community discussions."
—Van Dora Williams, Champlain College

"John Hatch's *Speaking to Reconciliation* will be a welcome addition to my undergraduate rhetoric curriculum. Distilling Kenneth Burke's frames of acceptance and directing its focus on reconciliation rhetorics, this book can help students craft connections across the humanities—in communication, religion, and politics. If my undergraduates can imagine a just and peace-building discourse in this increasingly divisive civic sphere, they will have the skills to engage and improve our world. Hatch's text skillfully provides both the theory and the practice for my students to understand that reconciliation."
—Camille K. Lewis, Visiting Professor, Department of Communication Studies, Furman University

"In *Speaking to Reconciliation*, John B. Hatch has assembled an important collection of voices that will illuminate efforts and conversations on racial reconciliation for years to come. As an Obama scholar, I found Hatch's analysis of Obama's eulogy following the terrorist attack at 'Mother Emanuel' in Charleston, South Carolina, to be especially valuable. I look forward to using this timely book in my research and teaching."
—Theon Hill, Assistant Professor of Communication, Wheaton College

"Hatch's book elucidates reconciliation as a process that exceeds the bounds of any single speech. This is especially evident in the book's final case: reconciliation between the United Church of Canada and First Nations people. By retracing speech-acts that occurred between the oppressed and a former oppressor over the course of a dozen years and beyond, Hatch shows us that reconciliation is not a destination, but a dialogic, embodied reality—a way of life."
—Naaman K. Wood, Assistant Professor of Media and Communication Studies, Redeemer University, Ontario

Speaking to Reconciliation

Speaking of Religion

Daniel S. Brown
Series Editor

Vol. 2

The Speaking of Religion series is part of the Peter Lang
Media and Communication list.
Every volume is peer reviewed and meets the
highest quality standards for content and production.

PETER LANG
New York • Bern • Berlin
Brussels • Vienna • Oxford • Warsaw

John B. Hatch

Speaking to Reconciliation

Voices of Faith Addressing
Racial and Cultural Divides

PETER LANG
New York • Bern • Berlin
Brussels • Vienna • Oxford • Warsaw

Library of Congress Cataloging-in-Publication Data

Names: Hatch, John B., author.
Title: Speaking to reconciliation: voices of faith addressing racial and
    cultural divides / John B. Hatch.
Description: New York: Peter Lang, 2020.
Series: Speaking of religion, vol. 2
ISSN 2575-9124 (print) | ISSN 2575-9132 (online)
Includes bibliographical references.
Identifiers: LCCN 2020007626 (print) | LCCN 2020007627 (ebook)
ISBN 978-1-4331-6232-9 (hardback) | ISBN 978-1-4331-6236-7 (paperback)
ISBN 978-1-4331-6233-6 (ebook pdf)
ISBN 978-1-4331-6234-3 (epub) | ISBN 978-1-4331-6235-0 (mobi)
Subjects: LCSH: Discourse analysis—Political aspects. | Discourse
    analysis—Religious aspects. | Rhetoric—Political aspects. |
    Rhetoric—Moral and ethical aspects. | Reconciliation—Political
    aspects. | Reconciliation—Philosophy. | Restorative justice. | Crimes
    against humanity. | Truth commissions.
Classification: LCC P302.77 .S64 2020 (print) | LCC P302.77 (ebook) | DDC 808.85—dc23
LC record available at https://lccn.loc.gov/2020007626
LC ebook record available at https://lccn.loc.gov/2020007627
DOI 10.3726/b14763

Bibliographic information published by **Die Deutsche Nationalbibliothek**.
Die Deutsche Nationalbibliothek lists this publication in the "Deutsche
Nationalbibliografie"; detailed bibliographic data are available
on the Internet at http://dnb.d-nb.de/.

© 2020 Peter Lang Publishing, Inc., New York
29 Broadway, 18th floor, New York, NY 10006
www.peterlang.com

All rights reserved.
Reprint or reproduction, even partially, in all forms such as microfilm,
xerography, microfiche, microcard, and offset strictly prohibited.

To the real experts on reconciliation:
brave souls who not only ruminate and write,
but also believe, listen, speak, and act as reconcilers
in the face of doubt and opposition—
at great personal cost.

Table of Contents

List of Figures ix
Foreword xi
Acknowledgments xiii

Introduction 1

Part I: Commending, Framing, and Explaining the Work of Reconciliation
Introduction to Part I 25
Chapter One: Reconciling a Divided Nation: Abraham Lincoln 29
    Second Inaugural Address 33
Chapter Two: Redressing a Grave Injustice: U.S. Rep. Thaddeus Stevens 37
    Remarks on the Slave Reparations Provision of H.R. 20 40
Chapter Three: Clearing the Way of Peace on Earth: Martin Luther King Jr. 43
    A Christmas Sermon on Peace 45
Chapter Four: Exposing Injustice against a Horizon of
    Reconciliation: Desmond Tutu 53
    1984 Nobel Lecture 55
Chapter Five: Framing South African Reconciliation: Desmond Tutu 63
    Address to the First Gathering of the TRC 65

Chapter Six: Religious Resources for Reconciliation in a Divided
 World: Miroslav Volf ... 69
 "After the Grave in the Air" ... 71
Chapter Seven: Mindfulness as a Key to Reconciliation: Thich Nhat Hanh ... 77
 "Leading with Courage and Compassion" ... 79
Chapter Eight: Rooting Reconciliation in a Shared Past: President Mary
 McAleese of Ireland ... 87
 Inaugural St. Patrick's Day Lecture at Armagh ... 90
Chapter Nine: Bridging America's Racial Divide: Barack Obama ... 97
 "A More Perfect Union" ... 100
Chapter Ten: Bridging a Divide between Civilizations: Barack Obama ... 111
 "A New Beginning" ... 113
Chapter Eleven: Bridging Religious Divides: King Abdullah II of Jordan ... 121
 Templeton Prize Acceptance Speech ... 123

Part II: Pursuing Reconciliation through Apology, Forgiveness,
 and Reparation
Introduction to Part II ... 127
Chapter Twelve: Remembering and Redressing Incomprehensible Evil:
 Elie Wiesel ... 139
 Address to the German Parliament at the Dedication of the Memorial
  to the Murdered Jews of Europe ... 142
Chapter Thirteen: Acknowledging a Heinous Historical Crime:
 George W. Bush ... 149
 Remarks on Goree Island ... 150
Chapter Fourteen: Explaining and Offering a Historical Apology: U.S. Rep.
 Tony Hall ... 155
 Apology to African Americans for Slavery ... 157
Chapter Fifteen: Commending the Grace of Forgiveness and
 Repentance: Barack Obama ... 163
 "Amazing Grace": Eulogy for the Honorable Reverend
  Clementa Pinckney ... 166
Chapter Sixteen: Reconciliation Unfolding: United Church of Canada ... 173
 1986 Apology to Indigenous Peoples ... 177
 1988 Response ... 177
 1998 Apology for Indian Residential Schools ... 178
Conclusion: The Ongoing Work of Reconciliation ... 181

List of Figures

Figure 1: The Tetrad of Values in Reconciliation (Pyramid Metaphor) 9
Figure 2: The Tetrad (Compass Metaphor) 12
Figure 3: The Tetrad as Complementary Moral Frames............... 17

Foreword

Speaking of Religion: A Book Series advances the important principle that religious words and ideas continue to hold authority and power in an increasingly secular world. The current volume joins other anthologies of speeches in the series, in which scholars demonstrate how rhetors have drawn substantially upon religious texts and traditions to address matters of public concern. One such public concern is social division that is rooted in a history of abuse and injustice. In recent decades, a growing number of public figures and organizations have responded to this exigency with a rhetoric of reconciliation. Such discourse is the focus of this volume.

Traditionally conceived of as a religious idea, reconciliation is today reoriented in public discourse for secular and at times even mercenary purposes. For sure, some of its roots lie in ideologies that are not explicitly religious. The concept of reconciliation is implicated, for example, in the word "Ubuntu." This African philosophical conception drives adherents to act morally for the greater good. Humans do not and cannot exist in isolation, for we are interconnected. The idea of Ubuntu is not born of religious tradition *per se*. It is, rather, a derivative of collectivistic cultures foregrounding this truth: Each person's actions have consequences for every other human being. National, corporate, and interpersonal relationships are meant, therefore, for Ubuntu—the ongoing state of being reconciled. While such philosophical assumptions inform the rhetoric of reconciliation, this book shows that *public discourse on social reconciliation continues to use the language and imagery of religion.*

Professor John Hatch is uniquely qualified to undertake this project. He is certainly one of the leading rhetorical scholars of reconciliation. His award-winning book, *Race and Reconciliation: Redressing Wounds of Injustice*,[1] is a landmark in the communication studies discipline. Hatch is the author of nearly twenty peer-reviewed articles and papers related to reconciliation. In addition, much of his published work examines contemporary religious discourse as it pertains to race, reconciliation, and other topics.

In this volume, Hatch builds on his previous work, extending our view of the rhetoric of reconciliation beyond religious observance to include reconciliation between nations and their historic adversaries, governments and their citizenries, churches and their parishioners, and, importantly, between individual perpetrators of political violence and their victims. Much of the rhetoric in today's public square may masquerade as post-modern naturalism, but the speeches in this volume show that faith is alive and well in discourse about social reconciliation.

Professor Martin Medhurst issued a call in 2001 for the modernization of the canon of public address. At the time, the oratorical canon was historical and designated by scholars of public address as the collection of "Great Speeches." Medhurst wrote that "individual discourse communities [should] … form their own canons through the process of rhetorical archaeology—the recovery of texts and discourses central to the self-understanding and public expression of specific groups and movements."[2] Hatch has answered Medhurst's challenge and done the hard work of recovering and curating artifacts central to the practice of reconciliation. What does the oratory of reconciliation look like? What are some important, representative speeches that have shaped diverse publics' view of reconciliation? This book is John Hatch's answer to these questions.

May we listen carefully and engage thoughtfully the language, the dreams, and the hopes embedded in these texts.

Daniel S. Brown, Jr.
Grove City, Pennsylvania

1. John B. Hatch, *Race and Reconciliation: Redressing Wounds of Injustice* (Lanham, MD: Lexington, 2008).
2. Martin. J. Medhurst, "The Contemporary Study of Public Address: Renewal, Recovery, and Reconfiguration," *Rhetoric & Public Affairs* 4, no. 3 (2001): 505, doi:10.1353/rap.2001.0048.

Acknowledgments

In the years since the publication of my scholarly monograph, *Race and Reconciliation*, I occasionally wondered if I should write a book on this subject at the intersection between rhetoric and religion for a wider audience. However, it wasn't until Dann Brown approached me about contributing a volume to the *Speaking of Religion* series that I embraced the idea. Compiling an anthology of faith-based reconciliation addresses not only afforded the opportunity to make my work more accessible, but also led to the discovery of significant speeches on reconciliation that I might otherwise not have encountered. For this, I am grateful.

Over the past decade and a half, Mark McPhail, David Frank, Aaron Gresson, and Marty Medhurst have been a tremendous support to my scholarship on racial reconciliation through their affirmations, collaborations, and venues for publication. I am in their debt. Gratitude is due as well to Robert Woods, whose encouragement and suggestions prepared me to embrace this opportunity when Dann approached me.

I would especially like to thank Eastern University for granting me a sabbatical to work on this book; my departmental colleagues for their encouragement and camaraderie; and my students for their openness to accompany me in exploring the intersections among faith, reason, justice, rhetoric, and culture. I am grateful to my editor at Peter Lang Publishing, Erika Hendrix, for her timely and enthusiastic assistance.

Finally, I thank my spouse and best friend, Christie Renae Hatch, for taking life in stride with a guy who seems always to be in front of a laptop; and our lovable beagle, Beau, for frequently pulling me from the realm of words and ideas into his earthy world of affection, play, and neighborhood jaunts.

John B. Hatch, Ph.D.
St. Davids, Pennsylvania

Introduction

"*The past is the past.*" "*Forgive and forget.*" "*No apologies, no regrets.*" "*Live in the present.*" "*The future is now.*" These popular aphorisms, and others like them, express an informal philosophy that is common in contemporary Western societies—especially the United States, one of the most individualistic and future-oriented nations in the world. These ideas can be quite liberating when one is facing interpersonal slights and offenses, regrets about past actions, or difficult career/business decisions. They encapsulate important truths; yet like many proverbs, the truths they convey are not universal principles as much as they are cultural nuggets of wisdom to apply judiciously in contexts where they fit. In this respect, they have much in common with *rhetoric* in the traditional sense of the word, as *public discourse designed to influence others*. As ancient Greek and Roman thinkers recognized, rhetoric draws upon *endoxa* or *sensus communis* (shared beliefs and values of a society), deals with human exigencies in specific times and places, and requires *phronesis*, or practical wisdom, for appropriate and effective application. In other words, rhetoric is situational.[1]

This book examines the use of rhetoric in situations and cultural contexts very different from the ones mentioned above—conditions in which collective social identity strongly shapes individuals' experiences, the weight of past wrongs by one group against another is too great to simply set aside, the injuries of injustice continue to handicap those who suffered them, and the future looks foreboding unless those wounds can be opened, dressed, and properly healed. For such exigencies, a different set of aphorisms would better apply:

> "The past is never dead. It's not even past."[2]
> "Never forget."
> "Those who cannot remember the past are condemned to repeat it."[3]
> "To forget the dead would be akin to killing them a second time."[4]
> "The one who throws the stone forgets; the one who is hit, remembers forever."

The last saying—an Angolan proverb—reminds us that some blows inflict a pain that can never be forgotten, a wound from which the victim cannot fully recover. For example, the unfathomable extermination of six million Jews during World War II by Germany—a nation known for its high culture, musical geniuses, and brilliant philosophers—left a massive scar on the psyche of the Jewish people as well as the moral self-confidence of Western societies. When public figures deny the Holocaust or minimize its import, they tear at that wound again, adding insult to injury.

All too often, there is a memory gap between perpetrators and victims, as captured in the proverb about the stone. In many cases, those who have abused others—or descendants of the abusers—are quick to justify or excuse these actions, minimize the harm they caused, or simply put this harm out of memory to avoid any unpleasant pangs of conscience or shame. Moreover, in order to commit the wrong in the first place, they (or their ancestors) had to desensitize themselves to the feelings and concerns of the other party. Those who have suffered a terrible wrong, by contrast, can hardly avoid feeling the pain and recognizing the injustice; and even if they try to forget, it frequently comes back to haunt them—unless and until the injustice is fully recognized, repented of, and redressed.

These dynamics have relational consequences. Just as a friend's lack of apology or corrective action after an offense creates tension in the friendship, so collective wrongs perpetrated by one group against another leave behind a legacy of resentment, tension, and division, for as long as the victimized group does not receive some form of apology and meaningful effort to repair the damage. To use a more specific interpersonal example, suppose someone has been spreading false rumors about their friend. If they stop spreading rumors, yet fail to apologize and inform everyone that the rumors were false, the damage continues to spread and the friendship may end. If a college student who has been "borrowing" cash from their roommate's desk drawer eventually stops stealing but doesn't repay their roommate and apologize, trust will never be restored; and even if they do repent and repay, restoring trust will take time and effort. In severe cases such as identity theft, wrongful imprisonment, or violent assault, the victim of wrongdoing may be left penniless or unable to earn a living. Worse still, multi-generational oppression of a group, such as the enslavement and segregation of African Americans or the theft of land and culture from Native American peoples, may leave their descendants with enduring material, cultural, political, and psychological disadvantages. Clearly, when an individual or group has been seriously wronged, it is not enough to stop harming the other party. The offender must go further, making a good-faith effort to repair the damage caused by past wrongs, restore the well-being of the victim, and respectfully work with the victim to heal their relationship. This process is called reconciliation.

Speaking to Reconciliation

The focus of this book is on public discourse concerning reconciliation, informed by religious traditions. The relevance of the religious angle on this subject requires some initial clarification, provided below. I then introduce a framework for critically examining reconciliation discourse, followed by a brief overview of the collection of speeches to follow.

At its core, reconciliation depends on communication, and when it involves public communication between representatives of groups, it is best understood through the lens of rhetoric. To orient the study of reconciliation in such cases, I define it as *"a dialogic rhetorical process of rectifying wrongs and healing relationships between parties, in ways that promote their common good."*[5] While the definition may sound simple enough, in truth it refers to a complex and messy human process of meaning-making and re-making. To clarify that complexity, let us compare this meaning of "reconciliation" to its sense in a different context.

In the field of accounting, reconciliation refers to the process of reviewing different records of past transactions and making sure that their bottom lines come out the same. When the numbers don't match up, the records must be checked for errors and corrected. Once corrected, the accounts are reconciled. In human affairs, however, reconciliation is less straightforward; it involves a complex web of ethical values and meanings, which are more subjective—or rather, inter-subjective, in the sense that they emerge from joint sense-making in communication with one another. Human meanings and values are deeply connected to identities, relationships, and communities. As such, they are central to our lives as personal, social beings. Moreover, human meaning-making and valuing are concerned with much more than just physical survival. A survey of human cultures across the world and across history suggests that we are innately religious creatures, even if we don't follow a formal religion. That is to say, we have a drive to understand the meaning of the universe, our place in it, and what is ultimately good or worthwhile.

Whenever someone violates our values, identities, or relationships, we hunger for a wholeness that has been shattered. Deep down, there is a sense that these social goods are sacred and should never be trampled upon or cast aside. Thus, the human search for meaning takes on especial urgency as it becomes a search for reconciliation—healing the rifts, filling the gaps, knitting the broken bones, putting the pieces of a broken moral order back together. Given its intrinsic connection to our most sacred values and our very selves, the work of reconciliation takes on a spiritual character. Little wonder, then, that we often turn to our faith traditions for frameworks and pathways of reconciliation. Religious faith is rich in discourse regarding ultimate reality, ultimate value, ethics and morals, sin and guilt, mercy and grace, atonement and forgiveness, sacrifice and restoration. The Judeo-Christian tradition, especially, features the theme of reconciliation, both vertical (divine-to-human) and horizontal (human-to-human).

Until recently, the study of reconciliation by Western scholars had been almost exclusively a theological pursuit, focused on unpacking the Biblical theme of reconciliation between God and humans. In the last three decades, however, the language of reconciliation has migrated from the pulpit and seminary into secular society and has substantially shifted in orientation from a primarily vertical concern to a frequently horizontal project addressing rifts and wounds in interpersonal, communal, and civic life. On this plane, it has been studied in a wide range of disciplines, including philosophy, political theology, psychology, sociology, political science, and communication. This multi-disciplinary scope attests to the richness and complexity of reconciliation as a process involving discourse and dialogue, taking shape in various forms and genres.

Given the persistence of unhealed rifts and long-festering social wounds in human societies around the world, there is much to be gained by studying the restorative elements and processes of reconciliation. At the very least, we can gain greater respect and appreciation for the multi-faceted challenge of reconciliation and for courageous efforts to promote it in our world. We may find occasion to support robust reconciliation initiatives, or to critique and challenge ill-conceived approaches. We may even feel called to take the lead in promoting reconciliation in our educational institutions, workplaces, churches, or local communities. If we take up this challenge, we might discover that this task requires not only social, political, and rhetorical resourcefulness, but also time-tested spiritual resources.

While reconciliation is now widely studied as a sociopolitical phenomenon, many of its proponents and practitioners still draw upon the deepest moral and spiritual wellsprings of their cultures—that is, religious traditions—for motivation, inspiration, wisdom, strength, and hope. There, they find direction and support on multiple levels: beliefs about the nature of the universe, humanity, morality, and divinity; values and morals that transcend personal feelings or political agendas; historical, poetic, and/or mythic narratives of redemption and restoration; symbols and saints that embody these beliefs, values, and narratives; rituals of cleansing, sacrifice, and reconciliation; practices of personal discipline; and vibrant spiritual connections that empower and sustain them through seemingly insurmountable difficulties and discouragements.

In this book, readers will encounter an array of speeches from political, religious, and cultural leaders who used rhetoric to promote reconciliation between races, peoples, political factions, religious groups, and civilizations—and in so doing, infused their rhetoric with beliefs, ethical principles, quotations, metaphors, and stories from their faith traditions. Each of these "snapshots" of reconciliation is only a piece of larger puzzle. By this I mean that each speech responded to a specific sociocultural or sociopolitical challenge in a particular time and place and can be fully understood only in relation to events, discourse, and actions preceding and following that speech. Thus, for each address included in this volume of the *Speaking of Religion* series, I provide an introduction orienting readers to its context and the shape and import of its text.

Above and beyond the speech-specific introductions, a big-picture orientation to the subject of this book is also needed. To understand, appreciate, and assess public addresses on reconciliation, we must develop a robust understanding of how it is constituted, how it works, and the standards by which its discourse may be evaluated. Thus, the next section presents a rhetorical framework originally developed in my book *Race and Reconciliation: Redressing Wounds of Injustice*.[6] Rooted in rhetorical theory, this framework is also deeply informed by theology and psychology, and it has been applied to various cases of reconciliation discourse in previous publications.[7]

A Rhetorical *Frame*-Work for Critically Examining Reconciliation

As indicated in the definition above, reconciliation is about rectifying wrongs and healing relationships between parties. Reconciliation becomes a matter for discussion only when coexisting or previously connected parties, whether individuals or groups, are alienated from one another. Something has come between them, obstructing harmonious interaction. In some cases, the parties are at war, whether in the form of violent conflict, litigation, or verbal aggression. If they are "at peace," it is a tense, superficial peace, filled with unspoken anger, fears, and resentments—more like a cold shoulder or a "cold war" than warm fellowship. Either way, the social good of harmony or genuine peace is lacking, having been displaced by enmity. This is the exigency that reconciliation rhetoric attempts to address.

A Values Restoration Project

If we talk to unreconciled parties about the reasons for their enmity, we soon discover that their lack of harmony is directly linked to a perceived absence of other social goods—values which have been violated by one or both of the parties. In some cases, it is a lack of truthfulness: someone has been ignoring, minimizing, or denying an important reality in the relationship. They may have lied or withheld vital information from the other party, causing a breach of trust; or they may have avoided facing the reality of challenges that one or both parties are dealing with; or they may refuse to admit to actions that have harmed the other party. Sometimes it is a matter of minimizing or rationalizing wrongful actions. Whatever the case, a lack of honesty strains a relationship by undermining the foundation of truth on which relational trust and well-being depend.

In many cases, disharmony stems from the fact that one or both of the parties feel that their power to make effective choices has been limited or taken away. For instance, liberty is one of the fundamental human rights for which American colonists fought their War of Independence; yet these white colonists, and the new nation they formed, deprived millions of African Americans of liberty, first through a century of slavery under the U.S. Constitution, and then through another century of racial segregation under various state and local laws. Although African Americans gained their rightful liberties under federal law through the Civil Rights Movement in the 1950s and 60s, their human agency—the capacity to shape their own destiny and better their lives—continued to be severely hindered by persistent prejudice, rampant poverty, redlining, lack of property and inherited capital, lack of education, lack of representation in government, lack of connections, and other disadvantages stemming from past enslavement and discrimination. While some African Americans managed to overcome these disadvantages through strength of will and good fortune, many others found that the psychological wounds and burdens left behind by generations of prejudice and oppression hamstrung their ability to hope for a better life and sapped their willpower to persevere amid the disadvantages mentioned above. Thus, for many black people today, a relative lack of agency stemming from the legacy of past racism fosters tension and resentment toward white people.

While both a lack of truth and a lack of agency tend to strain relations between individuals or groups, perhaps the most common cause of tension and strife between parties is a lack of justice. The aphorism "No justice, no peace" captures the linkage between these two social goods. "It's not fair!" "He hit me first!"

"Tit for tat." "An eye for an eye." "Turnabout is fair play." "Revenge is sweet." These common sayings express the human hunger for justice, a value associated with fairness or balance, as captured in the metaphor of balancing the scales. Justice is understood in various ways depending on the context. It may be defined in terms of strict equality or proportionate equity; it may pertain to retribution for crimes or a balanced distribution of goods; it may be measured in material/monetary value, or time spent behind bars, or symbolic rebalancing through words, memorials, etc. When one or both parties in a relationship believe that they are not getting their fair share, a debt has not been paid, or a wrong has not been righted, they will experience little harmony in their relationship until the injustice is properly redressed.

In the published literature about the nature and challenges of reconciliation, these values and the connections between them repeatedly come up in one form or another.[8] For instance, a number of nations with politically or culturally oppressive pasts have held *truth and reconciliation commissions* (TRC's), while some leaders have called for a truth and *conciliation* commission in the United States.[9] These phrases highlight how achieving a genuine and lasting peace between peoples or political factions depends upon unpacking the truth of oppressive practices in their history. Moreover, from 2007 to 2009, the U.S. House, Senate, and a number of state legislatures issued resolutions expressing "profound regret" or apology for the past enslavement and segregation of African Americans, each of which featured an extended historical review of the wrongs that were perpetrated against people of color under slavery and segregation.[10] Truth is foundational to reconciliation, yet it must be handled with care. Facing terrible truth about human cruelty inevitably sparks anger and fear; and attending to truth in isolation from other values can turn a fragile peace into a conflagration. As the author of a book on marital relationships observes, "Love without truth is sentimentality ... Truth without love is harshness."[11] A similar characterization can be made regarding peace and justice. While there can be no lasting peace without justice, the converse is true: without peace, there cannot be justice, because aggressive conflict escalates injustice on all sides and inevitably catches innocent victims in the crossfire.

The most famous and influential truth and reconciliation commission, the South African TRC, came about in an effort to avert the eruption of a bloody civil war over the oppressive system of racial segregation (*apartheid*) that had kept black Africans in fourth-class status within their own land for generations. The white masters of South African apartheid acceded to the creation of a new, racially inclusive democratic constitution in exchange for a grant of amnesty for any crimes against humanity committed by the government and its security forces in the name of official apartheid policy. Likewise, black activists who had committed crimes in the name of their liberation struggle would be granted amnesty rather than prosecution. In both cases, amnesty was not granted unless certain conditions were met: coming voluntarily before the TRC, making full disclosure of one's crimes, and convincing the TRC that these acts had been committed as part of a political agenda in the struggle for or against apartheid. In short, this amnesty arrangement relinquished criminal justice for past political crimes in exchange for a peaceful transition to a more just government; in the process, it also gained truth regarding heinous government actions and violent anti-government acts that had been planned or perpetrated outside of public view or accountability. As this case demonstrates, truth, justice, and peace are bound up together.

Reconciliation grapples with the value of agency as well.[12] As Kenneth Burke observes, human agency—the ability to reflect, choose, and act in ways that transcend our animal instincts—is rooted in our linguistic capacity.[13] Through language and rhetoric, we label and characterize situations, make more-or-less conscious choices to achieve goals, and evaluate our actions against social ideals and moral values. Thus, linguistic agency is the foundation of human dignity and morality, and in various religious traditions it is seen to be a divine gift.[14] Conversely, crimes against humanity, such as slavery, enforced segregation, and genocide, involve not only causing physical restriction, pain, or harm, but especially crushing the victims' power of speech and language.[15] For instance, Canada's Indian Residential School program not only forcibly removed native children from their families and villages to place them in boarding schools, but sought to stamp out their culture by forbidding them to speak in their native languages. In the United States, slaves were forbidden to learn how to read. In various repressive regimes around the world, the use of torture on political prisoners reduces their speech to the words their captors wish to extract from them (confession, information, etc.) or else wordless screams.

For this reason, key to restoring victims' agency is regenerating their capacity and freedom to speak for themselves, in their own personal/cultural voice, and give their own account of the wrongs done to them.[16] Such restoration of agency is essential to healing from the trauma of victimization. Moreover, when discussing reconciliation, many thinkers rightly argue that perpetrators or even third parties should not demand words of forgiveness from victims, as this demand would further deprive them of agency and deepen the hurt. Rather, forgiveness must be a free act. At the same time, psychologists studying forgiveness emphasize how the act of forgiving, when freely offered as part of a larger healing process, liberates the victim from being controlled by the pain of the victimizer's actions or poisoned by bitterness. (I say more about the nature of forgiveness in the introduction to Part II.)

On the part of the offending party, likewise, agency is an essential social good that reconciliation utilizes, realigns, and restores. It takes strength of will to choose repentance over the status quo, to expose and acknowledge wrongdoing, to open oneself up to the victim's anger, and to give up power and privilege that were unjustly gained somewhere along the line. Reconciliation is not about imposing punishment or removing liberty but about redeeming the oppressor's agency from the corruption of unjust power into the freedom of ethical responsibility—just as it relieves the victims' agency from the crushing weight of oppression, freeing them to act both for their own and others' well-being.

The Reconciliation Tetrad

In sum, reconciliation works not only to bring together alienated parties and restore their relationship, but also to restore interconnected social values that have been split apart or unbalanced through acts of violation. Above, I identified four cardinal values that must be restored and realigned in reconciliation: truth, agency, justice, and peace. I refer to them as the reconciliation *tetrad*. We might think of them as the four-cornered ethical foundation on which a healthy relationship or healthy society is built. We could also think of them as the corners of a pyramid with a triangular base (see Figure 1). This metaphor highlights how the values are each directly connected to one another—how they together constitute the shape of an ethical relationship.

As we go deeper into the forest of reconciliation discourse (often found within sacred writings or reflections on such writings), we find special terms that highlight how agency, truth, justice, and peace are interdependent. These special terms include *grace*, *restorative justice*, *restorative truth*, and the Hebrew word *shalom*. As seen in Figure 1, each of these concepts is closely linked to one of the cardinal values of the tetrad while also pulling together toward ethical wholeness at the heart of human relating.

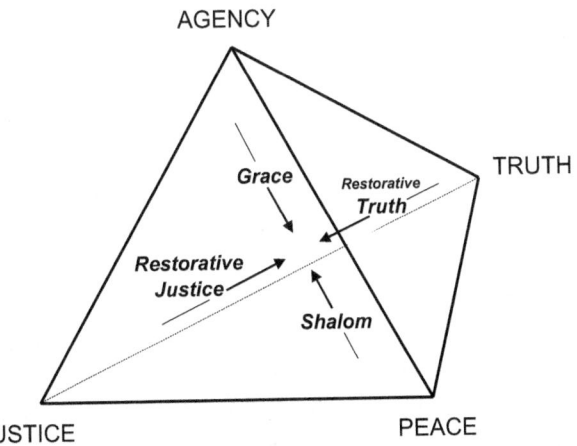

Figure 1. The Tetrad of Values in Reconciliation (Pyramid Metaphor). Source: Author

The first of these is *grace*—a disposition to give freely, even when the gift is not deserved. While grace is a major theme in Christian theology, English speakers of various religious and non-religious backgrounds also use this word in everyday human interactions. Communication scholar Julia Wood describes grace as "granting forgiveness, putting aside our needs, or helping another save face when no standard says we should or must do so. Rather than being prompted by rules or expectations, grace springs from a generosity of spirit."[17] Clearly, grace is an expression of agency—the capacity to act, to choose freely and put one's choice into effect. Yet grace is more specific: it involves *choosing not to impose the penalty of strict justice* after an infraction of rules or an infringement on someone's rights. When a student turns in a paper after the deadline and the professor waives the stated penalty for late submission because the student was facing difficult circumstances, the professor is showing grace. It is not that the deadline doesn't matter, but that the professor recognizes the complexity of life and has compassion on the student and therefore chooses not to deduct points in this case. When reconciliation grapples with serious injustice against a group, members of that group may express grace in choosing not to prosecute those who perpetrated injustice (e.g. amnesty); or they may personally forgive the perpetrators while still demanding prosecution or restitution. Thus, grace is not contrary to justice, but rather transcends justice even while recognizing and affirming its demands—typically because the person showing grace identifies with the offender in some way, recognizes their common bond of humanity or shared community, and feels empathy or compassion. Grace is informed by a desire for harmonious relation with the offending party; the grace-giver considers the well-being of that party, as well as the truth about wrongdoing and the demands of justice, and may take some of the costs of justice upon oneself so that the offender's humanity and the relationship may be restored.[18] While this is a central theme of the Bible,[19] it has powerful implications for contemporary human affairs, whether one identifies as Jewish, Muslim, Buddhist, Christian, Hindu, an adherent of another religion, an agnostic/atheist, or a "None."

A pyramid points upward, like a temple, church, or mosque. As such, the pyramid metaphor reminds us that human agents seeking reconciliation in the wake of serious wrongdoing often look to a divinity, higher power, or transcendent spiritual reality for inspiration, strength, and orienting vision. Religions are concerned with ultimate Truth, Justice, Peace—and above all, with divine Agent(s) or Agency. The placement of Agency (especially in the form of Grace) at the pinnacle of the tetrad highlights how reconciliation requires action that transcends other values and brings them together. It is agency—the power to choose and act accordingly—that creates the ground for moral judgment. It is grace that makes redemption possible and works to make a disjointed, fragmented moral order whole again.

While grace is an ancient concept with rich theological roots, "restorative justice" and "restorative truth" are concepts recently developed in the context of victim-offender mediation (VOM) processes and social reconciliation efforts.[20] Like grace, these terms speak to an intrinsic unity of values that transcends any situational opposition between them. For instance, while traditional criminal justice is concerned only with legal retribution for violating the laws of the state, *restorative justice* is concerned with the persons and social fabric that are damaged by wrongful acts; as such, it seeks to restore offender, victim, and relevant relationships to wholeness.[21] This means that restorative justice is broadly concerned with restoring the harmony and well-being of individuals and social relations, combining justice-oriented and peace-oriented perspectives for depth-perception to see a way through to enduring and meaningful justice.

Similarly, the notion of *restorative truth* implies that the bare facts alone, as well as the one-sided narrative truths of polarized individuals and groups, can tear the fabric of social relations and threaten the peace of society rather than restore it. For this reason, the South African Truth and Reconciliation Commission identified two additional types of truth as being essential to reconciliation: social/dialogue truth and restorative truth.[22] *Social/dialogue truth* has to do with coming together to listen to one another's individual and group stories to gain a many-sided picture of the unfolding social reality of oppression and suffering.[23] *Restorative truth*, on the other hand, refers to underlying truths that ground and motivate the difficult work of reconciliation. This is an area where religious traditions make a significant contribution. For instance, Buddhists' belief in the underlying oneness of all beings can function as a restorative truth. Jews' and Muslims' shared belief in one creator God and the obligation to love one's neighbor provides a basis for seeking reconciliation.[24] A key restorative truth for Christians is that Christ's willing self-sacrifice released divine grace into the world to forgive sins, redeem sinners, and break down the walls of enmity between groups—that is, that Christ died for reconciliation and made it possible for humans to reconcile despite the barriers and sacrifices involved.

Like "grace," the fourth special term comes from the Judeo-Christian tradition. In English, "peace" is a rather thin concept, suggesting the absence of conflict and perhaps the presence of tranquility. I have used the synonym "harmony" to suggest something richer than this: complementarity across differences, a beautiful and fluid blending of diverse elements. But if we translate "peace" into the Hebrew language, we get an even richer word, found both in the Bible and in modern usage: *shalom*. Used both as a greeting and a farewell, shalom identifies a particular kind of well-being, encompassing not only peace (in the sense of "the absence of agitation or discord") but also "completeness, wholeness, health … welfare, safety, soundness, tranquility, prosperity, perfectness, fullness, rest, harmony."[25] Rather than focusing on the individual in isolation from others, Jewish culture assumes that shalom is found in perfect community. Indeed, the city name "Jeru-salem" is derived from "shalom" and captures the dream of the ideal community. For a society to be characterized by shalom, there cannot be persistent injustice, oppression, or grinding poverty; there cannot be a pervasive lack of truth and trust; people cannot be deprived of liberty and agency over their lives. Thus, the concept of shalom reminds us that genuine, lasting peace is deeply connected with justice, truth, and agency.

While the metaphor of a four-pointed pyramid highlights the paradoxical unity of these values, a disadvantage of this metaphor is that it oversimplifies the assortment of social goods and values that people discuss and debate with regard to the work of reconciliation. To compensate, we might also think of justice, peace, truth, and agency as the four "compass points" of reconciliation, as seen in Figure 2.

This metaphor has two advantages. First, a compass is an orienting device that we carry with us, and it is sensitive to our context and position, redirecting us accordingly. Thus, if the pyramid evokes transcendent values and their connection to the sacred, the compass evokes the rhetorical nature of reconciliation in human society. Moreover, a compass in use is horizontal, like the relationship between parties in conflict, who must reorient themselves relative to one another in order to reconcile and move forward together. Second, a compass is round and encompasses many directions between north, east, south, and west. Similarly, each item in the tetrad is not one simple value, but a constellation of related values. Justice comes in a number of forms, as we have seen (fairness, equality, equity,

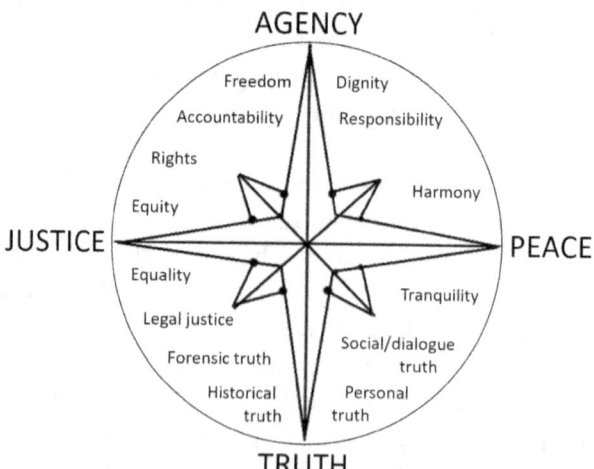

Figure 2. The Tetrad (Compass Metaphor). Source: Author

retribution, etc.); truth includes both objective facts and subjective perceptions/feelings; agency encompasses notions of freedom, liberty, and power; and peace ranges from the mere absence of conflict to the presence of harmony. Amid all this complexity, the simplicity of the tetrad—four cardinal values found in ethical relationships—helps to keep us oriented in our study of reconciliation.

The Four Values as Distinct Ethical Orientations (Frames)

Although reconciliation discourse often refers to certain values explicitly, it may not necessarily do so. Behind the words lies an ethical orientation, frame, or lens that shapes and colors how the *rhetor* (public communicator) presents the topic, whether consciously or not. For humans, reality is always somewhat filtered through our limited perception, and we act on our perceptions to create the social realities in which we live. This is true of values as well as facts. All of us desire that our relationships and societies be characterized by truthfulness, freedom of choice, justice, and peace—if not for others, then at least for ourselves. While we know that these values matter broadly, we tend to see the ethical quality of our relationships through our own limited and often egocentric (or ethnocentric) perspective. For instance, what one party sees as unfair in a given situation, another might believe to be perfectly just.

Severe and/or multi-generational violations perpetrated by one group against another have a way of exacerbating this natural perception gap, even after the violation has ended.[26] For instance, in the United States, many Caucasians perceive African Americans to be unnecessarily angry and pugnacious, disrupting the harmony of the nation by harping on race issues. Many African Americans, on the other hand, see white people as the beneficiaries of unjust privilege, complacent and oblivious to the ways in which past and present racial injustices still affect the lives of black people. Many whites believe firmly in the American Dream: that the United States is the land of freedom where anyone can be anything they choose to be—that is, they have tremendous agency over their own lives. Many black people look at the same nation and see a centuries-long nightmare of enslavement, segregation, lynching, and disenfranchisement, and the rubble of present-day prejudice and systemic poverty that still limits their agency to achieve a better life. We might say that many white people see their nation "through rose-colored glasses," while many black people "see red" as they survey the tragic scene of a nation pervaded by racial inequality, police shootings of unarmed black men, and so forth. And while many white people today make light of race and gravitate toward the idea of color-blindness (or seeing people in shades of grey), many black people still see a very black-and-white, racialized world around them—even when they wish it were not so.

If we critically reflect on these popular metaphors, we can discern that they refer to distinct value-orientations that color our social perceptions differently. When we say that someone is very "black-and-white" in their approach to the world, we mean that they make clear and simple distinctions between right and wrong, guilty and innocent, victim and victimizer; they have a strong sense of justice, or at least law and order. However, if someone sees in "shades of grey," they sense that human nature and moral choices are more complicated than that, and they are oriented toward finding common ground or harmony with others whose moral choices differ from theirs. When we say someone is "seeing red," we mean that they care passionately about justice and are very angry at some moral offense. If someone sees "through rose-colored glasses," they view the world as a beautiful place where people have agency to fulfill their dreams and everything turns out alright as long as they make good choices. Finally, if we say that someone "sees clearly," we mean that they face the truth even when it doesn't suit them—they see the world more or less for what it is, with minimal perceptual distortion. In reality, most of us see different issues in different ways; we may be very black-and-white about some issues, see shades of grey in other issues, view some situations through rose-colored glasses, and be clear-sighted realists about others.

Building upon the insights and terminology of one of the most important 20th-century rhetorical theorists, Kenneth Burke, I give the following labels to these broad ways of seeing:[27]

- *Tragic frame*—Justice-driven, seeing in black-and-white, or "seeing red" when there is injustice
- *Comic frame*—Peace-and-harmony oriented, seeing in shades of grey, with fuzzy lines
- *Romantic frame*—Agency-oriented, seeing through rose-colored glasses
- *Realistic frame*—Truth-oriented, trying to see through a clear window

Readers may wonder, why these terms? Simply put, Burke noted that different forms of drama and literature, such as tragedy and comedy, embody different generic ways in which humans may view (or "frame") their existence in society.[28] While literature is a form of art, Burke also regarded it to be "equipment for living,"[29] in the sense that it models ways in which we can approach the challenges of our existence with others. Such orientations emerged in cultural practice long ago, and came to be represented in the form of dramas and literary works as models of human engagement with the world. Burke recognized that although politicians and other rhetors speak in more prosaic forms, they draw upon such orientations to dramatize situations for audiences, knowingly or not. Depending on the frame chosen, they are more readily able to galvanize a certain kind of action from their audience to address a situation. For instance, if a politician portrays a political opponent as an evil villain and the audience buys into this tragic portrayal, they are more likely to seek that figure's removal from office. On the other hand, if the politician frames their opponent as an ignorant or misguided soul, the audience is more likely to tolerate that individual, at least until the next election.

Burke worried that humans were prone to overuse or misuse the most symbolically and emotionally compelling frame: the tragic.[30] Specifically, Burke saw the tragic frame causing much suffering and violence in human affairs, and he commended the comic frame as a corrective that would soften its hard edges.[31] As I explain in *Race and Reconciliation*:

> The tragic frame places human action under the rule of unyielding laws or principles, such that every violation inexorably leads to due punishment, whereas the comic frame casts wrongs as forgivable mistakes, misrecognitions that temporarily disrupt social harmony and the realization of the good. The tragic frame measures individuals by the blind, cold calculus of justice under the law (as duty, desert, or strict fairness—e.g., an eye for an eye); the comic frame presents parties who are blind to kinships that exist at a deeper level and eventually removes the scales from their eyes so they may enjoy the warmth of companionship and community.[32]

Many of us encounter the tragic and comic frames most frequently on television, in the form of two popular genres: the crime/detective show and the sitcom. Crime shows (so-called whodunit dramas) have a relentless focus on separating the guilty from the innocent and getting justice for victims by making sure that the perpetrators are caught and punished. Even when an episode reveals that the guilty party was driven to murder by sad circumstances, the focus of the story is not on pitying their humanity but on proving their guilt. This is in stark contrast with situation comedies, which focus on everyday life in some type of social group (family, friends, co-workers, neighbors, small community) and take a light-hearted look at the challenges which arise in relationships among different personalities and social identities. While every episode involves some kind of conflict or problem, it is presented as a mistake or misunderstanding to be empathized with or laughed about; viewers can relate to the characters' personal foibles and problems and are thus enabled to take their own challenges a bit more lightly. Reinforcing this positive outlook, in a sitcom the conflict is somewhat resolved by the end of the episode, no great harm is done, and harmony (or at least peaceful coexistence) is temporarily restored.

While sitcoms are humorous, it is important to note that "comedy" and "comic" have a deeper meaning beyond humor in the Western literary tradition—as captured in the title of Dante Alighieri's famous 14th century work, *The Divine Comedy*. This epic tale of a journey through hell and purgatory to heaven certainly cannot be characterized as funny (though it does contain some satire); nonetheless, it is a comedy in the deeper sense of *leading to a realization of oneness and well-being,* for its protagonist journeys from darkness to enlightenment, ultimately reaching a joyful vision of God and a state of personal alignment with divine love. This comports with the common medieval/Renaissance usage of "comedy" to refer to poems or stories with happy endings. In contemporary usage, the word *comity* refers to social harmony—much as a *comedy* typically ends with a resolution of conflict, and Burke's *comic* frame sees underlying connectedness among social actors as the ground for peace in human *community*.

While Burke's tragic and comic frames correspond with justice and peace in the reconciliation tetrad, literary theorist Northrop Frye identifies four paradigmatic literary forms across human literature (tragic, comic, ironic, and romantic); and for our purposes, the latter two can be identified as a truth orientation and an agency orientation, respectively. Adapting Frye's terminology, I identify the *realistic* frame as a perspective that dwells on the actual events and circumstances we must deal with (*truth* orientation), while the *romantic* frame highlights the human capacity to make choices that transcend one's circumstances and create a better world (*agency* orientation).[33] As a literary genre, *romance* can refer not only to a story about the pursuit of love, but also a narrative about a heroic quest, both of which involve overcoming obstacles to win the desired object.[34] Following Frye, I focus on the latter sense of romance, since reconciliation is a challenging quest that calls forth strength of character to overcome negative circumstances and emotions. In literature, heroic romance narratives tend to be imbued with a sense of wonder, mystery, and transcendence, sometimes involving the superhuman or supernatural. If a realistic perspective keeps us cautious and skeptical, a romantic perspective cues us to be courageous and hopeful—even to believe in the "impossible."

Figure 3 presents the tetrad as a combination of complementary frames through which to view relational conflict and reconciliation. Applying such terms as *tragic*, *comic*, and *romantic* to public reconciliation discourse may feel awkward at first. However, these terms have considerable advantages. Not only do they call our attention to the moral angle (or angles) from which a rhetor approaches the question of reconciliation in a given speech, but they also suggest the kind of *attitude* and *emotional tone* that this moral perspective brings to the subject. As suggested in our discussion of the "colored glasses" metaphor above, a tragic perspective confronts injustice with an attitude of condemnation, accompanied by such emotions as anger and anguish (if one is a member of the victim group) or regret and remorse (if a member of the victimizer group). In the context of reconciliation, a comic perspective is not humorous, but it does promote feelings of empathy, compassion, and relative calm as it highlights reasons to coexist peacefully and anticipates a

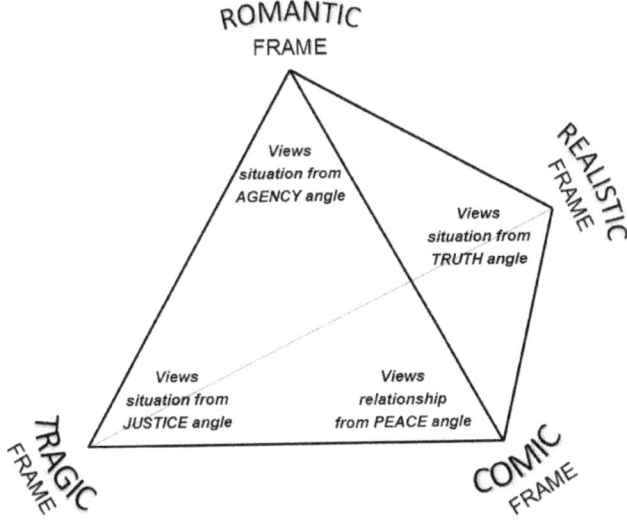

Figure 3. The Tetrad as Complementary Moral Frames. Source: Author

relatively happy ending. Romantically framed reconciliation discourse is colored with attitudes of faith and hope (and perhaps love, in the altruistic sense) and may be accompanied by excitement or joy at the prospect of healing society's wounds. A realistic perspective, on the other hand, is relatively dispassionate or emotionally neutral as the rhetor insists on good logic and factual truth.

Toward Moral Wholeness through the Work of Faith and Rhetorical Dialogue

While the frames in the tetrad are derived from the work of Burke and Frye, they originated with the ancient mythic, poetic, and religious narratives studied by these theorists. Sacred texts point toward a moral wholeness that presumably could be seen only from divine perspective and realized through divine power. Religions call their adherents to pursue such wholeness through faith in divine Agency, with the assumption that humans see only partially and cannot realize moral perfection by their own fallible efforts. It is for this reason that leaders, thinkers, and activists speaking to reconciliation often make allusions to sacred texts, symbols, and practices. While these speakers' rhetorical portrayals of reconciliation may somewhat capture the wholeness of the tetrad, they tend to be more partial when speaking to specific situations of conflict and injustice.

Often, one frame is emphasized—sometimes because the rhetor needs to stress values that have been neglected, but in other cases because the rhetor's perspective is incomplete (or is distorted by the effects of victimizing or being victimized).

Approaching reconciliation from just one angle of the tetrad not only puts that value front and center in our field of vision, but also causes us to see the other elements of the tetrad through the filter of that dominant value. For instance, when looking at reconciliation through the tragic frame (i.e., a justice filter), we will tend to perceive truth partially, in a way that fits our picture of the offender as evil and the situation as intolerably unjust; we will also notice the offender's power (and therefore responsibility) over their actions more than their weaknesses and extenuating circumstances, and we may see such stark differences between victimizer and victim that peace seems impossible—unless the victimizer pays a high price for wrongdoing. Conversely, the comic frame brings into focus truths about the parties' shared humanity; it emphasizes the weakness and fallibility of their agency when they act in opposition to one another (as versus their capacity to accomplish much good when acting cooperatively) and calls attention to the mixture of good and evil, justice and injustice, in both parties—which may obscure the fundamental difference between victimizing and being victimized. Fully understood, however, the way of reconciliation is not simply comic or tragic, but *tragicomic*; it is not simply romantic or realistic, but a combination of both—much as it takes two eyes to have depth perception of what one is examining. In robust reconciliation discourse, different framings come together and blend into holistic perspective. The question, then, is how alienated parties arrive at such depth and fullness of perception.

According to the definition given early in this introduction, reconciliation is a *rhetorical process*. That is to say, it entails framing a topic or situation in one way or another, so as to orient the audience toward certain beliefs, judgments, or actions with respect to that topic/situation. Going further, it entails a process of *re*-framing to overcome distorted or incomplete perspectives and reconstitute ethical wholeness in vision and practice. Because acts of wrongdoing and oppression stem from victimizers' distorted perspective and tend to misshape the moral perspectives of victims as well (and the perspectives of both parties' descendants), the reframing work of reconciliation best occurs in dialogue between these parties. Through *dialogic* rhetoric, parties are challenged to step back and view their relationship from different angles to gain a more holistic moral perspective on the conflict, its causes, and its remedies. Using our compass metaphor, we can say that they must circumnavigate their situation, viewing it from the four cardinal directions as well as points in between. A fully developed approach to reconciliation will encompass all four frames working to check and complement one another.

As emphasized in Part II, the dialogic rhetoric of reconciliation entails *listening* as well as speaking, to overcome distortions in perspective caused by involvement in victimizing or victimhood. It is especially incumbent on the party that perpetrated oppression to enter into *Other-centered* listening and verbal expression since acts of oppression, by their very nature, disrespect the human personhood of the other party, using them as an object for one's own gain. Correcting this wrong lies at the heart of repentance and apology. For victims, on the other hand, forgiveness is a process of liberation from victimhood to see themselves and the offender in a new light and let go of bitterness that poisons their existence. Here, Other-centered communication is not about accepting or excusing wrongdoing, but about recognizing the humanity of the oppressor despite the wrongdoing. The introduction to Part II explores these two sides of the reconciliation coin in greater depth, along with the important communicative work of coming together to address the material losses caused by the offense, negotiating some form of reparation or restoration to help compensate for these losses.

Analyzing and Evaluating Speeches on Reconciliation

The conceptual framework presented in this book provides lenses through which to examine, understand, and evaluate public address on reconciliation. The framework is rhetorical, in that it focuses attention on how speakers frame social division or conflict, either to orient their audiences' thinking and attitudes for the work of reconciliation or to facilitate reconciliation directly with an audience/stakeholder. As such, we can apply the tetrad and the concepts introduced in Part II to do *rhetorical criticism*—analysis and critique—of such discourse. This enterprise requires us to consider how (and how well) a given speech manages the tension between envisioning/promoting moral wholeness (as captured in the tetrad) and addressing the moral imbalances in the existing situation. Restoring balance requires not only emphasizing moral values that have been neglected or downplayed by one or more stakeholders within the audience, but also giving acknowledgment, respect, and voice to stakeholders whose perspective has heretofore been silenced or ignored.

While this is not a book of rhetorical criticism per se, my introductions to many of the speeches apply aspects of the critical framework presented above (and in the introduction to Part II) to help readers gain an initial understanding and appreciation of each speech artifact's unique strengths—and perhaps its weaknesses as well. These introductions provide crucial contextual information about the address and speaker, and note how the religious tradition invoked by the speaker distinctively points the way toward moral wholeness. In this way, each introduction constitutes a stepping-off point for anyone who may wish to analyze a given speech in greater depth. In so doing, they should remember that the tetrad constitutes an orienting device, not a map; it is the job of the analyst/critic to survey and appraise the artifact's textual features in relation to its context, the religious tradition upon which it draws, germane rhetorical concepts, and relevant critical standards.

Selection of Speeches

The guiding aim of this book is to introduce readers to the rhetoric of intergroup reconciliation expressed in public address informed by religious discourse. The artifacts included here exemplify how rhetors have used faith-infused speech to promote and explain reconciliation in their historical situation (the focus of Part I) or to make direct gestures of reconciliation (Part II). Some of the addresses are quite famous, others relatively obscure; nonetheless, all of them are significant exemplars of reconciliation rhetoric drawing on religious faith. With the exception of the address from Martin Luther King Jr., none of these speeches were sermons delivered in church, but they did take inspiration from religious discourse as they addressed social or political divides within a denomination, a nation, or the world.

It should be noted that some important reconciliation speeches were omitted from this collection because they did not frame reconciliation through a religious perspective. For example, in 1988 President Ronald Reagan gave an address apologizing to Japanese-Americans who had been held in internment/concentration camps by the U.S. government during World War II, and he explained why he was signing a bill that authorized monetary reparations for their mistreatment. While it is arguably one of the best exemplars of a reconciliation apology to date, the address did not qualify for inclusion in this volume because Reagan did not significantly draw upon any religious motif or trope. On the other hand, President Barack Obama spoke to reconciliation on numerous occasions during his presidency, and in several of these instances he substantially drew upon religious discourse. His three most significant addresses in this regard are included, as well as two important speeches by Republican presidents (Abraham Lincoln and George W. Bush) and one by a Republican congressman (Thaddeus Stevens).

As I gathered material for this book, I strove to locate artifacts representing a diversity of cultures, nations, genders, and religious perspectives. However, given the set page limit for the *Speaking of Religion* book series and the constraints of my own geographic, cultural, and linguistic location—as well as the relative rarity of speeches by major public figures addressing intergroup reconciliation from religious perspectives—most of the addresses I found were delivered by North American leaders, and all of them were delivered in English. Readers will also notice that most of the rhetors are males and many of the artifacts draw on the Judeo-Christian tradition. My search for addresses speaking to reconciliation in the public square from a religious perspective turned up comparatively few by women, and in the end only two made the cut. As for religious diversity, it should be noted that reconciliation is a prominent theme—arguably the central motif—of the Christian message, and much of the world's written and spoken discourse on social reconciliation in the last three decades bears the imprint of Biblical narratives and Christian theology. I had hoped to include a speech by the world's most famous Hindu social activist—Mohandas Gandhi (who significantly influenced Martin Luther King Jr.)—but most of his important ideas were expressed in his writings, and I did not find any substantial speeches that would qualify for inclusion here. This book does, however, include an address by one of the world's most prominent Buddhist leaders, another by the Muslim leader of an Arab nation, one by a Nobel Prize-winning Jewish writer, and another by a representative of Canada's indigenous First Nations peoples. Moreover, one address included here draws on texts from all three of the world's major monotheistic faiths: Judaism, Christianity, and Islam.

If the Judeo-Christian tradition exercises a significant influence on much of contemporary public discourse about reconciliation, the challenge of racial strife—especially between white people and black people—is one of the recurring issues that contemporary reconciliation discourse has addressed. As a result, many of the speeches in this book were delivered by black or white leaders in the United States or Africa speaking to racial injustice or enmity in some way.

Given the length constraints of this book series, I found it necessary to abridge some of the speech texts, omitting digressions and some portions that are less relevant to the topic of this book. This had the advantage of allowing me to include a wider diversity of reconciliation speech exemplars, as well as maintaining a tighter topical focus for readers. The disadvantage, of course, is that where a speech has been abridged, readers will miss some details and nuances of the rhetor's argument, style, use of examples, or connection with auditors. Therefore, readers who are interested in studying a given speech in greater depth are encouraged to locate and read the complete speech text. To that end, I have included endnotes indicating where the complete texts of abridged speeches can be accessed.

Organization of Book

This book is divided into two parts. The first part contains speeches that commended and explained the nature of reconciliation for their historical situation, informed by some or all of the value orientations found in the tetrad, in relation to a particular conflict or social divide. Each address found in Part I was designed to orient its audience to the work of reconciliation in its own cultural and political context, drawing on particular aspects of the speaker's and/or audience's faith tradition to address civic, racial, and cultural conflicts. The selected speeches range from the 19th century to the present and from North America to Europe and

Africa. The speakers include heads of state, religious thinkers/leaders/activists, and Nobel Prize winners.

Part II consists of speeches in which rhetors used public discourse to make direct gestures of reconciliation or commend such gestures. Some of these speeches focus mainly on facing the truth of a painful history that divides. Others apologize on behalf of a nation or institution. Some include the recipients' response to the apology. One speech represents the victims' perspective on a heinous historical act and includes a request for an apology. Another address eulogizes the victims of a mass shooting and celebrates the grace of forgiveness displayed by the family members. Part II concludes with a sequence of public speech-acts exchanged across a decade between representatives of victimized and victimizing parties—illustrating the unfolding dialogic process of reconciliation.

More detailed overviews of these two speech collections are found in the introductions to Part I and Part II. There is an introduction before each address as well, providing relevant information about the speaker and context and briefly analyzing the speech's approach to reconciliation in terms of the theoretical framework presented here.

Notes

1. By this, I mean both that human situations call for rhetoric and that rhetoric calls forth situations to address. See Lloyd F. Bitzer, "The Rhetorical Situation," *Philosophy & Rhetoric* 1 (1968): 1–14, Communication & Mass Media Complete; Richard E. Vatz, "The Myth of the Rhetorical Situation," *Philosophy & Rhetoric* 6 (1973): 154–61, Communication & Mass Media Complete.
2. William Faulkner, *Requiem for a Nun* (New York: Vintage International, 2011), 73.
3. George Santayana, *The Life of Reason* (Project Gutenberg eBook, 2005), https://www.gutenberg.org/files/15000/15000-h/15000-h.htm.
4. Elie Wiesel, *Night*, trans. Marion Wiesel (New York: Hill and Wang: 2006), xv.
5. John B. Hatch, *Race and Reconciliation: Redressing Wounds of Injustice* (Lanham, MD: Lexington, 2008), 7.
6. Ibid.
7. For example, see John B. Hatch, "Reconciliation: Building a Bridge from Complicity to Coherence in the Rhetoric of Race Relations," *Rhetoric & Public Affairs* 6 (2003): 739–66, doi:10.1353/rap.2004.0008; John B. Hatch, "Beyond *Apologia*: Racial Reconciliation and Apologies for Slavery," *Western Journal of Communication* 70, no. 3 (July 2006): 186–211, doi:10.1080/10570310600843496; John B. Hatch, "Dialogic Rhetoric in *Letters Across the Divide*: A Dance of (Good) Faith toward Racial Reconciliation," *Rhetoric & Public Affairs* 12 (2009): 485–532, https://doi.org/10.1353/rap.0.0118; John B. Hatch, "'Accidental Racist:' Stumbling through the Motions of Racial Reconciliation," *Communication Quarterly* 64 (2016): 93–118, doi:10.1080/01463373.2015.1103281.
8. See Hatch, *Race and Reconciliation*, 99–117 and 128–36.

9. Native American activist Mark Charles and theologian Soong-Chan Rah argue for the latter term (omitting *re-*) in cases where the relationship between alienated parties was never genuinely truthful, just, or peaceful from the start, such as between white European colonizers and Native Americans in the Americas. See Mark Charles and Soong-Chan Rah, *Unsettling Truths: The Ongoing, Dehumanizing Legacy of the Doctrine of Discovery* (Downers Grove, IL: InterVarsity Press, 2019).
10. For an examination of the first three state resolutions apologizing for slavery and segregation, see Hatch, *Race and Reconciliation*, 321–34.
11. Timothy J. Keller, *The Meaning of Marriage: Facing the Complexities of Commitment with the Wisdom of God* (New York: Penguin Books, 2011), 48.
12. For a detailed exploration of agency as a social good in reconciliation, see Hatch, *Race and Reconciliation*, 111–16.
13. See Kenneth Burke, "Dramatism," in *International Encyclopedia of the Social Sciences*, ed. David L. Sills (New York: MacMillan, 1968), 445–52; Kenneth Burke, *The Rhetoric of Religion: Studies in Logology* (Berkeley: University of California Press, 1970), 16.
14. For example, in the Biblical account of the creation of the world, humans are made "in the image of God" (Genesis 1:27–28), which suggests that they have the capacity to name things (the first recorded human action in the Bible), create, make choices, and order their world.
15. See Teresa G. Phelps, *Shattered Voices: Language, Violence, and the Work of Truth Commissions* (Philadelphia: University of Pennsylvania Press, 2004), 42–50.
16. See ibid., 58–59.
17. Julia T. Wood, *Communication Mosaics: An Introduction to the Field of Communication*, 7th ed. (Boston: Wadsworth, 2014), 151.
18. For further explanation of the nature of grace, see Hatch, *Race and Reconciliation*, 116–17.
19. The writings of the Christian New Testament teach that even though humans have repeatedly violated divine justice, God in Christ willingly suffered for them and bore the consequences of their sin in order to loose divine grace into a broken world. It is this costly grace that reconciles humans to God and to one another, breaking down the dividing walls between races and genders and classes, insiders and outsiders. See Romans 5:6–10; Ephesians 2:14–16.
20. See Howard Zehr, *Changing Lenses: A New Focus for Crime and Justice*, 3d ed. (Harrisonburg, VA: Herald Press, 2005). See also Charles Villa-Vicencio, "Restorative Justice: Dealing with the Past Differently," in *Looking Back, Reaching Forward: Reflections on the Truth and Reconciliation Commission of South Africa*, ed. Charles Villa-Vicencio and Wilhelm Verwoerd (Cape Town, SA: University of Cape Town Press, 2000), 68–76.
21. See Zehr.
22. See John de Gruchy, *Reconciliation: Restoring Justice* (Minneapolis: Fortress Press, 2002), 155; Alex Boraine, "Truth and Reconciliation in South Africa: The Third Way," in *Truth V. Justice: The Morality of Truth Commissions*, ed. Robert I. Rotberg and Dennis Thompson (Princeton, NJ: Princeton University Press, 2000), 151–53.
23. See Charles Villa-Vicencio, Telling One Another Stories: Toward a Theology of Reconciliation," in *The Reconciliation of Peoples: Challenge to the Churches*, ed. Gregory Baum and Harold Wells (Maryknoll, NY: Orbis, 1997).
24. The mystical branches within the Christian and Islamic traditions somewhat overlap with Buddhism in seeking to apprehend ultimate Oneness through meditation, although they differ from Buddhism in seeing a *personal, loving* divinity at the heart of all things.
25. James Strong, *Strong's Exhaustive Concordance of the Bible with Greek and Hebrew Dictionaries* (Nashville: Royal Publishers, 1979), no. 7965.

26. See Hatch, *Race and Reconciliation*, 95–98.
27. See ibid., 145–49.
28. See Kenneth Burke, *Attitudes Toward History*, 3d ed. (Berkeley: University of California Press, 1984), 34–91.
29. Kenneth Burke, *The Philosophy of Literary Form: Studies in Symbolic Action*, 3d ed. (Berkeley: University of California Press, 1984), 293.
30. See Burke, *Attitudes Toward History*, 188–89; Kenneth Burke, *Permanence and Change: An Anatomy of Purpose*, 3d ed. (Berkeley: University of California Press, 1984), 74–75; Kenneth Burke, *The Rhetoric of Religion: Studies in Logology* (Berkeley: University of California Press, 1970), 4–5 and 181–82.
31. See Burke, *Attitudes Toward History*, 41–42 and 166–71.
32. Hatch, *Race and Reconciliation*, 25.
33. See the first and third essays in Northrop Frye, *Anatomy of Criticism: Four Essays* (Princeton, NJ: Princeton University Press, 1957). For further clarification on how I bring Burke's frames and Frye's mythic forms/modes together and how I understand the nature of these four frames, see Hatch, *Race and Reconciliation*, 145–49.
34. See Camille K. Lewis, *Romancing the Difference: Kenneth Burke, Bob Jones University, and the Rhetoric of Religious Fundamentalism*, Studies in Rhetoric and Religion (Waco, TX: Baylor University Press, 2007), 7–9; John B. Hatch, "Towards a Fuller Moral Act: Refiguring the Romantic" (paper presented at National Communication Association Convention, Chicago, November 2009).

PART I

COMMENDING, FRAMING, AND EXPLAINING THE WORK OF RECONCILIATION

Introduction to Part I

Part I consists of public addresses that promoted and explained reconciliation in their own historical contexts. Depending on the rhetor's vision of reconciliation and purpose in speaking, each address embodies a somewhat distinct value orientation in framing social conflict and its remedy. In addition, the speeches draw upon different aspects of the rhetor's and/or audience's religious traditions to warrant their claims and give specific shape to their visions of reconciliation.

We begin in 19th-century America, with the Second Inaugural Address of Abraham Lincoln. Having just been elected to a second presidential term after four years of civil war, and knowing that victory over the South is now at hand, Lincoln lays the groundwork for national reconciliation. With great rhetorical care and skill, he steps back to take in a wider historical and theological view, framing the conflict in a way that makes reconciliation between the North and South appear both necessary and possible—despite the terrible bloodshed between them. Following Lincoln's second inaugural is a speech given two years later by Rep. Thaddeus Stevens, urging Congress to pass a law that would, among other things, provide land reparations to former slaves so that they would have a reasonable opportunity to thrive as free citizens of the United States and live at peace with their white neighbors.

Although an uneasy reconciliation between North and South was eventually achieved, it came at African Americans' expense, as Stevens's proposal was not accepted by Congress. Instead, slavery was followed by repressive segregation laws and practices in the South, as well as rampant discrimination in the North. A century later, a young minister named Martin Luther King Jr. became the leader and spokesman of the civil rights movement, which worked to finally gain black people's full rights as American citizens. While King is most famous for his March on Washington Speech ("I Have a Dream"), this book features "A Christmas Sermon on Peace," in which King offers a fuller account of how reconciliation between races and nations is possible. Speaking four years after the March on Washington, King not only explains his faith-informed philosophy of peace-making but also revisits the vision of reconciliation expressed at the end of "I Have a Dream," reviving the hope expressed in that speech despite setbacks and barriers on the way to achieving that dream.

Next come two speeches by Desmond Tutu, an Anglican spiritual leader in South Africa who repeatedly spoke out against that nation's racially segregated apartheid system and later headed its Truth and Reconciliation Commission. In 1984, Tutu was awarded the Nobel Peace Prize for his efforts to expose the injustice of apartheid and bring about its abolition by peaceful means. In his Nobel Lecture, he thoroughly explained the unjust nature of apartheid, set against an African understanding of interdependent humanity and a Christian vision of diverse individuals and cultures living together in dignity, justice, and harmony. Two decades later, South Africa finally transitioned from apartheid to a full democracy, and the Truth and Reconciliation Commission was instituted to address the violence committed by apartheid agents and anti-apartheid activists prior to the transition. Tutu was appointed chair of the TRC, and when the members of the Commission met for the first time to discuss the work ahead, he delivered some remarks on the moral purpose and spiritual nature of their task. Excerpts from that opening address are included here.

After Tutu's speeches, the next two addresses are loosely connected with the 9/11 terrorist attacks in the United States, although they have a much broader focus. On September 11, 2001, one of the world's leading theologians, Miroslav Volf, gave an important address to members of the United Nations on the insights that religion, specifically the Christian tradition, offers for working toward reconciliation in the world. Volf also clarified the factors that turn religion toward justifying violence instead of promoting reconciliation. Ironically, it was during this talk that two jetliners hijacked by al-Qaeda terrorists plunged into the World Trade Center just a few blocks away. Although neither Volf nor the attendees became aware of the attack until after the meeting, it lent especial urgency to his message. It also created occasion for ongoing consideration of this issue. Two years later, on the eve of the second anniversary of 9/11, Vietnamese Buddhist leader Thich Nhat Hanh delivered an address to members of the U.S. Congress on how to lead the nation with mindfulness and compassion, qualities that make reconciliation possible not only between family members and political parties, but even between enemies.

The next speech takes us across the Atlantic Ocean to Ireland, a land torn by a tangle of religious and political violence for centuries, especially in Northern Ireland in the second half of the 20th century. During this period, known as "The Troubles," many people died in shootings and bombings perpetrated by Protestant and Catholic paramilitary groups. Thankfully, in the late 1990s, the sides worked through a peace process that resulted in the 1998 Good Friday Agreement. Nonetheless, deep divisions between Northern Irish Catholics and Protestants persisted, and in 2001, President Mary McAleese of Ireland spoke to this challenge in the inaugural St. Patrick's Day Lecture at Armagh, drawing on the example of St. Patrick's life and passages from Irish literature to cast a vision of reconciliation rooted in Irish culture.

America's first biracial president, Barack Obama, had several occasions to speak to racial or cultural division, both within and beyond the United States. In so doing, he not only clarified the nature of those divides but also articulated bridges toward reconciliation, often drawing on religious beliefs and traditions. That is why this book includes three speeches by Obama (two of them in Part I). The first of these, "A More Perfect Union," was delivered during his 2008 presidential campaign, in response to a crisis of racial division that threatened to derail his path to the presidency. In this speech, he not only defused the crisis but articulated, perhaps better than any president up to that point in history, the nature of the racial divide in the United States and the way it could be overcome. The second speech by Obama looks outside the nation's borders. In the first year of his presidency, Obama gave an important speech designed to overcome enmity between the United States and Muslims worldwide (which had grown through the 9/11 attacks and the Iraq War) and promote a "new beginning" of cooperation. In this address, Obama sheds the light of truth on the causes of their divisions and casts a vision of reconciliation and cooperation between the two parties by highlighting the cultural and religious values and traditions they hold in common.

The final speech in Part I was delivered by a political leader from the Muslim world—His Majesty King Abdullah II of Jordan. In 2018, Abdullah II was awarded the prestigious Templeton Prize for having "done more to seek religious harmony within Islam and between Islam and other religions than any other living political leader."[1] His acceptance speech affirms the common roots and common ethical principles of Judaism, Christianity, and Islam as the basis for harmony between adherents of these faiths.

Notes

1. "King Abdullah II of Jordan Awarded 2018 Templeton Prize," *PR Newswire*, June 27, 2018, https://www.prnewswire.com/news-releases/king-abdullah-ii-of-jordan-awarded-2018-templeton-prize-300671672.html.

CHAPTER ONE

Reconciling a Divided Nation: Abraham Lincoln

On March 4, 1865, Abraham Lincoln was inaugurated for his second term as President of the United States. Although the Union and Confederacy were still at war, it was now evident that the Union would soon prevail. Lincoln could have used his inaugural address to herald the voters' affirmation of his presidency, praise the Union's military successes, predict victory over the Confederacy, and set forth policies for rebuilding the nation. Instead, he directed attention to the bigger moral picture: the cause of the war, its meaning, and the work of healing that would soon be needed. Deceptively brief, his Second Inaugural proved to be one of the greatest speeches in U.S. history; it has been studied at length by numerous rhetoric scholars and merits a comparatively lengthy introduction here.[1]

As Andrew C. Hansen notes, Lincoln's Second Inaugural Address stands apart for its strict attention to establishing "the proper moral stance toward and positioning of his audience."[2] Specifically, Lincoln here focused on *framing the Civil War* for his audience—the divided nation—through a *particular moral perspective* that simultaneously indicted the injustice of slavery and established ground for reconciliation between the North and South. The perspective he offered was overtly religious in character. Frederick Douglass, the former slave turned eloquent abolitionist, remarked that the speech "sounded more like a sermon than a state paper,"[3] and he applauded its "sacred" quality in framing the Civil War as a divine judgment on American slavery.[4] Because of its clear indictment of the Peculiar

Institution, the Second Inaugural was well received by African Americans in the audience.[5] Nonetheless, Lincoln's failure to recognize them as *moral agents* in this address arguably foreshadowed their ultimate marginalization from the reconciliation that unfolded after the war—and exemplified the limitations of political leaders' agency to promote morally robust reconciliation when their primary constituency is resistant to it.

After brief prefatory remarks contrasting the exigency of his second inauguration with that of the first, Lincoln's address begins in earnest by reviewing the root cause of the Civil War: division over the issue of slavery. With rhetorical finesse, Lincoln walks a tightrope between finding common ground with the South and blaming them for the war. In so doing, he applies both the comic and tragic frames. As explained in the introduction to this book, reconciliation requires that rhetors both condemn injustice (tragic framing) and recognize common ground between victims and perpetrators as fallible human beings (comic framing). The comic frame is quite evident in the middle of the third paragraph, where Lincoln observes that both sides "read the same Bible, and pray to the same God" and "[invoke] His aid against the other." Calling it "strange" that anyone would ask God's assistance in keeping other human beings enslaved, he then adds, "let us judge not that we be not judged."[6] This is a classic instance of a "comic corrective"[7]—seeing the adversary as mistaken rather than evil, while also recognizing one's own side as fallible, with its own errors to account for. In this way, Lincoln seems to make light of the moral difference between the North and South with regard to slavery.

However, Lincoln's portrayal of slavery and the war now becomes heavy with a form of tragic framing. As explained by communication scholar Gregory Desilet, *synagonal tragedy* recognizes that both sides of a conflict are complicit in evil and must therefore suffer the consequences together.[8] Unlike factional tragedy (in which one faction or party views the other as evil, thus driving the two sides apart),[9] this kind of tragic framing tends to draw the two sides together by focusing on their shared guilt and suffering. Steeped in the Bible (like most men of his age), Lincoln achieves this synagonal perspective by shifting to a "providential" or "God's-eye" view and alluding to Christ's warning that human offenses inevitably occur (given the corruptibility of human nature) and will be punished in due time. Lincoln regards American slavery as one of these terrible wrongs that must be punished: it was allowed by God to occur for a time, but the people of the United States (both North and South) have failed to end this atrocity for almost a century since the nation's birth, so divine patience has reached the end of its rope.

In the dramatic scenario constructed by Lincoln, the divine judgment comes in the form of human action—war—as a natural outgrowth of the fact that the Southern half of the nation refused even to limit the spread of slavery. Yet in Lincoln's synagonal telling, the blame does not fall on the South alone; for the Northern states have been complicit in America's Peculiar Institution, as the president well knows. Not only did they ratify a Constitution that allowed slavery, but their shipping merchants profited from the slave trade, and the capitol in Washington D.C. was built with slave labor. Thus, the "scourge of war" between the states, which has inflicted horrible suffering and death on soldiers from both sides, serves as a kind of ironic punishment on both South and North for having propagated and tolerated the cruel institution of slavery. Lincoln alludes to the fact that the war was not short-lived as everyone expected. (Indeed, it had dragged on for four years, cost the nation billions of dollars, and taken the lives of more than half a million soldiers.) This tragic reality draws Lincoln's attention to the millions of slaves whose labor has never been compensated and whose bodies have bled under the whips of their masters. In this light, he feels compelled to view the long and bloody war as a criminal sentence passed on the nation's citizens by God.

Because both sides have shared in the offense of slavery, Lincoln is able to conclude the speech by turning his attention to reconciliation in tragicomic perspective, with "malice toward none" and "charity toward all"—even though he believes that the South is more in the wrong. Rather than nurturing hatred, he commends an attitude of grace (charity) toward the people of the Confederacy, even while acknowledging that the cause of the North is right. Although the work of winning military victory is not yet finished, Lincoln focuses on what will be needed afterward: healing the wounds of war and working toward a just and lasting peace.

In hindsight, although Lincoln's tragicomic framing of the war did lay rhetorical groundwork for rebuilding the North and South as a reconciled nation, his vision of a just and enduring peace was undermined by insufficient attention to the matter of *racial* justice. Notice that when Lincoln identifies the presence of "colored slaves" as the reason for the war, he refers to them three times thereafter as an "interest"—an impersonal, economic motivating factor—and only once as "men." In this address, Lincoln frames African Americans as passive subjects of white citizens' good or evil desires and actions, not persons with agency and voices of their own. His focus is on white people, their actions, their suffering, and their healing. Indeed, Frederick Douglass later observed that Lincoln "was pre-eminently the white man's President, entirely devoted to the welfare of white men."[10] Yet Douglass also acknowledged: "Measuring him by the sentiment of his country, a sentiment he was bound as a statesman to consult, he was swift, zealous, radical, and determined" to abolish slavery.[11]

Similarly, rhetorician Kirt H. Wilson both acknowledges Lincoln's shortcomings and credits him for working toward emancipation in a way that took into account the limitations of his political and rhetorical agency. Neither Lincoln nor his party could single-handedly bring an end to slavery in the entire United States; the South would not abandon slavery on its own, and the long war eroded commitment to the abolitionist cause in the North. Thus, during his presidency, Lincoln "was neither a reluctant participant nor a leader of emancipation. He was, instead, a mediator, a dialogic rhetorician who seemed intent on prompting others to discussion and action."[12] "In numerous letters and speeches," Wilson notes, Lincoln "deferred his material and symbolic agency, emphasizing, instead, the rhetorical agency of others" to find an effectual way to achieve the goal of emancipation.[13] Indeed, Lincoln increasingly "effaced himself" from his rhetoric as his presidency unfolded; Edwin Black explains that "he withdrew from his public discourses any representations of his own personality. And in the place of his vanished ego, he proposed a set of principles of which he became the personification."[14]

This is consummately true of the Second Inaugural, in which Lincoln offers a moral and theological vision in place of the expected celebration of personal, political, and (in this case) military victory. Although its portrayal of vain human aspirations is deeply realistic, the Second Inaugural evinces neither cynicism nor fatalism; rather, it affirms the personhood and agency of a "just" and "Living" God who shepherds wayward human agents toward the fulfillment of a divine purpose.[15] In this mutedly romantic light, Lincoln is able to encourage the Union to finish achieving its just cause and then bend its efforts toward reconciliation. The shortcoming of the Second Inaugural's moral vision—its elision of black Americans' agency—says as much (or more) about moral blindness among many of Lincoln's white compatriots as it does about Lincoln himself.

Indeed, after Lee's surrender and Lincoln's assassination, the North and South ultimately achieved reconciliation at African Americans' expense. For one thing, the former slaves never received any kind of restitution for their uncompensated labor, nor did the nation ever deliver on the promise that they would receive "40 acres and a mule" to make a life for themselves as free people. Once Reconstruction ended—the period when agents from the North worked to rebuild the South—Southern states and communities quickly passed laws and established practices to hold African Americans in a "separate and unequal" status of virtual slavery. Racial prejudice and discrimination were rampant in the North as well. It would take another century for the U.S. government to finally overturn segregation laws and outlaw lynching. This is a reminder that the task of reconciliation is not a simple, one-time act but a messy process that may need to be revisited and corrected. Indeed, racial reconciliation and reparations are still matters of serious discussion and debate in the United States today.

Lincoln's Second Inaugural demonstrates the power of rhetoric to promote reconciliation on one level while potentially undermining it on another. It reveals that even when such rhetoric is sensitive to the Other, we should ask which "other" is in focus, and whether some relevant "other" has been relegated to the edge of the frame—or left out altogether. It also reminds us that politics is "the art of the possible"; the political agency of leaders in a democracy is somewhat constrained by the beliefs and interests of their constituents, and the moral vision presented in their rhetoric tends to reflect these constraints, especially when trying to reconcile widely divergent stakeholders. Finally, it illustrates the importance of considering not only what a rhetor literally says (e.g. talking about such values as justice, peace, truth, and agency), but how the rhetor frames the matter at hand.

Second Inaugural Address

Washington DC
March 4, 1865
Fellow Countrymen:

    At this second appearing to take the oath of the presidential office, there is less occasion for an extended address than there was at the first. Then a statement, somewhat in detail, of a course to be pursued, seemed fitting and proper. Now, at the expiration of four years, during which public declarations have been constantly called forth on every point and phase of the great contest which still absorbs the attention and engrosses the energies of the nation,[16] little that is new could be presented. The progress of our arms, upon which all else chiefly depends, is as well known to the public as to myself; and it is, I trust, reasonably satisfactory and encouraging to all. With high hope for the future, no prediction in regard to it is ventured.

    On the occasion corresponding to this four years ago, all thoughts were anxiously directed to an impending civil war. All dreaded it—all sought to avert it. While the inaugural address was being delivered from this place, devoted altogether to *saving* the Union without war, insurgent agents were in the city seeking to *destroy* it without war[17]—seeking to dissolve the Union, and divide effects, by negotiation. Both parties deprecated war; but one of them would *make* war rather than let the nation survive; and the other would *accept* war rather than let it perish. And the war came.

    One eighth of the whole population were colored slaves, not distributed generally over the Union, but localized in the Southern part of it. These slaves constituted a peculiar and powerful interest. All knew that this interest was, somehow, the cause of the war. To strengthen, perpetuate, and extend this interest was the object for which the insurgents would rend the Union, even by war; while the government claimed no right to do more than to restrict the territorial enlargement of it. Neither party expected for the war the magnitude, or the duration, which it has already attained. Neither anticipated that the *cause* of the conflict might cease with, or even before, the conflict itself should cease.[18] Each looked for an easier triumph, and a result less fundamental and astounding. Both read the same Bible, and pray to the same God; and each invokes His aid against the other. It may seem strange that any men should dare to ask a just God's assistance in wringing their bread from the sweat of other men's faces; but let us judge not that we be not judged. The prayers of both could not be answered; that of neither has been answered fully. The Almighty has His own purposes. "Woe unto the world because of offences! for it must needs be that offences come; but woe to that man by whom the offence cometh!"[19] If we shall suppose that American slavery is one of those offences which, in the providence of God, must needs come, but which, having continued through His appointed time, He now wills to remove, and that He gives to both North and South this terrible war, as the woe due to those by whom the offence came, shall we discern therein any departure from those divine attributes which the believers in a Living God always ascribe to Him? Fondly do we hope—fervently do we pray—that this mighty scourge of war may speedily pass away. Yet, if God wills that it continue, until all the wealth piled by the bondman's two hundred and fifty years of unrequited toil shall be sunk, and until every drop of blood drawn with the lash shall be paid by another drawn with the sword, as was said three thousand years ago, so still it must be said "the judgments of the Lord are true and righteous altogether."[20]

With malice toward none; with charity for all; with firmness in the right, as God gives us to see the right, let us strive on to finish the work we are in; to bind up the nation's wounds; to care for him who shall have borne the battle, and for his widow, and his orphan—to do all which may achieve and cherish a just, and a lasting peace, among ourselves, and with all nations.

Notes

1. For example, the very first issue of *Communication Reports* (vol. 1, 1988) featured five articles on Lincoln's Second Inaugural. Other in-depth rhetorical/historical analyses of the speech include Amy Slagell, "Anatomy of a Masterpiece," *Communication Studies* 42, no. 2 (1991): 155–71, doi:10.1080/10510979109368330; Edwin Black, "The Ultimate Voice of Lincoln," *Rhetoric and Public Affairs* 3, no. 1 (2000): 49–57, doi:10.1353/rap.2010.0125; Andrew C. Hansen, "Dimensions of Agency in Lincoln's Second Inaugural," *Philosophy and Rhetoric* 37, no. 3 (2004), 223–54, doi:10.1353/par.2004.0021; Don J. Kramer, "'It May Seem Strange': Strategic Exclusions in Lincoln's Second Inaugural," *Rhetoric Review* 27, no. 2 (2008): 165–84,

doi:10.1080/07350190801921776; Ronald C. White Jr., *Lincoln's Greatest Speech: The Second Inaugural* (New York: Simon & Schuster, 2002).
2. Hansen, 251.
3. Frederick Douglass, *Autobiographies* (New York: Library of America, 1994; reprint of 1893 ed.), 801, qtd. in White, 184.
4. See White, 184, 199.
5. Ibid., 182.
6. This is an allusion to Matthew 7:1.
7. Kenneth Burke, *Attitudes Toward History*, 3rd ed. (Berkeley: University of California Press, 1984), 166.
8. Gregory Desilet, *Our Faith in Evil: Melodrama and the Effects of Entertainment Violence* (Jefferson, NC: McFarland, 2006).
9. See Burke, *Attitudes Toward History*, 188–89.
10. Frederick Douglass, "Oration by Frederick Douglass Delivered on the Occasion of the Unveiling of the Freedman's Monument in Memory of Abraham Lincoln," April 14, 1876 (Washington DC: Gibson Brothers, 1876), 5, Frederick Douglass Papers, Library of Congress, https://cdn.loc.gov/service/rbc/lcrbmrp/t0c12/t0c12.pdf.
11. Ibid., 10.
12. Kirt H. Wilson, "Debating the Great Emancipator: Abraham Lincoln and Our Public Memory," *Rhetoric & Public Affairs* 13 (2010), 460.
13. Ibid., 462.
14. Black, 51.
15. See White, 133–49.
16. By "contest," Lincoln means the Civil War.
17. This refers to Southern legislators who were working on terms of political secession from the Union.
18. Here Lincoln is alluding to the Emancipation Proclamation, a wartime executive order that had freed slaves in Confederate states, giving the Union an economic and military advantage (since many slaves then joined the Union army as it advanced).
19. Matthew 18:7 (King James Version).
20. Psalm 19:9 (King James Version).

CHAPTER TWO

Redressing a Grave Injustice: U.S. Rep. Thaddeus Stevens

If Lincoln was committed above all to restoring national unity after the Civil War, his Republican colleague in the House of Representatives, Thaddeus Stevens, was a firebrand for justice. A member of the Radical Republican faction, Stevens not only fiercely opposed slavery but also strongly advocated for the equal rights of African Americans. His vision of post-war reconstruction focused less on "charity for all" than justice for the North and for black Americans, as he sought from the Confederacy a recompense for the costs of the war and a redistribution of property to freed slaves, who otherwise would have no means of economic survival (apart from employment by their former masters, which would mean virtual slavery).

When Lincoln ran for reelection as a Republican in 1864, he chose a Southern Democrat, Andrew Johnson, as his running mate. A Tennessean and former slaveholder, Johnson had remained loyal to the Union even after his state joined the Confederacy in 1861. His inclusion on the presidential ticket was designed to signal a commitment to reunifying the North and South. During the campaign, Johnson promised that he would be black Americans' "Moses," leading them out of bondage. When Lincoln was tragically assassinated on April 15, 1865—less than a week after the Union victory over the Confederacy—Johnson ascended to the presidency, and it fell to him to spearhead Reconstruction. As a Southern Democrat, Johnson worked to bring Southern states back into the Union quickly, mostly on their own terms, letting them determine the rights of former slaves within their borders. Although he granted amnesty and pardon to many Confederate leaders and allowed them to regain much of their former power, Johnson opposed voting rights for African Americans, and at one point suggested that they should return to Africa to establish their own colony—belying his claim to be their "Moses." White leaders in the South quickly took advantage of this situation, imposing harsh laws and taxes on black people. Moreover, in 1866 race riots broke out against newly freed African Americans in various places, especially in Memphis and New Orleans, and many were killed.

The following year, in an effort to ensure the well-being of former slaves, wounded Union soldiers, and other victims of the Confederacy, Pennsylvania Congressman Thaddeus Stevens introduced bill H.R. 20 in the House of Representatives. While the bill did not succeed in becoming law, Stevens's speech in its defense explains his Radical Republican vision of *justice through reparation* in a morally reconciled nation. H.R. 20 authorizes the federal government to confiscate some of the property of "belligerent traitors" (Confederates), not only as "a punishment for the great crime of war to destroy the Republic," but also for three reparative purposes: to provide more adequate pensions for wounded Union soldiers who were no longer able to work for a living; to provide compensation to loyal Unionists from both North and South whose property had been confiscated or destroyed by "rebel raiders and rebel legislatures"; and finally, to provide former slaves with land of their own so that they could realize their human rights to *life, liberty, and the pursuit of happiness* rather than being forced to work as virtual slaves on the plantations of their former masters. On the whole, Stevens frames national reconstruction through a tragic frame of injustice and due punishment—while nodding to the hope of peace between North and South, black and white, because of their civic and economic interdependence.

From Stevens's lengthy speech, just the section on reparations to former slaves is excerpted below. While endnotes clarify the meanings of archaic word usages, some of his remarks require contextual clarification here. First, Stevens makes sarcastic allusions to Andrew Johnson's claim to be black Americans' "Moses," since Johnson had proved to be nothing of the sort. Second, the vast majority of slaves were illiterate, had received no formal education of any kind, and were never taught how to work for themselves and compete in a free market. Thus, while Stevens firmly believes in African Americans' equality as human beings and their entitlement to equal rights (including the right to vote), he takes a pragmatic view of their situation, arguing that the first order of business for the government is to designate parcels of land to be held in trust for the former slaves, allowing them to work this land until they have enough knowledge and experience to become its full owners and fend for themselves without being easily taken advantage of. Since property owners and heads of households traditionally were men, Stevens specifies that each adult male freedman receive 40 acres of land. General Sherman of the Union army had promised that when the war ended, liberated slaves would be given "40 acres and a mule"; this idea actually had emerged through conversations with Stevens and his abolitionist colleagues. In H.R. 20, the mule provision was replaced with a proposal that $100 be allocated "to build a dwelling" on the land.

Besides arguing that former slaves need their own land so they can live and work as free citizens, Stevens's speech offers three other arguments. First, he cites President Andrew Johnson's expressed fears that a race war might come if former slaves were given full rights as Americans. Turning Johnson's argument on its head, Stevens suggests that *failure* to give black people their rights will lead to war by putting them in a position where they must take up arms to defend themselves from abuse. Second, he makes an argument from human interdependence: if black people are allowed to work for themselves, they will be industrious and productive, which will not only make them good citizens but also benefit the South economically by fully farming its land—a benefit that will be lost if they are sent back to Africa.

Third, in response to other politicians' religious arguments against slave reparations, Stevens makes a passionate argument *for* reparations from the Bible, citing both the principle of justice and the story of the Jews' liberation from Egyptian slavery as evidence that reparation is owed to slaves. If the Jews, who suffered under a much less severe form of bondage, were commanded by the divine Judge to request valuables from their Egyptian neighbors to support them on their freedom journey, how much more should former slaves in America expect remuneration for their long years of unpaid service? Turning the tables on opponents' claim that giving land as compensation to former slaves is a "Satanic" idea, Stevens suggests that rejecting this obligation would in fact be "blasphemy" against God. Lincoln had cast the Civil War as a form of divine punishment for slavery; Stevens now warns that failure to make reparation to the liberated slaves will lead to divine punishment through disease or war. He ends with a plea not to be distracted from justice by an empty comparison between defeated Southern rebels and the repentant Prodigal Son (of the parable told by Jesus), whose father welcomed him back with forgiveness and a feast ("the fatted calf").

If Andrew Johnson erred on the side of welcoming back Southern states without justice for black people, some have faulted Stevens with being vindictive toward the South. In his defense, historian Hans L. Trefousse argues that Stevens was primarily motivated by the goal of racial equality,[1] a claim confirmed by Stevens's plea that at least the slave reparations provision of H.R. 20 must pass, even if Congress would reject the other provisions. Unfortunately, it did not gain enough support to become law. Instead, cruel and unequal treatment of black people soon settled like a dark cloud over the nation and remained for another century. Jim Crow segregation in the South, housing and job discrimination in the North, and the resulting legacy of black poverty in the present have extended the moral mandate of reparations to today's descendants of African-American slaves. Since 1989, a bill that would authorize the creation of a Commission to Study Reparation Proposals for African-Americans has been introduced in Congress, year after year. Its identifying code, H.R. 40, alludes to the number of acres originally promised to ex-slaves. At the time of this writing, it has never gained passage.

Remarks on the Slave Reparations Provision[2] of H.R. 20

U.S. Capitol, Washington, DC
March 19, 1867

.... The fourth section provides, first, that out of the lands thus confiscated, each liberated slave who is a male adult, or the head of a family, shall have assigned to him a homestead of 40 acres of land (with $100 to build a dwelling), which shall be held for them by trustees during their pupilage.[3] Let us consider whether this is a just and politic provision.

Whatever may be the fate of the rest of the bill, I must earnestly pray that this may not be defeated. On its success, in my judgment, depends not only the happiness and respectability of the colored race, but their very existence. Homesteads to them are far more valuable than the immediate right of suffrage,[4] though both are their due.

Four million of persons have just been freed from a condition of dependence, wholly unacquainted with business transactions, kept systematically in ignorance of all their rights and of the common elements of education, without which none of any race are competent to earn an honest living, to guard against the frauds which will always be practiced on the ignorant, or to judge of the most judicious manner of applying their labor. But few of them are mechanics, and none of them skilled manufacturers. They must, therefore, be the servants and victims of others, unless they are made in some measure independent of their wiser neighbors.[5] The guardianship of the Freedmen's Bureau,[6] that benevolent institution, cannot be expected long to protect them. It encounters the hostility of the old slaveholders, whether in official or private station, because it deprives these dethroned tyrants of the luxury of despotism. In its nature it is not calculated for a permanent institution.[7] Withdraw that protection and leave them a prey to the legislation and treatment of their former masters, and the evidence already furnished shows that they will soon become extinct, or driven to defend themselves by civil war.[8]

Withhold from them all their rights, and leave them destitute of the means of earning a livelihood, the victims of the hatred or cupidity[9] of the rebels whom they helped to conquer, and it seems probable that the war of races might ensue which the President feared would arise from kind treatment and the restoration of their rights. I doubt not that hundreds of thousands would annually be deposited in secret, unknown graves. Such is already the course of their rebel murderers; and it is done with impunity ...[10]

Make them independent of their old masters, so that they may not be compelled to work for them upon unfair terms, which can only be done by giving them a small tract of land to cultivate for themselves, and you remove all this danger. You also elevate the character of the freedman. Nothing is so likely to make a man a good citizen as to make him a freeholder.[11] Nothing will so multiply the productions of the South as to divide it into small farms. Nothing will make men so industrious and moral as to let them feel that they are above want and are the owners of the soil which they till. It will also be of service to the white inhabitants. They will have constantly among them industrious laborers, anxious to work for fair wages. How is it possible for them to cultivate their lands if these people were expelled? If "Moses" should lead or drive them into exile,[12] or carry out the absurd idea of colonizing them,[13] the South would become a barren waste.

.... They and their ancestors have toiled,[14] not for years, but for ages, without one farthing of recompense.[15] They have earned for their masters this very land and much more. Will not he who denies them compensation now be accursed, for he is an unjust man? Have we not upon this subject the recorded decision of a Judge who never erred? Four million Jews were held in bondage in Egypt. Their slavery was mild compared with the slavery inflicted by Christians. For of all recorded slavery—pagan, heathen, or Mohammedan[16]—Christian slavery has been the most cruel and heartless; and of all Christian slavery, American slavery has been the worst. God, through no pretended, but a true Moses,[17] led them out of bondage, as in our case, through a Red sea, at the cost, as in our case, of the first born of every household of the oppressor. Did he advise them to take no remuneration for their years of labor? No! He understood too well what was due to justice. He commanded the men and the women to borrow[18] from their confiding[19] neighbors "jewels of silver and jewels of gold and raiment."[20] They obeyed him amply, and spoiled[21] the Egyptians, and went forth full-handed. There was no blasphemer then to question God's decree of confiscation. This doctrine then was not "Satanic." He who questions it now will be a blasphemer, whom God will bring to judgment. If we refuse to this down-trodden and oppressed race the rights which Heaven decreed them, and the remuneration which they have earned through long years of hopeless oppression, how can we hope to escape still further punishment if

God is just and omnipotent? It may come in the shape of plagues or of internecine wars—race against race, the oppressed against the oppressor. But come it will. Seek not to divert our attention from justice by a puerile cry of fatted calves![22]

Notes

1. Hans L. Trefousse, *Thaddeus Stevens: Nineteenth-Century Egalitarian* (Chapel Hill, NC: University of North Carolina Press, 1997).
2. An image of the complete text of Stevens's speech as originally published is found at https://archive.org/details/speechofhontstev01stev/page/n6. A digitized (and unedited) version of that text is available at https://archive.org/stream/speechofhontstev01stev/speechofhontstev01stev_djvu.txt.
3. In other words, until they learn how to make a living as free men.
4. I.e., the right to vote.
5. By "wiser," Stevens means more educated or experienced in the ways of business.
6. The Freedmen's Bureau was a temporary federal agency created in 1865 to make sure that freed slaves and other refugees of the Civil War were provided with basic amenities and protection.
7. Although the Bureau's authorization had been renewed beyond the original one-year period, and it continued until 1872, by design it was only a temporary agency.
8. Here and in the next sentence, where Stevens starts with an imperative verb ("Withdraw that protection," "Withhold from them,") he is not giving a direction or suggestion; he is using an implicit form of the construction "If you do x, then y will happen." In short, he is warning against these actions.
9. In other words, *greed*.
10. Here, a technical detail has been omitted and a paragraph break inserted for ease of comprehension.
11. I.e., a landowner.
12. Stevens is making a sarcastic reference to President Andrew Johnson's promise to be "Moses."
13. I.e., make them return to Africa to live in a colony there.
14. In the full speech transcript, this paragraph begins with an extended example from Russian history to illustrate the wisdom of land reparations to former slaves.
15. A farthing is one-quarter of a penny in British currency.
16. Here, using the archaic terminology of his day, Stevens is referring to peoples who worshipped idols, peoples who practiced "primitive" religions, and Muslims, respectively.
17. Here, Stevens is contrasting the real Moses with Andrew Johnson's empty claim to be "Moses" to black Americans.
18. I.e., "ask."
19. I.e., "nearby."
20. Here, Stevens is quoting Exodus 3:22 in the Bible translation of his day (King James Version). "Raiment" means clothing.
21. I.e., "plundered."
22. In the parable of the Prodigal Son, the father was so overjoyed at his wayward son's return that he ordered the slaughter of his best (fattest) calf for a celebration feast.

CHAPTER THREE

Clearing the Way of Peace on Earth: Martin Luther King Jr.

Nearly a century after Lincoln gave his Second Inaugural Address, Martin Luther King Jr. delivered his famous "I Have a Dream" speech from the steps of the Lincoln Memorial. It was the final address of the 1963 March on Washington, aimed at galvanizing the civil rights movement, explaining the rationale and goals of the movement to the nation, and giving politicians in Washington, DC added impetus to pass civil rights legislation.

While "I Have a Dream" is King's most famous address (and one of the greatest speeches in U.S. history),[1] for this book a different speech has been selected—"A Christmas Sermon on Peace"—because of its clear articulation of the philosophy underlying King's pursuit of reconciliation and social justice in the world. Delivered on Christmas Eve, 1967, in Ebenezer Baptist Church (where King was co-pastor), this sermon was broadcast live by the Canadian Broadcasting Corporation (CBC) as part of their prestigious Massey Lectures series.[2] In an interesting twist, at the end of the speech King revisits his "I Have a Dream" motif, adapting and renewing it in light of what he had seen happen across the nation in the four years following the March on Washington.

King uses the famous Christmas story of the angels singing "Peace on earth, and good will to men" as a springboard to explore the conditions that make for peace. Speaking at the height of the Cold War in an age of nuclear weapons, King regards this to be an especially pressing question. True to his philosophy of personalism and nonviolence,[3] King forges a strong connection between *ontology* (philosophical understandings of the ultimate nature of reality, including human nature) and *axiology* (conceptions of what is ultimately right or good). For King, certain actions are good and right because they align with the very nature of the world—if not on the surface level of day-to-day material existence, then at a deeper, spiritual level.

First, King argues, we must widen our loyalties beyond those who are just like us and become committed to all human beings as brothers and sisters. His reason for this is an ontological premise: *all humans are interconnected*. As King famously puts it, "We are all caught in an inescapable network of mutuality, tied in a single garment of destiny." King gives examples from everyday life to help his listeners see how interdependent they are with people from around the world. Notice how this perspective aligns with the comic frame, focusing on the commonality and connections underlying people's differences and divisions. In working for racial justice, King's ultimate aim was *Beloved Community*, "a global vision, in which all people can share in the wealth of the earth ... poverty, hunger and homelessness will not be tolerated ... Racism and all forms of discrimination, bigotry and prejudice will be replaced by an all-inclusive spirit of sisterhood and brotherhood."[4] King had cast this kind of vision in his March on Washington address, imagining a time when diverse people would "sit down together at the table of brotherhood" and "all of God's children" would join hands to sing "Free at Last."[5]

Next, King addresses a question of axiology: What is the right way to go about achieving peace? In response, King argues that the means of achieving a good end must be part and parcel of that end. Here, he transcends the gap between two approaches to ethics: *deontological* (based on the idea that we should do only what is intrinsically right, regardless of the outcome) and *consequentialist* (that we should do whatever would produce the best outcome—or, in its cruder form, "The end justifies the means"). King argues that when it comes to the goal of justice, only peaceful/nonviolent means can actually achieve that end, "because the means represent the seed and the end represents the tree." Only a nonviolent approach to resolving conflicts and injustice can remove the injustice of violence and lead to lasting peace. This idea relates to the reconciliation tetrad, in which peace and justice are essentially connected; therefore, one cannot coherently promote justice without simultaneously promoting peace.

King's third point is related to his first: to achieve peace, we must recognize that every person has sacred value as a child of God. Since they *are* of such value in their very nature (ontology), we *should recognize* their intrinsic worth (axiology). In terms of the tetrad, human agency should be protected; all humans should be treated not as things to be used but as persons to be respected and loved, bearers of divine grace. King elaborates on this idea by talking about three types of love.

The sacredness of humanity, he says, does not require that we *like* everyone, which would be impossible, especially with those who abuse or oppress us. What we can and should do, however, is practice a kind of love that the New Testament, in its original Greek text, refers to as *agape*—which King defines as "understanding, creative, redemptive good will for all [people]." (This idea closely aligns with *grace*, the capacity to will and act for another's well-being, regardless of any bad they may have done.) Notice that King here affirms the need to continue pursuing justice, to "work passionately and unrelentingly ... to remove every vestige of segregation and discrimination from our nation." Rather than contradicting justice, *agape* love—like grace—lends empathy, dignity, creativity, and redemption to the pursuit of justice. This means confronting injustice nonviolently, with "soul force" as King puts it, even when oppressors inflict violence on those who do so. By meeting strong hate with a stronger love, "We will not only win freedom for ourselves; we will so appeal to your heart and conscience that we will win you in the process, and our victory will be a double victory."

The final condition King identifies for achieving peace in the world is an ontological belief in "the ultimate morality of the universe ... that all reality hinges on moral foundations." As a Christian minister, King cites the death and resurrection of Christ as proof that "no lie can live forever" and good must ultimately triumph over evil. It is this confidence, he argues, that makes it possible to love one's enemies and keep up the nonviolent struggle for justice in the face of violent injustice.

King concludes by revisiting the theme of "I Have a Dream." In the years since that speech, King confesses, he has seen his dream of equality and brotherhood turn into a nightmare: violent backlash from vicious racists, unresolved poverty in urban ghettos, misguided rioting by angry black communities, and the escalation of the war in Vietnam. (Indeed, scholars have noted that King's rhetoric grew more tragic in tone during those later years.[6]) Facing these challenges realistically, he reaffirms his dream nonetheless, recycling a number of phrases from his most famous speech—many of which are taken from Scripture. Armed with the philosophical and theological faith he has so eloquently articulated, King refuses to let go of the romantic vision of Beloved Community he had immortalized at the 1963 March on Washington.

A Christmas Sermon on Peace[7]

Ebenezer Baptist Church, Atlanta, Georgia
December 24, 1967

"Peace on earth." This Christmas season finds us a rather bewildered human race. We neither have peace within nor peace without. Everywhere paralyzing fears

harrow people by day and haunt them by night. Our world is sick with war; everywhere we turn we see its ominous possibilities. And yet, my friends, the Christmas hope for peace and good will toward all men can no longer be dismissed as a kind of pious dream of some utopian hoper. If we don't have good will toward men in this world, we will destroy ourselves by the misuse of our own instruments and our own power. Wisdom born of experience should tell us that war is obsolete. There may have been a time when war served as a negative good by preventing the spread and growth of an evil force, but the very destructive power of modern weapons of warfare eliminates even the possibility that war may any longer serve as a negative good. So, if we assume that life is worth living, if we assume that mankind has a right to survive, then we must find an alternative to war. And so let us this morning explore the conditions for peace. And as we explore these conditions, I would like to suggest that modern man really go all out to study the meaning of nonviolence, its philosophy, and its strategy.

We have experimented with the meaning of nonviolence in our struggle for racial justice in the United States, but now the time has come for man to experiment with nonviolence in all areas of human conflict, and that means nonviolence on an international scale.

Now let me suggest first that if we are to have peace on earth, our loyalties must become ecumenical rather than sectional. Our loyalties must transcend our race, our tribe, our class, and our nation; and this means we must develop a world perspective.[8] No individual can live alone; no nation can live alone, and as long as we try, the more we are going to have war in this world. Now the judgment of God is upon us, and we must either learn to live together as brothers or we are all going to perish together as fools....[9]

It really boils down to this: that all life is interrelated. We are all caught in an inescapable network of mutuality, tied in a single garment of destiny—that whatever affects one directly, affects all indirectly. We are made to live together because of the interrelated structure of reality. Did you ever stop to think that you can't leave for your job in the morning without being dependent on most of the world? You get up in the morning and go to the bathroom and reach over for the sponge, and that's handed to you by a Pacific islander. You reach for the bar of soap, and that's given to you at the hands of a Frenchman. And then you go in the kitchen to drink your coffee for the morning, and that's poured in your cup by a South American. And maybe you want tea: that's poured in your cup by a Chinese. Or maybe you're desirous of having cocoa for breakfast, and that's poured in your cup by a West African. And then you reach over for your toast, and that's given to you at the hands of an English-speaking farmer, not to mention the baker. And before you finish eating breakfast in the morning, you've depended on more than half of the world. This is the way our universe is structured; it is its interrelated quality. We aren't going to have peace on earth until we recognize this basic fact of the interrelated structure of all reality.

Now let me say, secondly, that if we are to have peace in the world, men and nations must embrace the nonviolent affirmation that ends and means must cohere. One of the great philosophical debates of history has been over the whole question of means and ends. And there have always been those who argued that the end justifies the means, that the means really aren't important. The important thing is to get to the end, you see. So, if you're seeking to develop a just society, the important thing is to get there, and the means are really unimportant; any means will do as long as they get you there. They may be violent, they may be untruthful means; they may even be unjust means to get to a just end. There have been those who have argued this throughout history. But we will never have peace in the world until men everywhere recognize that ends are not cut off from means, because the means represent the ideal in the making, and the end in process, and ultimately you can't reach good ends through evil means, because the means represent the seed and the end represents the tree.

It's one of the strangest things that all the great military geniuses of the world have talked about peace. The conquerors of old came killing in pursuit of peace. Alexander, Julius Caesar, Charlemagne, and Napoleon were akin in seeking a peaceful world order. And do you know, if you will read *Mein Kampf* closely enough, Hitler contended that everything he did in Germany was for peace. And the leaders of the world today talk eloquently about peace. Every time we drop our bombs in North Vietnam, President Johnson is talking eloquently about peace. What is the problem? They are talking about peace as a distant goal, as an end we seek, but one day we must come to see that peace is not merely a distant goal that we seek, but it is a means by which we arrive at that goal. We must pursue peaceful ends through peaceful means. All of this is saying that, in the final analysis, means and ends must cohere because the end is preexistent in the means, and ultimately destructive means cannot bring about constructive ends.

Now let me say that the next thing we must be concerned about if we are to have peace on earth and good will toward men must be the nonviolent affirmation of the sacredness of all human life. Life is sacred. Every man is somebody because he is a child of God. And so when we say "Thou shalt not kill," we're really saying that human life is too sacred to be killed on the battlefields of the world. Man is more than a tiny vagary of whirling electrons or a wisp of smoke from a limitless smoldering. Man is a child of God, made in His image, and therefore must be respected as such. Until men see this everywhere, until nations see this everywhere, we will be fighting wars. One day somebody should remind us that even though there may be political and ideological differences between us, the Vietnamese are our brothers, the Russians are our brothers, the Chinese are our brothers; and one day we've got to sit down together at the table of brotherhood. But in Christ there is neither Jew nor Gentile. In Christ there is neither male nor female. In Christ there is neither communist nor capitalist. In Christ, somehow, there is neither bound nor free. We are all one in Christ Jesus. And when we truly believe in the sacredness of human personality, we won't exploit people, we won't trample over people with the iron feet of oppression, we won't kill anybody.

There are three words for "love" in the Greek New Testament; one is the word "*eros.*" *Eros* is a sort of aesthetic, romantic love. Plato used to talk about it a great deal in his dialogues, the yearning of the soul for the realm of the divine. And there is and can always be something beautiful about *eros*, even in its expressions of romance. Some of the most beautiful love in all of the world has been expressed this way.

Then the Greek language talks about "*phileo,*" which is another word for love, and *phileo* is a kind of intimate love between personal friends. This is the kind of love that you have for those people that you get along with well; and those that you like on this level you love because you are loved. You love those people that appeal to you and those that you like.

Then the Greek language comes up with another word for love; it is the word "*agape.*" *Agape* is more than romantic love, it is more than friendship. *Agape* is understanding, creative, redemptive good will for all men. *Agape* is an overflowing love which seeks nothing in return. Theologians would say that it is the love of God operating in the human heart. And so, when you rise to love on this level, you love all men not because you like them, not because their ways appeal to you, but you love every man because God loves them. This is what Jesus meant when he said, "Love your enemies." And I'm happy that he didn't say, "Like your enemies," because there are some people that I find it pretty difficult to like. *Like* is an affectionate emotion, and I can't like anybody bombing my home. I can't like anybody who would exploit me. I can't like anybody who would trample over me with injustices. I can't like them. I can't like anybody who threatens to kill me day in and day out. But Jesus reminds us that *love* is greater than *like*. Love is understanding, creative, redemptive good will for all men. And I think this is where we are, as a people, in our struggle for racial justice. We can't ever give up. We must work passionately and unrelentingly for first-class citizenship. We must never let up in our determination to remove every vestige of segregation and discrimination from our nation, but we shall not in the process relinquish our privilege to love.

I've seen too much hate to want to hate, myself, and I've seen hate on the faces of too many sheriffs, too many White Citizens' Councilors, and too many

Klansmen of the South to want to hate, myself; and every time I see it, I say to myself, hate is too great a burden to bear. Somehow we must be able to stand up before our most bitter opponents and say: "We shall match your capacity to inflict suffering by our capacity to endure suffering. We will meet your physical force with soul force. Do to us what you will and we will still love you. We cannot in all good conscience obey your unjust laws and abide by the unjust system, because non-cooperation with evil is as much a moral obligation as is cooperation with good, and so throw us in jail and we will still love you. Bomb our homes and threaten our children, and, as difficult as it is, we will still love you. Send your hooded perpetrators of violence into our communities at the midnight hour and drag us out on some wayside road and leave us half-dead as you beat us, and we will still love you. Send your propaganda agents around the country, and make it appear that we are not fit, culturally and otherwise, for integration, and we'll still love you. But be assured that we will wear you down by our capacity to suffer, and one day we will win our freedom. We will not only win freedom for ourselves; we will so appeal to your heart and conscience that we will win you in the process, and our victory will be a double victory."

If there is to be peace on earth and good will toward men, we must finally believe in the ultimate morality of the universe, and believe that all reality hinges on moral foundations. Something must remind us of this as we somehow stand in the Christmas season and think of the Easter season simultaneously, for the two somehow go together. Christ came to show us the way. Men love darkness rather than the light, and they crucified him, and there on Good Friday on the cross it was still dark, but then Easter came, and Easter is an eternal reminder of the fact that the truth-crushed earth will rise again. Easter justifies Carlyle in saying, "No lie can live forever." And so this is our faith, as we continue to hope for peace on earth and good will toward men: let us know that in the process we have cosmic companionship.

In 1963, on a sweltering August afternoon, we stood in Washington, D.C., and we talked to the nation about many things. Toward the end of that afternoon, I tried to talk to the nation about a dream that I had had, and I must confess to you today that not long after talking about that dream I started seeing it turn into a nightmare. I remember the first time I saw that dream turned into a nightmare, just a few weeks after I had talked about it. It was when four beautiful, unoffending, innocent Negro girls were murdered in a church in Birmingham, Alabama. I watched that dream turn into a nightmare as I moved through the ghettos of the nation and saw my black brothers and sisters perishing on a lonely island of poverty in the midst of a vast ocean of material prosperity, and saw the nation really doing nothing to grapple with the Negro's problem of poverty. I saw that dream turn into a nightmare as I watched my black brothers and sisters in the midst of anger and understandable outrage, in the midst of their hurt, in the midst of their disappointment, turn to misguided riots to try to solve that problem. I saw that dream turn to a nightmare as I watched the war in Vietnam escalating, and as I saw so-called military advisors, sixteen thousand strong, turn into fighting soldiers until today some five hundred thousand American boys are fighting on Asian soil. Yes, I am personally the victim of deferred dreams, of blasted hopes, but in spite of that I close today by saying I still have a dream, because, you know, you can't give up in life. If you lose hope, somehow you lose that vitality that keeps life moving, you lose that courage to be, that quality that helps you to go on "in spite of."

And so today I still have a dream that men will rise up and come to see that they are made to live together as brothers. I still have a dream this morning that one day every Negro in this country, every colored person in the world, will be judged on the basis of the content of his character rather than the color of his skin, and every man will respect the dignity and worth of human personality. I still have a dream today that one day the idle industries of Appalachia will be revitalized, the empty stomachs of Mississippi will be filled, and brotherhood will be more than a few words at the end of a prayer, but the first order of business on every legislative agenda. I still have a dream today that one day justice will roll down like waters, and righteousness like a mighty stream.[10] I still have a dream today that in all of our state houses and city halls men will be elected to go there who will do justly and love mercy and walk humbly with their God.[11] I still have a dream today that one day war will come to an end, and men will beat their swords into plowshares and their spears into pruning hooks, and nations will no longer rise up against nations, neither will they study war any more.[12] I still have a dream today that one day the lamb and the lion will lie down together and every man will sit under his own vine and fig tree and none shall be afraid.[13] I still have a dream today that one day every valley shall be exalted and every mountain and hill will be made low, the rough places will be made plain and the crooked places straight, the glory of the Lord shall be revealed, and all flesh shall see it together.[14] I still have a dream that with this faith we will be able to adjourn the councils of despair and bring new light into the dark chambers of pessimism. With this faith we will be able to speed up the day when there will be peace on earth and good will toward men.[15] It will be a glorious day, the morning stars will sing together, and the sons of God will shout for joy.[16]

Notes

1. Numerous rhetoric scholars have examined "I Have a Dream" in depth. Studies of the religious/theological elements of the speech include John H. Patton, "'I Have a Dream': The Performance of Theology Fused with the Power of Orality," in *Martin Luther King Jr. and the Sermonic Power of Public Discourse*, ed. Carolyn Calloway-Thomas and John L. Lucaites (Tuscaloosa: University of Alabama Press, 1993), 104–26; David Bobbitt and Harold Mixon, "Prophecy and Apocalypse in the Rhetoric of Martin Luther King, Jr.," *Journal of Communication & Religion* 17, no. 1 (1994): 27–38; Mark Vail, "The 'Integrative' Rhetoric of Martin Luther King Jr.'s 'I Have a Dream' Speech, *Rhetoric & Public Affairs* 9, no. 1 (2006): 51–78, doi:10.1353/rap.2006.0032; Keith D. Miller, "Second Isaiah Lands in Washington, DC: Martin Luther King, Jr.'s 'I Have a Dream' as Biblical Narrative and Biblical Hermeneutic," *Rhetoric Review* 26, no. 4 (2007): 405–24, doi:10.1080/07350190701577926.
2. King gave five Massey lectures that year, which were later compiled in Martin Luther King Jr., *The Trumpet of Conscience* (Boston: Beacon Press, 2010).
3. For a brief synopsis of King's philosophy, see John B. Hatch, "Martin Luther King, Jr.," *An Encyclopedia of Communication Ethics: Goods in Contention* (New York: Peter Lang, 2018), 263–67.
4. "The King Philosophy," *The King Center*, https://thekingcenter.org/king-philosophy/.
5. Martin Luther King Jr., "I Have a Dream," speech delivered August 28, 1963, *American Rhetoric*, https://www.americanrhetoric.com/speeches/mlkihaveadream.htm.
6. For example, see Edward C. Appel, "The Rhetoric of Dr. Martin Luther King, Jr.: Comedy and Context in Tragic Collision," *Western Journal of Communication* 61, no. 4 (1997): 376–402, doi:0.1080/10570319709374586; Andre E. Johnson and Anthony J. Stone Jr., "'The Most Dangerous Negro in America': Rhetoric, Race and the Prophetic Pessimism of Martin Luther King Jr.," *Journal of Communication & Religion* 41, no. 1 (2018): 8–22.
7. A complete text of the speech is found in King, *The Trumpet of Conscience*, 67–80; it is reprinted here (with abridgement of one paragraph) by arrangement with The Heirs to the Estate of Martin Luther King Jr., c/o Writers House as agent for the proprietor, New York, NY (© 1967 Martin Luther King, Jr. © renewed 1995 Coretta Scott King). For this book, minor corrections have been made to the wording of the originally published version to more accurately match King's oral delivery, found at https://www.youtube.com/watch?v=1jeyIAH3bUI.
8. In the accessed recording of King's delivery, this sentence is omitted.
9. In a paragraph omitted here, King digresses to talk about his visit to India, the rampant desperate poverty he witnessed there, and his realization that the United States had enough surplus food to feed the hungry of the world.
10. Amos 5:24.
11. Micah 6:8.
12. Micah 4:3.
13. Isaiah 11:6; Micah 4:4.
14. Isaiah 40:4–5.
15. Luke 2:14.
16. Job 38:7.

CHAPTER FOUR

Exposing Injustice against a Horizon of Reconciliation: Desmond Tutu

If the American South was infamous for its policy of racial segregation until the 1960s, the Republic of South Africa was similarly infamous for its system of *apartheid*—enforced racial separateness—until the 1990s. Unlike African Americans, blacks in South Africa were indigenous inhabitants, like Native Americans in the United States. As Dutch and British settlers colonized the territory over two and a half centuries, black Africans increasingly lost control of their land, and eventually a system of "pass laws" restricted their movements. When South Africa transitioned to full independence from the United Kingdom in the first decades of the 20th century, only white citizens were granted voting rights, and laws were passed to further restrict black freedom and property ownership. Residents of East Indian descent—including a young lawyer named Mohandas Gandhi—were similarly subjected to restrictions, and it was in South Africa that Gandhi began to develop and practice the philosophy of nonviolent resistance that he eventually applied on a mass scale in India's independence movement.

After South Africa's National Party came into power in 1948, the government began to implement a thoroughgoing system of apartheid that legally separated all South Africans into four races and apportioned unequal rights and limitations to these races, including the forced removal of many black South Africans from their homes in urban centers to undesirable "bantustan homelands" or "reserves," similar to American Indian reservations. As non-white South Africans increasingly resisted these oppressive measures in the 1960s–1980s, police responded to mass protests with violent massacres, and many anti-apartheid activists were imprisoned, including Nelson Mandela.

It was during this period of unrest and repression that a black cleric in the Anglican Church, Desmond Mpilo Tutu, rose to prominence as a leader in several multi-racial Christian institutions and a vocal opponent of apartheid. Influenced by Scripture, black theology, and African conceptions of humanity, Tutu spoke out on behalf of activists who were struggling against apartheid (he insisted on a nonviolent approach but acknowledged the justice of their cause and the reasons they resorted to violent resistance); endorsed an international economic boycott against South Africa over its racist policies; appealed directly to government leaders in his country and other nations to work to end apartheid; and suffered both arrest and temporary confiscation of his passport for doing so. As a result, Tutu became an icon of black South Africans' struggle for racial equality, and in 1984, he was awarded the Nobel Peace Prize for his efforts. In his Nobel Lecture (below), he explained the South African situation and his vision of just reconciliation to an international audience.

Tutu begins his speech in the midst of the cruel violence plaguing South Africa under apartheid, giving two heartrending examples in which children were slain—one black, one white. He goes on to detail another example of apartheid's cruelty: black wives from rural areas were not allowed to live with or near their husbands in the urban areas where the men had gone to find work. (These male employees were forced to live in single-sex hostels or else lose their jobs.) Stepping back for a moment to create a contrast, Tutu describes the natural beauty and bounty of his beloved land. He then quickly populates this scene with the brutal realities of South Africa's white supremacist government, laws, and policies. He contrasts the abundance of the land with the selfishness and meanness of apartheid. As Tutu details the sufferings of native black Africans under white rule, he presents this situation both in a tragic frame of justice—highlighting gross inequalities actively imposed by the apartheid government—and a comic frame of interdependence, virtually identical to that in King's "A Christmas Sermon on Peace." Like King, Tutu's perspective is deeply theological, premised on the belief that all people are made in God's image.

The bulk of this speech details the heinous facts of South African apartheid. Tutu views apartheid policies through a tragic lens of moral condemnation, decrying them as "selfish," "discriminatory," "racist," "wasteful," "iniquitous," "repressive," and "evil"; moreover, he compares apartheid to cancer, Hitler's Final Solution, and even blasphemy against God. In this tragic moral frame, Tutu notes that this evil system sows the seeds of its own destruction—a kind of built-in punishment.

Although the tragic frame dominates this speech, Tutu applies it only to the impersonal system of apartheid, not to the human beings who misguidedly manage that system. That is because Tutu's view of humanity, highlighted toward the end of the speech, can be characterized as *comic* in the serious sense of the term, emphasizing the interdependence and vulnerability of all persons. It is based on the African concept of *ubuntu*, which Tutu explains as follows in his book *No Future Without Forgiveness*: "We say, 'A person is a person through other persons.' It is not, 'I think therefore I am.' It says rather: 'I am human because I belong. I participate, I share.'"[1] In this light, Tutu can somewhat empathize with the human agents of oppression, pitying them for foolishly hurting themselves.

Like two eyes working together for depth perception, Tutu joins comic and tragic lenses when he declares, "We are not made for an exclusive self-sufficiency but for interdependence [comic frame], and we break the law of our being at our peril [tragic frame]." His concluding challenge reinforces such framing: "If we want peace, so we have been told, let us work for justice." Beyond these two values, reconciliation entails a host of ethical goods coming together, as captured in the Jewish notion of *shalom*. True to his faith as a Christian minister, Tutu envisions shalom being realized in the Biblical image of "all nations and kindreds and peoples and tongues" joyously gathered before God at the consummation of history—a vision akin to King's Beloved Community. Because of his faith in an ultimate Agent who freely created and redeemed the world, Tutu ends on a romantic note of praise and gratitude, in words quoted from the final book of the Bible.

1984 Nobel Lecture[2]

Oslo, Norway
December 11, 1984
Ladies and Gentlemen,

Before I left South Africa, a land I love passionately, we had an emergency meeting of the Executive Committee of the South African Council of Churches with the leaders of our member churches. We called the meeting because of the deepening crisis in our land, which has claimed nearly 200 lives this year alone. We visited some of the trouble-spots on the Witwatersrand. I went with others to the East Rand. We visited the home of an old lady. She told us that she looked after her grandson and the children of neighbors while their parents were at work. One day the police chased some pupils who had been boycotting classes, but they disappeared between the township houses. The police drove down the old lady's street. She was sitting at the back of the house in her kitchen, whilst her charges were playing in the front of the house in the yard. Her daughter rushed into the house, calling out to her to come quickly. The old lady dashed out of the kitchen into the living room. Her grandson had fallen just inside the door, dead. He had been shot in the back by the police. He was six years old. A few weeks later, a white mother, trying to register her black servant for work, drove through a black township. Black rioters stoned her car and killed her baby of a few months old, the first white casualty of the current unrest in South Africa. Such deaths are two too many. These are part of the high cost of apartheid.

Every day in a squatter camp near Cape Town called K.T.C., the authorities have been demolishing flimsy plastic shelters which black mothers have erected because they were taking their marriage vows seriously. They have been reduced to sitting on soaking mattresses, with their household effects strewn round their feet, and whimpering babies on their laps, in the cold Cape winter rain. Every day the authorities have carried out these callous demolitions. What heinous crime have these women committed, to be hounded like criminals in this manner? All they have wanted is to be with their husbands, the fathers of their children. Everywhere else in the world they would be highly commended, but in South Africa, a land which claims to be Christian, and which boasts a public holiday called Family Day, these gallant women are treated so inhumanely, and yet all they want is to have a decent and stable family life. Unfortunately, in the land of their birth, it is a criminal offence for them to live happily with their husbands and the fathers of their children. Black family life is thus being undermined, not accidentally, but by deliberate government policy. It is part of the price human beings, God's children, are called to pay for apartheid. An unacceptable price.

I come from a beautiful land, richly endowed by God with wonderful natural resources, wide expanses, rolling mountains, singing birds, bright shining stars out of blue skies, with radiant sunshine, golden sunshine. There is enough of the good things that come from God's bounty, there is enough for everyone, but apartheid has confirmed some in their selfishness, causing them to grasp greedily a disproportionate share, the lion's share, because of their power. They have taken 87% of the land, though being only about 20% of our population. The rest have had to make do with the remaining 13%. Apartheid has decreed the politics of exclusion. Seventy-three percent of the population is excluded from any meaningful participation in the political decision-making processes of the land of their birth. The new constitution, making provision of three chambers, for whites, coloreds, and Indians, mentions blacks only once, and thereafter ignores them completely. Thus this new constitution, lauded in parts of the West as a step in the right direction, entrenches racism and ethnicity. The constitutional committees are composed in the ratio of four whites to two coloreds and one Indian. *Zero black.* Two plus one can never equal, let alone be more than, four. Hence this constitution perpetuates by law and entrenches white minority rule. Blacks are expected to exercise their political ambitions in unviable, poverty-stricken, arid, bantustan homelands, ghettoes of misery, inexhaustible reservoirs of cheap black labor, bantustans into which South Africa is being balkanized. Blacks are systematically being stripped of their South African citizenship and being turned into aliens in the land of their birth. This is apartheid's final solution, just as Nazism had its final solution for the Jews in Hitler's Aryan madness. The South African Government is smart. Aliens can claim but very few rights, least of all political rights.

In pursuance of apartheid's ideological racist dream, over three million of God's children have been uprooted from their homes, which have been demolished, whilst they have then been dumped in the bantustan homeland resettlement camps. I say dumped advisedly: only things or rubbish is dumped, not human beings. Apartheid has, however, ensured that God's children, just because they are black, should be treated as if they were things, and not as of infinite value as being created in the image of God. These dumping grounds are far from where work and food can be procured easily. Children starve, suffer from the often-irreversible consequences of malnutrition—this happens to them not accidentally, but by deliberate government policy. They starve in a land that could be the bread basket of Africa, a land that normally is a net exporter of food.

The father leaves his family in the bantustan homeland, there eking out a miserable existence, whilst he, if he is lucky, goes to the so-called white man's town as a migrant, to live an unnatural life in a single-sex hostel for 11 months of the year, being prey there to prostitution, drunkenness, and worse. This migratory labor policy is declared government policy, and has been condemned, even by the white Dutch Reformed Church, not noted for being quick to criticize the government, as a cancer in our society. This cancer, eating away at the vitals of black family life, is deliberate government policy. It is part of the cost of apartheid, exorbitant in terms of human suffering.

Apartheid has spawned discriminatory education, such as Bantu Education, education for serfdom, ensuring that the government spends only about one tenth on one black child per annum for education what it spends on a white child. It is education that is decidedly separate and unequal. It is to be wantonly wasteful of human resources, because so many of God's children are prevented, by deliberate government policy, from attaining to their fullest potential. South Africa is paying a heavy price already for this iniquitous policy because there is a desperate shortage of skilled manpower, a direct result of the short-sighted schemes of the racist regime. It is a moral universe that we inhabit, and good and right and equity matter in the universe of the God we worship. And so, in this matter, the South

African Government and its supporters are being properly hoisted with their own petard.

Apartheid is upheld by a phalanx of iniquitous laws, such as the Population Registration Act, which decrees that all South Africans must be classified ethnically, and duly registered according to these race categories. Many times, in the same family one child has been classified white whilst another, with a slightly darker hue, has been classified colored, with all the horrible consequences for the latter of being shut out from membership of a greatly privileged caste. There have, as a result, been several child suicides. This is too high a price to pay for racial purity, for it is doubtful whether any end, however desirable, can justify such a means. There are laws, such as the Prohibition of Mixed Marriages Act, which regard marriages between a white and a person of another race as illegal. Race becomes an impediment to a valid marriage. Two persons who have fallen in love are prevented by race from consummating their love in the marriage bond. Something beautiful is made to be sordid and ugly. The Immorality Act decrees that fornication and adultery are illegal if they happen between a white and one of another race. The police are reduced to the level of peeping Toms to catch couples red-handed. Many whites have committed suicide rather than face the disastrous consequences that follow in the train of even just being charged under this law. The cost is too great and intolerable.

Such an evil system, totally indefensible by normally acceptable methods, relies on a whole phalanx of draconian laws such as the security legislation which is almost peculiar to South Africa. There are the laws which permit the indefinite detention of persons whom the Minister of Law and Order has decided are a threat to the security of the State. They are detained at his pleasure, in solitary confinement, without access to their family, their own doctor, or a lawyer. That is severe punishment when the evidence apparently available to the Minister has not been tested in an open court—perhaps it could stand up to such rigorous scrutiny, perhaps not; we are never to know. It is a far too convenient device for a repressive regime, and the minister would have to be extra special not to succumb to the temptation to circumvent the awkward process of testing his evidence in an open court, and thus he lets his power under the law to be open to the abuse where he is both judge and prosecutor. Many, too many, have died mysteriously in detention. All this is too costly in terms of human lives. The minister is able, too, to place people under banning orders without being subjected to the annoyance of the checks and balances of due process. A banned person for three or five years becomes a non-person, who cannot be quoted during the period of her banning order. She cannot attend a "gathering," which means more than one other person. Two persons together talking to a banned person are a gathering! She cannot attend the wedding or funeral of even her own child without special permission. She must be at home from 6:00 p.m. of one day to 6:00 a.m. of the next and on all public holidays, and from 6:00 p.m. on Fridays until 6:00 a.m. on Mondays for three years. She cannot go on holiday outside the magisterial area to which she has been confined. She cannot go to the cinema, nor to a picnic. That is severe punishment, inflicted without the evidence allegedly justifying it being made available to the banned person, nor having it scrutinized in a court of law. It is a serious erosion and violation of basic human rights, of which blacks have precious few in the land of their birth. They do not enjoy the rights of freedom of movement and association. They do not enjoy freedom of security of tenure, the right to participate in the making of decisions that affect their lives. In short, this land, richly endowed in so many ways, is sadly lacking in justice.

Once a Zambian and a South African, it is said, were talking. The Zambian then boasted about their Minister of Naval Affairs. The South African asked, "But you have no navy, no access to the sea. How then can you have a Minister of Naval Affairs?" The Zambian retorted, "Well, in South Africa you have a Minister of Justice, don't you?"

It is against this system that our people have sought to protest peacefully since 1912 at least, with the founding of the African National Congress. They have used the conventional methods of peaceful protest—petitions, demonstrations, deputations, and even a passive resistance campaign. A tribute to our people's commitment to peaceful change is the fact that the only South Africans to win the Nobel Peace Prize are both black. Our people are peace-loving to a fault. The response of the authorities has been an escalating intransigence and violence, the violence of police dogs, tear gas, detention without trial, exile, and even death. Our people protested peacefully against the Pass Laws in 1960, and 69 of them were killed on March 21, 1960, at Sharpeville, many shot in the back running away. Our children protested against inferior education, singing songs and displaying placards and marching peacefully. Many in 1976, on June 16th and subsequent times, were killed or imprisoned. Over 500 people died in that uprising. Many children went into exile. The whereabouts of many are unknown to their parents. At present, to protest that self-same discriminatory education, and the exclusion of blacks from the new constitutional dispensation, the sham local black government, rising unemployment, increased rents and General Sales Tax, our people have boycotted and demonstrated. They have staged a successful two-day stay away. Over 150 people have been killed. It is far too high a price to pay. There has been little revulsion or outrage at this wanton destruction of human life in the West. In parenthesis, can somebody please explain to me something that has puzzled me. When a priest goes missing and is subsequently found dead, the media in the West carry his story in very extensive coverage. I am glad that the death of one person can cause so much concern. But in the self-same week when this priest is found dead, the South African police kill 24 blacks who had been participating in the protest, and 6,000 blacks are sacked[3] for being similarly involved, and you are lucky to get that much coverage. Are we being told something I do not want to believe, that we blacks are expendable and that blood is thicker than water, that when it comes to the crunch, you cannot trust whites, that they will club together against us? I don't want to believe that is the message being conveyed to us.

Be that as it may, we see before us a land bereft of much justice, and therefore without peace and security. Unrest is endemic, and will remain an unchanging feature of the South African scene until apartheid, the root cause of it all, is finally dismantled. At this time, the Army is being quartered on the civilian population. There is a civil war being waged. South Africans are on either side. When the African National Congress and the Pan-Africanist Congress were banned in 1960, they declared that they had no option but to carry out the armed struggle. We in the South African Council of Churches have said we are opposed to all forms of violence—that of a repressive and unjust system, and that of those who seek to overthrow that system. However, we have added that we understand those who say they have had to adopt what is a last resort for them. Violence is not being introduced into the South African situation *de novo* from outside by those who are called terrorists or freedom fighters, depending on whether you are oppressed or an oppressor. The South African situation is violent already, and the primary violence is that of apartheid, the violence of forced population removals, of inferior education, of detention without trial, of the migratory labor system, etc.

There is war on the border of our country. South African faces fellow South African. South African soldiers are fighting against Namibians who oppose the illegal occupation of their country by South Africa, which has sought to extend its repressive system of apartheid, unjust and exploitative.

There is no peace in Southern Africa. There is no peace because there is no justice. There can be no real peace and security until there be first justice enjoyed by all the inhabitants of that beautiful land. The Bible knows nothing about peace without justice, for that would be crying "peace, peace, where there is no peace." God's shalom, peace, involves inevitably righteousness, justice, wholeness, fullness of life, participation in decision-making, goodness, laughter, joy, compassion, sharing and reconciliation.

I have spoken extensively about South Africa, first because it is the land I know best, but because it is also a microcosm of the world and an example of what is to be found in other lands in differing degree—when there is injustice, invariably peace becomes a casualty. In El Salvador, in Nicaragua, and elsewhere in Latin America, there have been repressive regimes which have aroused opposition in those countries. Fellow citizens are pitted against one another, sometimes attracting the unhelpful attention and interest of outside powers, who want to extend their spheres of influence. We see this in the Middle East, in Korea, in the Philippines, in Kampuchea, in Vietnam, in Ulster, in Afghanistan, in Mozambique, in Angola, in Zimbabwe, behind the Iron Curtain.

Because there is global insecurity, nations are engaged in a mad arms race, spending billions of dollars wastefully on instruments of destruction, when millions are starving. And yet, just a fraction of what is expended so obscenely on defense budgets would make the difference in enabling God's children to fill their stomachs, be educated, and given the chance to lead fulfilled and happy lives. We have the capacity to feed ourselves several times over, but we are daily haunted by the spectacle of the gaunt dregs of humanity shuffling along in endless queues, with bowls to collect what the charity of the world has provided, too little too late. When will we learn, when will the people of the world get up and say, "Enough is enough!" God created us for fellowship. God created us so that we should form the human family, existing together because we were made for one another. We are not made for an exclusive self-sufficiency but for interdependence, and we break the law of our being at our peril. When will we learn that an escalated arms race merely escalates global insecurity? We are now much closer to a nuclear holocaust than when our technology and our spending were less.

Unless we work assiduously so that all of God's children, our brothers and sisters, members of our one human family, all will enjoy basic human rights, the right to a fulfilled life, the right of movement, of work, the freedom to be fully human, with a humanity measured by nothing less than the humanity of Jesus Christ Himself, then we are on the road inexorably to self-destruction, we are not far from global suicide; and yet it could be so different.

When will we learn that human beings are of infinite value because they have been created in the image of God, and that it is a blasphemy to treat them as if they were less than this and to do so ultimately recoils on those who do this? In dehumanizing others, they are themselves dehumanized. Perhaps oppression dehumanizes the oppressor as much as, if not more than, the oppressed. They need each other to become truly free, to become human. We can be human only in fellowship, in community, in *koinonia*, in peace.

Let us work to be peacemakers, those given a wonderful share in our Lord's ministry of reconciliation. If we want peace, so we have been told, let us work for justice. Let us beat our swords into ploughshares.

God calls us to be fellow workers with Him, so that we can extend His Kingdom of Shalom, of justice, of goodness, of compassion, of caring, of sharing, of laughter, joy and reconciliation, so that the kingdoms of this world will become the Kingdom of our God and of His Christ, and He shall reign forever and ever.[4] Amen. Then there will be a fulfillment of the wonderful vision in the Revelation of St. John the Divine:

> After this I beheld, and lo, a great multitude, which no man could number, of all nations and kindreds and peoples and tongues, stood before the throne and before the Lamb, clothed with white robes, and palms in their hands, and cried with a loud voice saying, "Salvation to our God, who sitteth upon the throne, and unto the Lamb"…[5]

Notes

1. Desmond Tutu, *No Future Without Forgiveness* (New York: Doubleday, 1999), 31.
2. © 1984 The Nobel Foundation. Used with permission.
3. In South Africa's English dialect (as in Great Britain), this word means "fired."
4. Revelation 11:15.
5. Holy Bible, King James Version, Revelation 7:9–12. (Verses 11–12 have been omitted for brevity.)

CHAPTER FIVE

Framing South African Reconciliation: Desmond Tutu

As explained in the previous speech and introduction, South Africa's system of apartheid caused terrible suffering and sparked various forms of resistance. By the early 1990s, tensions had escalated to the point that the white government and black militants seeking liberation from apartheid were poised on the brink of a bloody civil war. To avert this eventuality, President F. W. de Klerk and Nelson Mandela (whom de Klerk had released from prison in 1990) spearheaded peace negotiations, from which emerged an interim constitution with a bill rights for all South Africans, as well as the nation's first fully democratic elections. During negotiations, constituents of the white apartheid government refused to accept the interim constitution without a guarantee of amnesty (pardon) for any past political actions that might be deemed as crimes against human rights. This demand was eventually accepted by Mandela and his allies, with the proviso that once elections were held, the newly elected government would determine the conditions and process for granting amnesty.[1]

Free, non-racial elections were held for the first time in April 1994, and Mandela's party, the African National Congress, won a sweeping victory that put it in control of the South African Parliament. The Parliament then formally elected Mandela as the nation's first black president. Over the next year, his government solicited input from various civic and religious organizations, human rights lawyers, and victims of the apartheid era to determine how best to deal with the nation's past and move forward. This process of dialogue resulted in the passage of the Promotion of National Unity and Reconciliation Act of 1995, the law that instituted the Truth and Reconciliation Commission. It charged the TRC with the following purpose:

> To provide for the investigation and the establishment of as complete a picture as possible of the nature, causes and extent of gross violations of human rights committed during the period from 1 March 1960 to the cut-off date contemplated in the Constitution, within or outside the Republic, emanating from the conflicts of the past, and the fate or whereabouts of the victims of such violations; the granting of amnesty to persons who make full disclosure of all the relevant facts relating to acts associated with a political objective committed in the course of the conflicts of the past during the said period; affording victims an opportunity to relate the violations they suffered; the taking of measures aimed at the granting of reparation to, and the rehabilitation and the restoration of the human and civil dignity of, victims of violations of human rights; reporting to the Nation about such violations and victims; the making of recommendations aimed at the prevention of the commission of gross violations of human rights.[2]

During apartheid, many violations of human rights were committed in the dark of night or on remote country roads, in police stations or in jail cells, away from public view. Anti-apartheid activists were murdered by the police or simply disappeared. Conversely, some of these activists not only committed acts of terrorism against white institutions or government agents but also harmed members of their own community whom they perceived as disloyal to the cause. Under the amnesty rules stated above, anyone who had perpetrated violence or other human rights abuses in the struggle for/against apartheid would be granted political amnesty only if they voluntarily came forward to the TRC and fulfilled two conditions: to make full disclosure of their crimes, and to convince the Commission they had committed these acts as part of a political agenda in the struggle for or against apartheid. Although this arrangement somewhat sacrificed criminal justice for the sake of peace, it did bring truth to light, as those responsible for political crimes came forward, were exposed, and experienced a kind of retribution in the form of public shame for their deeds. If the conditions for amnesty were not met, perpetrators could be tried under criminal law.[3]

By the end of the year, Mandela had selected 17 prominent individuals from a wide array of races, religions, and political persuasions to serve as the commissioners of the TRC. Desmond Tutu, now an archbishop in the Anglican Church, was appointed its chair. The day after the members of the TRC were officially announced by President Mandela, they met together for the first time to begin preparing themselves for the work ahead.[4] As chair, Tutu hosted the commissioners at Bishopscourt, his official residence as Anglican Archbishop of Cape Town, and he delivered a series of remarks orienting them for this difficult task. While most of the address focused on the nuts and bolts of the TRC process (not included below), its second section and conclusion spoke to the beliefs, principles, vision, and energy undergirding the work of the TRC.

In the excerpts below, Tutu steps back to highlight the TRC's moral purpose and what he sees to be its spiritual character. Given South Africa's recent transformation and the Commission's purpose, the tragic tone of his Nobel Lecture has given way to comic and romantic hues, featuring such language as "happy coincidence," "providentially significant," "healing," "forgiving," "divine blessings," "miracle," "spectacular victory," "transcend," "glorious future," and "scintillating success." Early on, Tutu emphasizes that the TRC is *not* a "witch-hunt hell-bent" on vengeance against whites. Nonetheless, he insists on realism about the dark past and the difficult task ahead. True to his *ubuntu* theology,[5] Tutu recognizes that all South Africans, both oppressors and oppressed, have been wounded in some way, caught up together in a web of injustice and violence. For healing to occur, he argues, truth must be brought to light. Perpetrators seeking amnesty from the TRC will have to describe their harmful deeds in detail and explain the political motivations behind these acts. Both telling and hearing such painful truths in a spirit of reconciliation requires especial strength, for which Tutu commends the resources of faith and prayer. He ends on a romantic note, celebrating South Africa's "miracle" and exhorting citizens to ensure that its promise is fully realized.

Address to the First Gathering of the TRC[6]

Cape Town, South Africa
December 16, 1995
[***Preamble omitted***]

Delicate and Critical Task

Everyone is aware that we have been assigned a delicate task whose execution, successful or otherwise, will have critical and far-reaching consequences for our land and nation. It is an awesome responsibility.

It is important to bear constantly in mind the title of the act that has brought us into being—the Promotion of National Unity and Reconciliation. What a happy coincidence, how providentially significant, that our very first meeting takes place on the day designated in our calendar as the Day of Reconciliation. Absolutely central to our concern in the work of our Commission is helping our land and people to achieve genuine, real and not cheap and spurious reconciliation. Some view the Commission with considerable misgiving and indeed suspicion and even hostility because they have convinced themselves that the Commission is going to degenerate into an Inquisition, a witch-hunt hell-bent on bringing miscreants to book and the assumption is that it would be miscreants from one side only.

We must scotch that rumor or suspicion from the outset. We are meant to be a part of the process of the healing of our nation, of our people, all of us, since every South African has to some extent or other been traumatized. We are a wounded people because of the conflict of the past, no matter on which side we stood. We all stand in need of healing. We on the Commission are no superhuman exceptions. We too need forgiving and to forgive. I hope that our churches, mosques, synagogues and temples will be able to provide liturgies for corporate confession and absolution.

We are privileged to be on this Commission to assist our land, our people to come to terms with our dark past once and for all. They say that those who suffer from amnesia, those who forget the past, are doomed to repeat it. It is not dealing with the past to say facilely, let bygones be bygones, for then they won't be bygones. Our country, our society would be doomed to the instability of uncertainty—the uncertainty engendered by not knowing when yet another scandal of the past would hit the headlines, when another skeleton would be dragged out of the cupboard.

We will be engaging in what should be a corporate nationwide process of healing through contrition, confession and forgiveness. To be able to forgive one needs to know whom one is forgiving and why. That is why the truth is so central to this whole exercise.

But we will be engaging in something that is ultimately deeply spiritual, deeply personal. That is why I have been appealing to all our people—this is not something just for the Commission alone. We are in it, all of us together, black and white, colored and Indian, we this rainbow people of God. That is why I have appealed to our different communities of faith (Christian, Muslim, Jewish, Hindu, etc.) to uphold the Commission in fervent prayer and intercession that we may be showered with the divine blessings of wisdom, courage and discernment.

That is why I have asked religious communities of monks and nuns around the world to soak our Commission and its deliberations in fervent volumes of prayer. That is why I want to suggest that all our activities should be started if not by prayer then by a substantial silence, and that we should start our work with a retreat together for the replenishment of our spiritual resources. Our work is going to be harrowing and demanding. We will need counselling periodically to recoup.

[***Third and fourth sections omitted***]

Conclusion

We have seen a miracle unfold before our very eyes and the world has marveled as South Africans, all South Africans, have won this spectacular victory over injustice, oppression and evil. The miracle must endure. Freedom and justice must become realities for all our people and we have the privilege of helping to heal the hurts of the past, to transcend the alienations and the hostilities of that past so that we can close the door on that past and concentrate in the present and our glorious future.

We have it in us as South Africans to become a scintillating success. God bless us in our high calling.

Notes

1. For a thorough examination of these negotiations, see Erik Doxtader, *With Faith in the Works of Words: The Beginnings of Reconciliation in South Africa, 1985–1995* (Lansing: Michigan State University Press, 2009).
2. South Africa Parliament, *Promotion of National Unity and Reconciliation Act*, no. 34, 1995, https://www.justice.gov.za/legislation/acts/1995-034.pdf.
3. See Tutu, *No Future Without Forgiveness* (New York: Doubleday, 1999); Antjie Krog, *Country of My Skull: Guilt, Sorrow, and the Limits of Forgiveness in the New South Africa* (New York: Three Rivers, 2000); Philippe-Joseph Salazar, *An African Athens: Rhetoric and the Shaping of Democracy in South Africa* (Mahwah, NJ: Lawrence Erlbaum Associates, 2002); Erik Doxtader, "Making Rhetorical History in a Time of Transition: The Occasion, Constitution, and Representation of South African Reconciliation," *Rhetoric & Public Affairs* 4, no. 2 (Summer 2001): 223–60, doi:10.1353/rap.2001.0023.
4. See Tutu, *No Future Without Forgiveness*, chapter 5.
5. For an in-depth look at Tutu's theology of interdependence, see Michael Battle, *Reconciliation: The Ubuntu Theology of Desmond Tutu* (Cleveland, The Pilgrim Press, 1997). For a reflection on the relevance of theology to the work of the TRC, see Tutu, *No Future Without Forgiveness*, 80–87.
6. Reprinted with permission from South Africa's Department of Justice and Constitutional Development. The full speech can be found at https://www.justice.gov.za/trc/media/pr/1995/p951216a.htm.

CHAPTER SIX

Religious Resources for Reconciliation in a Divided World: Miroslav Volf

Born and raised in Yugoslavia, and theologically trained in the United States and Germany, Croatian theologian Miroslav Volf saw his country torn apart in the early 1990s by the horrors of civil war and genocide. In response, Volf wrote an important work entitled *Exclusion and Embrace: A Theological Exploration of Identity, Otherness, and Reconciliation*.[1] On the strength of this award-winning book and other works, Volf rose to prominence as one of the world's foremost public theologians. As such, he was invited to speak at the 16th Annual International Prayer Breakfast at the United Nations, held on September 11, 2001—a date soon to be infamously known as 9/11. While Volf was in the midst of delivering his address on reconciliation to ambassadors and others at the U.N., terrorist hijackers flew two airliners into the World Trade Center just a few blocks away. Neither Volf nor the audience became aware of the attacks until after the meeting ended;[2] still, the speech's prominent image of "a grave in the air" uncannily captures the horror that the world witnessed at Manhattan's Twin Towers, and this calamity lends especial urgency to Volf's message about how religion can either fuel violence or foster reconciliation.

In his speech, Volf refines ideas originally developed in *Exclusion and Embrace* regarding the relations among justice, love, and grace.[3] He begins with a tone of tragic realism by reciting a stanza from a famous poem about life in a Nazi death camp penned by Holocaust survivor Paul Celan. (In Part II of this book, another famous Holocaust survivor, Elie Wiesel, quotes this poem as well.) Highlighting its images of "the unbridgeable gap created by unspeakable evil," and noting that similar horrors are still occurring in various parts of the world, Volf asks whether reconciliation is even possible. In answer, he calls attention to some resources for promoting peace and reconciliation from the Christian faith. Before unpacking these resources, he addresses an objection some people understandably raise: that Christianity, and religions in general, are more a source of conflict than peace. After clarifying the conditions under which Christianity does and does not cause conflicts, Volf proceeds to critique two unacceptable forms of reconciliation and draw four principles from the central narrative and symbol of his faith: the cross of Christ. These principles of reconciliation connect with ideas presented in the introduction of this book.

First, notice that justice and peace go hand in hand in Volf's account of reconciliation. To work for peace without addressing injustice is "cheap reconciliation," he says, and it goes against the Christian faith, which cries out against injustice. On the other hand, similar to King's argument that peaceful ends must be pursued by peaceful means, Volf argues that those who put peace-making on the back burner until they win the struggle for justice are bound to fail; they will never arrive at justice, since it is intrinsically connected with reconciliation; nor will they ever reach peace, since strict justice tends to divide parties further. Like King and Tutu, Volf highlights a recognition of human interdependence as the root of peace.

As Volf continues, another element of the tetrad comes into prominent view. The "will" to pursue reconciliation, he says, does not depend on the other party doing justice, for it is a matter of *grace* (i.e., agency freely directed toward the restoration of the other party and the relationship). Yet the "actual embrace" of reconciliation cannot be accomplished by one party's free will alone; it requires both parties to address truth and justice together. With truth added to the picture, the tetrad is complete; however, grace takes precedence in Volf's account, for he insists that the "*will to embrace*" (i.e., grace) constitutes "*the framework of the search for truth and justice.*" In terms of the reconciliation tetrad, we might say that the various frames of reconciliation are gathered within a master "romantic frame"—that is, oriented above all by a faith that healing can occur, a love for other human beings (in the agape sense highlighted by King), and a hope that goodness will triumph in the end.

Given that grace is the key to the Christian account of reconciliation, it makes sense that Volf ends his speech with an "invitation to creativity" in pursuing reconciliation. Creativity involves giftedness, free association, freewheeling exploration, and making something new, not strictly bound by past history or rules. Truth and justice are essential when pursuing a horizon of peace, but arguably it is grace that leads the way.

"After the Grave in the Air"[4]

Address to 16th Annual International Prayer Breakfast at the U.N. September 11, 2001

Mr. President, Mr. Minister, Excellencies, Ladies and Gentlemen: It is indeed my honor to address you today on the day of the opening of a new session of the General Assembly. It is appropriate, in this place where you do such important and tireless work to resolve many of the conflicts that rage around our world, for us to come before God and ask for God's wisdom and God's guidance. It is also appropriate, I think, for the theme of my talk to be reconciliation. I thank you for your attention as I reflect on this theme.

Allow me to start by drawing your attention to the character of the world in which we live. I will not do so by quoting statistics about many dangers and sufferings in our world, statistics that you know better than I do; instead I will offer a meditative text written by a young Jewish poet immediately after World War II. It is a poem with unpredictable rhythms, a poem with grim metaphors, a poem with a startling combination of tenderness and brutality. Here is the first stanza.

> Black milk of daybreak we drink it at evening
> we drink it at midday and morning we drink it at night.
> we drink and we drink
> we shovel a grave in the air there you won't lie all too cramped
> A man lives in the house he plays with his vipers he writes
> he writes when it grows dark to Germany of your golden-haired Margareta
> he writes it and steps out of doors and the stars are all sparkling
> he whistles his hounds to come close
> he whistles his Jews into rows has them shovel a grave in the ground
> he commands us play up for the dance[5]

This poem must be one of the most remarkable literary creations about the most infamous event of the 20th century. The event is the Holocaust; the poem is Paul Celan's "Deathfugue." Behind the outlandish images of digging graves "in the air" and "in the ground" and about "playing up for the dance" lies a brutal reality. It was common practice in Nazi concentration camps to order one group of prisoners to play or sing nostalgic tunes while others dug graves or were executed. Young German men who were cultivated enough to occupy themselves with writing, and who were tender enough to daydream about their girlfriends' golden hair, were masters of death.

Now the Holocaust is in many ways unique, perhaps not so much in its scale and brutality as in its technological sophistication and the single-mindedness with which murderous intentions were directed against particular people. But the reason that I read this poem to you is because in so many places in the world today, similar things are happening. In many respects, the Holocaust is not an anomaly in the world in which we live. Death is not just a blue-eyed master from Germany.

Rivers of blood have flowed and mountains of corpses have grown most recently in my own country, Croatia, as also in Macedonia, Bosnia, Rwanda, and other places—you name them, you know them all better than I do. They all bear horrifying testimony to the fact that the world in which we live is also a world in which the most brutal practices of exclusion are the order of the day. And I have not even mentioned living rooms. You may know that, statistically, most of the violence in this world does not happen on battlefields but in homes, between estranged spouses, parents and children, and siblings.

The poem that I quoted, "Deathfugue," ends with the following line: "Your golden hair, Margareta—your ashen hair, Shulamite." It is clear who "Margareta" is: the blond-haired German girl, the romantic ideal drawn from Goethe's poetry, of whom the executioner tenderly daydreams. But who is "Shulamite"? Shulamite is no ash blonde, but the black and comely maiden of the Song of Songs, whose hair has grown pale because the ash of burning has fallen on it. Shulamite is the Jewish people, experiencing the most horrid events in their history. When, in "Deathfugue," Paul Celan puts together Margareta and Shulamite, nothing can reconcile them—they stand next to each other as symbols of the unbridgeable gap created by unspeakable evil.

Now it is understandable why this would be so for Celan; when he wrote this poem, the ovens that had sent his own parents and many of his kin into their grave in the air had barely cooled down. But the issue remains for us today. Can we simply leave Margareta and Shulamite side by side as symbols of the unreconciliation that governs so prominently in our world? Or can we do something to reconcile estranged individuals and peoples? Sometimes it feels as if very little—almost nothing—can be done to make our world a more peaceful place, nothing except maybe to keep "containing the situation"—until the next outburst of violence.

I want to draw your attention to the resources offered by the Christian faith for fostering more peaceful social environments. One such resource is signaled in the theme of my talk: the theme of reconciliation—the reconciliation of humanity to God and the reconciliation of peoples and individuals to one another.

Now some of you might object—that objection has been in fact mentioned already today—that religion often is *not* a positive influence in the world of social relations. Religion, Christianity included, can and does cause conflicts.

In my experience, however, Christianity is a factor in conflict (1) when it is regarded as primarily a *cultural resource*, a marker of a particular group's identity, in the name of which they then struggle against another group, rather than as the living faith of individuals and of whole communities; and (2) when there is only a superficial (though not necessarily lukewarm!) relationship to that faith, when one has not been inducted into, sustained and nurtured by a longstanding tradition of that faith. Those who have been nurtured in the Christian tradition are more likely to become agents of peace than perpetrators of violence. That is a controversial claim, I know. But there are recent studies that have shown that to be the case. A similar claim could probably be made by other religions, but, at any rate, I think it stands for the Christian religion.

So it is important to look at the resources for creating more peaceful social environments that lie at the center of the Christian faith. One of them, as I mentioned, is the notion of reconciliation. I want first to dispose of two *unacceptable* notions of reconciliation and then to advocate a third one.

One unacceptable notion of reconciliation is what some people have called *cheap reconciliation*. Cheap reconciliation sets in contrast justice and peace. To pursue this sort of "reconciliation" means to give up the struggle for freedom, to give up the pursuit of justice. It means to put up with oppression. If we were to pursue such cheap reconciliation, it is clear that this would amount to the betrayal of those who suffer injustice, violence, and deception. But I think also that this would amount to the betrayal of the Christian faith. As I read the Christian message, a prophetic strand which denounces injustice has a prominent place in it. You cannot take away that prophetic strand from the Christian faith without gravely distorting it.

Cheap reconciliation, I think, is what has taken place in many countries in recent decades. Oppressive regimes have been replaced by more just governments, but those who committed crimes were never brought to justice—in the name of national reconciliation. The strategy was: do not rock the boat. That kind of strategy has its own virtues but has significant disadvantages as well, above all disregard for the suffering of the oppressed.

If I see things rightly, in western cultures, cheap reconciliation is not so much of a problem. If anything, we are tempted to pursue justice without even asking the question of reconciliation. That brings me to the second unacceptable notion of reconciliation. This might be described as follows: *first justice, then reconciliation*. Once the requirements of justice have been satisfied, then we can sit around the table and talk about reconciliation. I suggest that this way of going about "reconciliation" suffers from at least three major problems.

First, taken seriously, this stance, *first justice, then reconciliation*, is impossible. As Nietzsche—not a theologian but nonetheless a valuable dialogue partner for theologians—rightly noted, given the nature of human interaction, all pursuit of justice not only rests upon partial injustices but also creates new injustices.

Moreover, all accounts of what is "just" are to some extent relative to a particular group and therefore invariably contested by rival groups. Those of you who have two or more children know exactly what I am talking about. How do you get to the bottom of the little quarrels that happen between children? It's virtually impossible, because each of them has their own perspective. Multiply that in a certain way, and you get the situation of nations. So no peace is possible within the over-arching framework of strict justice for the simple reason that no strict justice is possible.

Second, even if justice could be done, it would be insufficient, because justice done would not really bring people together. In order to have healing, you have to have people brought together and reconciled.

One of the reasons why this is so is because our identities, our personal and collective identities, are not simply self-contained and internally determined; rather, they are always shaped by interaction with other people. I am Miroslav Volf, not only because I am distinct from my wife, Judy Gundry-Volf, but also because over the past 20 years, I have been shaped by a relationship with her. This holds true also for nations. I was talking to the Ambassador from my native Croatia this morning. It just happens to be the case that to be a Croatian means to have Serbs as your neighbors. You may not like it, and we Croatians certainly have not liked it at certain points because it was a difficult relationship. But that is the way it is. So because the other is part of my own identity, my own healing depends on healing of the relationship with the other.

Thirdly, justice pursued first—in addition to being strictly impossible and anyway insufficient—would also be undesirable. Recall the Old Testament law "An eye for an eye and a tooth for a tooth." We think that is very excessive, very harsh; and yet when you think about it, it's not sufficiently just. Say somebody breaks my tooth. How can it be just if, in recompense, I or somebody else breaks only one of that person's teeth? Our relationship is asymmetrical: I haven't done any wrong to that person. So it would seem that at least two of his teeth ought to be broken! Then we might have something like justice! But it should be clear that if we pursue "street" justice in such ways, the result will be a maimed and finally humanly unsustainable world.

As an alternative to these two unacceptable ways to understand reconciliation by relating it to justice, I want to look at the resources that lie at the very heart of the Christian tradition. At this center we find the narrative, the story, the event of the cross of Christ as an act of reconciliation of God with humanity. On the cross of Christ, God is manifested as the God who, though in no way indifferent toward the distinction between good and evil, nonetheless lets the sun shine on both the good and the evil; as the God of infinite and indiscriminate love who died for the ungodly in order to bring them into divine communion; the God who offers grace even to the vilest evildoer.

I want to draw four implications from this Christian account of who God is for our understanding of inter-human relations.

First, *the will to embrace another person is unconditional.* The starting point must be the primacy of the will to embrace. Since the God of Christian belief is the God of unconditional love and the God who died for the ungodly, the will to embrace the other, even the evil other, is a fundamental Christian obligation. The will to give ourselves to others and "welcome" them, the will to readjust our identities to make space for them, is prior to any judgment about others, except that of identifying them in their humanity. The will to embrace precedes any "truth" about others and any construction of their "justice." This will is absolutely indiscriminate and strictly immutable; it transcends the moral mapping of the social world into "good" and "evil."

This is a scandal when you think about it. But it is qualified by my second point. *Truth and justice are preconditions of actual embrace.* Notice that I have described *the will* to embrace as unconditional and indiscriminate, not the embrace itself. A genuine embrace—an embrace that neither play-acts acceptance nor crushes the other—cannot take place until the truth has been said and justice established. Hence the will to embrace includes in itself the will to find out what is the case and the will to determine what is just; the will to embrace includes the will to rectify the wrongs that have been done and the will to reshape relationships so as to correspond to truth and justice.

But does this not bring us back to the unacceptable *first justice, then reconciliation?* Not quite. For, third, *the will to embrace is the framework of the search for truth and justice.* How do we find what has transpired between people so as to be able to pursue truth and justice in a particular case? My argument is this: Unless you will to embrace the other and be reconciled to her, you will not find what is truth and what is justice. For you can always interpret somebody's outwardly generous action as a covertly violent action—as a bouquet of flowers in which a dagger is hidden. You have to want to see the other's goodness in order actually to perceive it—provided, of course, that the other actually does manifest goodness.

Fourth and finally, *embrace is the horizon of the struggle for justice.* As in many of our activities, so in the struggle for justice: much depends on the *telos*, on the goal of that struggle. Toward what is it oriented? Is it oriented simply toward ensuring that everyone gets what one deserves? Or is it oriented toward the larger goal of healing relationships? My contention is that it must be oriented precisely toward the latter. The reason is simple. You will have justice only if you strive for something greater than justice, only if you strive after love.

My time is up. In addition to emphasizing the priority of embrace while not disregarding justice, I want to leave you with an invitation to creativity. I don't have time to suggest how you would acquire the will to embrace or practice embrace in concrete situations, whether in your personal or in your more communal lives. I pray that God will grant you wisdom to find creative ways to practice embrace in our world shot through with violence.

Notes

1. Miroslav Volf, *Exclusion and Embrace: A Theological Exploration of Identity, Otherness, and Reconciliation* (Nashville: Abingdon, 1996).
2. Miroslav Volf, "After the Grave in the Air," *Christianity Today*, September 1, 2001, https://www.christianitytoday.com/ct/2001/septemberweb-only/9-17-54.0.html.
3. See Volf, *Exclusion and Embrace*, 220–25. Volf's 9/11 speech more closely mirrors his later articulation of these ideas in Miroslav Volf, "Forgiveness, Reconciliation, & Justice: A Christian Contribution to a More Peaceful Environment," in *Forgiveness and Reconciliation: Religion, Public Policy, and Conflict Transformation*, ed. Raymond G. Helmick and Rodney L. Peterson (Philadelphia: Templeton Foundation, 2001), 27–49.
4. This speech was originally published in *Christianity Today* (Volf, "After the Grave in the Air"). It is reprinted here with the permission of the speaker.
5. Here Volf appears to have been quoting from Felstiner's translation of the poem, while adapting the wording in a few places. See John Felstiner, *Paul Celan: Poet, Survivor, Jew* (New Haven, CT: Yale University Press, 2001), 31.

CHAPTER SEVEN

Mindfulness as a Key to Reconciliation: Thich Nhat Hanh

The next speech draws upon an Eastern religious tradition to speak to the challenges of reconciliation in the West and beyond. In 1926, a boy named Nguyen Xuan Bao was born in Vietnam. Drawn to a life of contemplation, he entered a Zen Buddhist monastery at the age of 16 and took his full vows as a monk a decade later, at which time he received the name Thich Nhat Hanh. Gifted with a brilliant mind and a passion for social activism, he responded to Vietnam's war in the 1950s by founding the Engaged Buddhism movement, which aims to "apply Buddhist teachings and practice to the real-world suffering caused by war, social injustice, and political oppression."[1] In the 1960s, Thich Nhat Hanh spent time in the United States, studying and teaching at prominent universities and working to promote peace as a second war escalated in his homeland, this time between communist forces and anti-communist forces supported by the U.S. military. During this period, he had meetings with two important American religious figures: Thomas Merton, a famous monk and contemplative in the Roman Catholic tradition, and Martin Luther King Jr, the leading voice of the civil rights movement. King's philosophy and practice of nonviolent resistance had inspired Hanh and other Vietnamese Buddhists working for peace in their homeland; conversely, Hanh's thoughts on nonviolence and the Vietnam conflict moved King to speak out against U.S. military action in Vietnam. King was so impressed with Hanh that he nominated him for the Nobel Peace Prize.

Thich Nhat Hanh became a world-renowned spiritual leader, establishing a new order of Buddhist monasteries and developing an approach to meditation called *mindfulness*, which combines ancient Buddhist traditions with ideas from Western psychology. In 2003, he was invited to address members of the U.S. Congress on the eve of the second anniversary of 9/11. Delivering his speech in the Library of Congress, Hanh offered insights from Engaged Buddhism in hope of helping legislators better serve the citizens they represented and "heal the wounds that have divided our nation and the world."

In the text of his address to U.S. legislators, he wastes no time getting to the topic of mindfulness. While it might appear at first to be merely a matter of regulating one's own mental state, Hanh soon shows how mindfulness prepares us to relate to others with compassion, even when they do things that would normally provoke us to anger. Mindfulness does not focus on seizing control of life to achieve a desired future, nor on fighting against pain and those who cause it, but rather on accepting, understanding, and appreciating life in the present moment, with its gifts and challenges. In this way, mindfulness enables one to have compassion on oneself when suffering, and thus to have compassion on others—even on those who have caused the hurt—for they too are suffering in some way.

To live one's life and lead one's nation mindfully, Thich Nhat Hanh recommends four specific practices: mindful breathing, deep/compassionate listening, loving speech, and mindful consumption. He notes that these and other forms of mindfulness are practiced in the spiritual community called Plum Village, a Buddhist monastery he founded in France, where visitors come for times of retreat and reorientation to better face the challenges in their world. Hanh tells of Israelis and Palestinians spending time at Plum Village and returning to their country prepared to be compassionate peacemakers. Likewise, he challenges the legislators in his audience to practice mindfulness so that they might transcend partisanship, collaborate better to solve common problems, and move beyond relying on force to achieve political and national goals.

In contrast with other speeches in this book, Hanh's address to members of Congress seems to downplay the importance of justice. That is because a fixation on getting justice often masks a deeper issue: an inability to deal with our own suffering, recognize others' suffering, and realize our commonality and interdependence with them. While justice focuses on dealing with parties in their separateness—making sure each party gets its fair share, and dividing the guilty from the innocent—Buddhism focuses on recognizing the underlying oneness or interconnectedness of all things. In other words, mindfulness is rather like working to see life through a comic frame, learning to treat more lightly the differences and divisions that irritate us.

In relation to this idea, notice Hanh's description of mindful breathing: "Breathing in, I know I am alive. Breathing out, *I smile to life*."² Readers may recall seeing statues of the Buddha and noticing that this figure is always seated in a meditative position with a gentle, serene smile on its face. This smiling pose represents a state of *satori*, or "enlightenment," which in Buddhism means apprehending universal Oneness and thus transcending the illusions of separate/insular egos, with their limited perceptions and desires that cause suffering. In Hanh's speech, we see this influence in his multiple references to "wrong perceptions." Similarly, in the comic frame of Western literature and drama, conflicts are resolved by correcting misunderstandings and mistaken identities, rather than by punishing villains. We might think of the Buddhist vision as "comic consciousness on a cosmic scale." As "comedy" in the Middle Ages referred to any story that ends happily, so Buddhism pursues the goal of happiness, in the sense of contentment and inner tranquility through enlightenment—rooted not in the outcome of unfolding circumstances, but in the heart of reality itself. As Burke's comic frame valorizes peace by focusing on the hidden oneness underlying surface conflict, so Buddhist meditation seeks equanimity, or peace of mind, through apprehension of ultimate oneness. While this may sound like an avoidance of real problems and pain, it actually takes hard work. Indeed, Thich Nhat Hanh's Engaged Buddhism strives not so much to be light-hearted as to bear and lighten others' heavy burdens. With deep mindfulness and compassion, it enters into people's suffering and seeks to ameliorate both the causes and effects of oppression and injustice.

Although Martin Luther King Jr. spoke from the Christian tradition and Hanh from the Buddhist tradition, attentive readers may notice some strong conceptual parallels between statements in Hanh's speech and King's Christmas Sermon on Peace concerning the interconnected nature of reality and the way in which peace can be realized.

"Leading with Courage and Compassion"³

U.S. Library of Congress, Washington, DC
September 10, 2003
Distinguished Members of Congress, Ladies and Gentlemen, Dear Friends:

It is my pleasure to have this opportunity to talk with you about how we can share our insight, our compassion and our understanding in order to better serve those we want to serve and help heal the wounds that have divided our nation and the world.

When you sit in your car on the way to work, you might like to use that time to come home to yourself and touch the wonders of life. Instead of allowing yourself to think of the future, you might like to pay attention to your breath and come home to the present moment. We breathe in and out all day, but we are not aware that we are breathing in and breathing out. The practice of bringing our attention to our breath is called mindful breathing: Breathing in, I know I am alive. Breathing out, I smile to life. This is a very simple practice. If we go home to our in-breath and out-breath and breathe mindfully, we become fully alive in the here and now.

In our daily lives, our bodies are present, but our minds might be elsewhere, caught in our projects, our worries and our anxieties. Life is only available in the present moment. The past is already gone; the future is not yet here. When we establish ourselves in the present moment we are able to live our moments deeply and to get in touch with the healing, refreshing and nourishing elements that are always within us and around us.

With this energy of mindfulness, we can recognize our pain and embrace it tenderly like a mother whose baby is crying. When a baby cries, the mother stops everything she is doing and holds the baby tenderly in her arms. The energy of the mother will penetrate into the baby and the baby will feel relief. The same thing happens when we recognize and embrace our own pain and sorrow. If we can hold our anger, our sorrow and our fear with the energy of mindfulness, we will be able to recognize the roots of our suffering. We will be able to recognize the suffering in the people we love as well.

Mindfulness helps us to not be angry at our loved ones, because when we are mindful, we understand that our loved ones are suffering as well. The person you love has a lot of suffering and has not had a chance to be listened to. It is very important to take the time to sit down and listen with compassion. We call this practice "deep listening." Deep listening can be used with the practice of loving speech to help restore communication with the people you care about. To listen like this is to give the other person a chance to empty his or her heart. If you can keep your compassion alive during that time—even if what the other person says is full of accusations and bitterness—it will not touch off irritation and anger in you. Listen in order to help the other person to suffer less.

When you communicate with compassion, you are using language that does not have the elements of anger and irritation in it. In this way we can help each other remove wrong perceptions. All the energies of anger, hatred, fear and violence come from wrong perceptions. Wrong perceptions result in a lot of anger, mistrust, suspicion, hate and terrorism. You cannot remove wrong perceptions through punishment. You have to do it with the tools of deep and compassionate listening and loving speech. With deep, compassionate listening and loving speech, we can bring harmony to our families, and our communities can become communities of understanding, peace and happiness.

When I was in India a number of years ago, I spoke to Mr. R. K. Narayan, a member of the Indian parliament, about the practice of deep listening and compassionate dialogue in legislative bodies. When you represent the people, you are expected to offer the people the best of your understanding and compassion. I said that a legislative assembly could become a community with a lot of mutual understanding and compassion. It could have strong collective insight to support the decision-making process and the people of the nation. Here in Washington, before a session of Congress, one person could read a short meditation: "Dear colleagues, we are elected by our people and our people expect us to listen to each other deeply and to use the kind of language that can convey our wisdom and insight. Let us bring together our individual experiences and wisdom so that we can offer our collective insight and make the best decisions for the country and the people."

When a member of Congress is speaking from her insight with this kind of language, she is offering the best of herself. If we only act and speak the party line, then we are not offering the best compassion and understanding we have.

Members of Congress are very concerned about the levels of violence in our families, in our schools and in our society. Each concerned person may have his or her own ideas and insights about how to bring down that level of violence. If we can combine all our insights and experiences we will have the collective insight that will help to decrease the amount of violence in our society. If we are not able to listen to our colleagues with a free heart, though—if we only consider and support ideas from our own party—we are harming the foundation of our democracy. That is why we need to transform our community—in this case the Congress—into a compassionate community. Everyone would be considered a brother or sister to everyone else. Congress would be a place where we learn to listen to everyone with equal interest and concern. The practice of deep and compassionate listening and loving speech can help to build brotherhood, can remove discrimination and can bring about the kind of insight that will be liberating to our country and to our people.

Two days after the events of September 11th, I spoke to 4,000 people in Berkeley, California. I said that our emotions are very strong right now, and we should calm ourselves down. With lucidity and calm we would know what to do and what not to do in order not to make the situation worse. I said that the terrorists who attacked the World Trade Center must have been very angry. They must have hated America a lot. They must have thought of America as having tried to destroy them as individual people, as a religion, as a nation, and as a culture. I said that we had to find out why they did such a thing to America.

America's political leaders can ask the question, calmly and with clarity: "What have we done that has made you suffer so much?" America's political leaders can say, "We want to know about your suffering and why you hate us. We may have said something or done something that gave you the impression that we wanted to destroy you. But that is not the case. We are confused, and that is why we want you to help us understand why you have done such a thing to us."

We call this loving or gentle speech. If we are honest and sincere, they will tell us how they feel. Then we will recognize the wrong perceptions they have about themselves and about us. We can try to help them to remove their wrong perceptions. All these acts of terrorism and violence come from wrong perceptions. Wrong perceptions are the ground for anger, violence and hate. You cannot remove wrong perceptions with a gun.

When we listen deeply to another person, we not only recognize their wrong perceptions, but we also identify our own wrong perceptions about ourselves and about the other person. That is why mindful dialogue and mindful communication is crucial to removing anger and violence.

It is my deepest hope that our political leaders can make use of such instruments to bring peace to the world. I believe that using force and violence can only make the situation worse. Since September 11th, America has not been able to decrease the level of hate and violence on the part of the terrorists. In fact, the level of hate and violence has increased. It is time for us to go back to the situation, to look deeply and to find another less costly way to bring peace to us and to them. Violence cannot remove violence—everyone knows that. Only with the practice of deep listening and gentle communication can we help remove wrong perceptions that are at the foundation of violence.

America has a lot of difficulty in Iraq. I think that America is caught in Iraq in the same way that America was caught in Vietnam. We have the idea that we have to go and destroy the enemy. That idea will never give us a chance to do the right thing to end violence. During the Vietnam War, America thought that it had to go to North Vietnam to bomb. The more America bombed, the more communists they created. I am afraid that the same thing is happening in Iraq. I think that it is very difficult for America to withdraw now from Iraq. Even if they want to leave, it is very difficult.

The only way for America to free itself from this situation is to help build the United Nations into a real body of peace so that the United Nations will take over the problem of Iraq and of the Middle East. America is powerful enough to make this happen. America should allow other nations to contribute positively to building the United Nations into a true organization for peace with enough authority to do its job. To me, that is the only way out of our current situation.

We have to wake up to the fact that everything is connected to everything else. Our safety and well-being cannot be individual matters anymore. If they are not safe, there is no way that we can be safe. Taking care of other people's safety is taking care of our own safety. To take care of their well-being is to take care of our own well-being. It is the mind of discrimination and separation that is at the foundation of all violence and hate.

My right hand has written all the poems that I have composed. My left hand has not written a single poem. But my right hand does not think, "Left Hand, you are good for nothing." My right hand does not have a superiority complex. That is why it is very happy. My left hand does not have any complex at all. In my two hands there is the kind of wisdom called the wisdom of nondiscrimination. One day I was hammering a nail and my right hand was not very accurate and instead of pounding on the nail it pounded on my finger. It put the hammer down and took care of the left hand in a very tender way, as if it were taking care of itself. It did not say, "Left Hand, you have to remember that I have taken good care of you and you have to pay me back in the future." There was no such thinking. And my left hand did not say, "Right Hand, you have done me a lot of harm—give me that hammer, I want justice." My two hands know that they are members of one body; they are in each other.

I think that if Israelis and Palestinians knew that they were brothers and sisters—that they are like my two hands—they would not try to punish each other anymore. The world community has not helped them to see that. If Israelis and Palestinians—and Muslims and Hindus—knew that discrimination was at the base of our suffering, they would know how to touch the seed of nondiscrimination in themselves. That kind of awakening—that kind of deep understanding—brings about reconciliation and well-being.

I believe that in America there are many people who are awakened to the fact that violence cannot remove violence. They realize there is no way to peace: peace itself is the way. Those people must come together and voice their concern strongly and offer their collective wisdom to the nation so the nation can get out of this current situation. Every one of us has the duty to bring together that collective insight. With that insight, compassion will make us strong and courageous enough to bring about a solution for the world.

Every time we breathe in, go home to ourselves and bring the element of harmony and peace into ourselves, that is an act of peace. Every time we know how to look at another living being and recognize the suffering in him that has made him speak or act like that, we are able to see that he is the victim of his own suffering. When that understanding is in us, we can look at this other person with the eyes of understanding and compassion. When we can look with the eyes of compassion, we don't suffer and we don't make the other person suffer. These are the actions of peace that can be shared with other people.

At Plum Village, there are several hundred people living together like a family in a very simple way. At Plum Village, we have had the opportunity to practice together as a community. We are able to build up brotherhood and sisterhood. Although we live simply, we have a lot of joy because of the amount of understanding and compassion that we can generate. We are able to go to many countries to offer mindfulness retreats so that people may have a chance to heal, transform and to reconcile. Healing, transformation and reconciliation always happen during our retreats. That can be very nourishing.

We have invited Israelis and Palestinians to Plum Village to practice with us. When they come they bring anger, suspicion, fear and hate. But after a week or two of the practices of mindful walking, mindful breathing, mindful eating and mindful sitting, they are able to recognize their pain, embrace it and find relief. When they are initiated to the practice of deep listening, they are able to listen to others and realize that people from the other groups suffer as they do. When you know that they also suffer from violence, from hate, from fear and despair, you begin to look at them with the eyes of compassion. At that moment you suffer less and you make them suffer less. Communication becomes possible with the use of loving speech and deep listening.

The Israelis and Palestinians always come together as a group at the end of their stay in Plum Village. They always report the success of their practice. They always go back to the Middle East intending to continue the practice and invite others to join them, so that those others might suffer less and help others to suffer less too.

I believe that if this practice could be done on the national level, it would bring about the same kind of effect. Unfortunately, our political leaders have not been trained in these practices of mindful breathing, mindful walking and embracing pain and sorrow to transform their suffering. They have been trained only in political science.

So I think we should all bring a spiritual dimension into our daily lives. We should be awakened to the fact that happiness cannot be found in the direction of power, fame, wealth and sex. If we look deeply around us, we see many people with plenty of these things, but they suffer very deeply. When you have understanding and compassion in you, you don't suffer. You can relate very well to other people around you and to other living beings also. That is why a collective awakening about that reality is crucial....[4]

My strongest desire is that the members of Congress will have time to look into these matters and look deeply into the roots of their own suffering, the suffering of this nation, and the suffering around the world. This suffering does not have to continue. We already have the compassion and understanding necessary to heal the world.

Notes

1. Lindsay Kite., "The Life of Thich Nhat Hanh," *Lion's Roar*, October 11, 2018, https://www.lionsroar.com/the-life-of-thich-nhat-hanh/.
2. Italics added.
3. Words of Thich Nhat Hanh © Plum Village Community of Engaged Buddhism.
4. Here, two paragraphs on mindful consumption of food, entertainment, and material things have been omitted due to relevance and space considerations. The unabridged transcript is available at https://plumvillage.org/about/thich-nhat-hanh/letters/thich-nhat-hanh-address-to-us-congress-september-10-2003/.

CHAPTER EIGHT

Rooting Reconciliation in a Shared Past: President Mary McAleese of Ireland

One of the most protracted civil conflicts of the 20th century was the turmoil between Catholics and Protestants in Northern Ireland, known by the Irish simply as "the Troubles." With roots going back through centuries of British rule in Ireland, the Troubles involved a complex intertwining of political and religious identities with resentments fueled by discriminatory policies, harsh policing, economic hardships, and military conflicts in Irish history.[1] The conflict between Catholics and Protestants was less about differences in religious belief and practice than the connections between religious and national identity and political control. In this way, the Troubles confirm Miroslav Volf's claim (in his speech in this book) that religion fuels conflict "when it is regarded as primarily a cultural resource, a marker of a particular group's identity, in the name of which they then struggle against another group."

While Catholics constitute the vast majority of the Irish population, the six counties of Ulster that comprise Northern Ireland have long had a Protestant majority because many English and Scottish people settled there over the centuries, and for this reason they wanted to remain under British rule rather than join the Republic of Ireland to the south (which became independent in 1949). Because of their allegiance to the United Kingdom, these Protestants were known as "unionists" or "loyalists," and they supported such political parties as the Ulster Unionists and the Democratic Unionist Party. Meanwhile, the Catholic minority in Northern Ireland felt that they were unfairly targeted by British security forces and treated as second-class citizens by the majority-Protestant government in Ulster. Most of these Catholics supported Sinn Féin, the largest political party representing Irish nationalism.

Amid these political struggles, the Troubles involved severe social tensions, creating social and physical barriers across communities in Northern Ireland and spawning violence in the form of riots, shootings, and terrorist bombings. Much of the violence was spearheaded by paramilitary/terrorist groups, including the Irish Republican Army (IRA) on the Catholic/nationalist side and the Ulster Volunteer Force (UVF) on the Protestant/loyalist side. During the 1970s, annual deaths often numbered in the hundreds, and through 1988 more than 50 people died every year.[2]

In the 1990s, with help from U.S. Senator George Mitchell (who was sent by President Bill Clinton), peace negotiations gradually unfolded among representatives of various parties, including the British government, the Republic of Ireland, Sinn Féin, the IRA, and Protestant loyalists. In 1997, the IRA declared an unconditional cease-fire. The peace process culminated in an agreement by all political stakeholders on Good Friday, 1998. In recognition of this achievement, a joint Nobel Peace Prize was awarded to David Trimble (of the Ulster Unionist Party) and John Hume (of the main Catholic nationalist party).

Although the Good Friday Agreement brought the Troubles to an end politically, it could not eliminate the psychological scars and festering social wounds from many decades of hatred, division, and violence between Catholic nationalists and Protestant loyalists. Indeed, in August of that year, a renegade splinter group of the IRA set off a car bomb in the town of Omagh in Northern Ireland, killing 29 people and injuring 220 others, making it the single deadliest incident of the Troubles. While the ensuing decade was, thankfully, free of high-profile bombings, sectarian-motivated killings of individuals still occurred. Moreover, the number of "peace lines"—high walls cutting through city districts and streets to protect Catholic and Protestant neighborhoods from each other—grew in number, and the vast majority of children in Northern Ireland still attended segregated schools. While life was more peaceful than before, meaningful reconciliation was hardly possible with so little interaction across the divide.[3]

In 2010, the President of the Republic of Ireland, Mary McAleese, spoke to the challenge of Irish reconciliation from an insider's perspective. Born in Belfast, Northern Ireland, McAleese had come of age in the heart of the Troubles. Although her Roman Catholic family had been forced to move from their home by Protestant loyalist mobs, they held fast in their commitment to Christian love, refusing to succumb to resentment or violence. After earning her law degree, McAleese taught at Trinity College in the Republic of Ireland and later worked as a journalist for the national television service. In 1987, she returned to Belfast to become Director of the Institute of Professional Legal Studies at Queen's University, and eventually became the Pro-Vice Chancellor of that institution. A devout Roman Catholic, McAleese was involved in various delegations of her church and an outspoken advocate for increasing inclusiveness within Catholicism.[4]

In 1997, McAleese was elected president of the Republic of Ireland, making her not only the first native of Northern Ireland to become president of the Irish republic, but also the first woman in world history to succeed another woman (Mary Robinson) as an elected head of state. In accord with her presidential theme of "building bridges,"[5] McAleese made regular visits to Northern Ireland, formed positive relations with both the Protestant and Catholic communities, made a symbolic gesture of interdenominational unity by participating in Eucharist at the Protestant Church of Ireland, and made the Twelfth of July (an important day for Ulster Protestants) an official holiday in the majority-Catholic Republic of Ireland. With her strong and inclusive Christian faith, her commitment to a spirituality of love,[6] and her political savvy, McAleese played a pivotal role in promoting Irish reconciliation and building the cultural infrastructure for a unified future. In 2010, the City of Armagh, known as the ecclesiastical capital of Ireland, invited the president to give the first annual St. Patrick's Day lecture. The speech she delivered is eloquent and inspiring with its comic-romantic celebration of Ireland's peaceful transformation, its allusions to shared Irish history and literature, and its vivid and rhythmic language.

President McAleese's lecture exemplifies how a deeply divided society may find bedrock for reconciliation by digging down to "a shared heritage, a shared memory"—a unifying tradition, story, or historical figure from the past. In this case, the tradition is ancient Irish Christianity, and the figure is St. Patrick. Since reconciliation is multi-faceted and challenging, people often find it necessary to draw inspiration from the stories of heroes who embodied reconciliation. St. Patrick serves as the perfect choice for McAleese's address, not only because he is such an iconic figure for Irish culture, but also because his life story is one of being brutally mistreated and yet eventually overcoming the past through forgiveness, to build a new future for the culture that had abused him—much as the people of today's Ireland suffered both political oppression and sectarian violence during the Troubles and must find a way to overcome the pain of this past. The son of a wealthy Christian family living in the Roman-controlled part of Great Britain around the 5th century C.E., Patricius (Patrick) was captured by Irish pirates at the age of 16 and taken to their country, where he was held as a slave until his escape six years later. His trials led him to lean on the God of his upbringing, become a devoted Christian, and eventually enter the priesthood. A few years later, he experienced a vision calling him back to Ireland, this time to spread Christian faith among the people who had once captured and oppressed him.

As McAleese draws on key facets of St. Patrick's life, notice how she relates his experiences to those of the modern-day Irish people. If they are to find strength for reconciliation in Patrick's story, it is vital that they be able to identify with him. Although St. Patrick is a towering figure of history and legend, McAleese quotes a passage from his autobiography that makes him relatable to ordinary people in their struggles: "'I am the sinner Patrick. I am the most unsophisticated of people, the least of Christians.'" She uses this statement to empower her audience: "He was an ordinary man who found in himself the capacity for extraordinary, heroic things. Every community needs such people." Identification with a historic figure is strengthened when one can connect with that individual's history concretely. Accordingly, McAleese highlights the fact that the city where she is delivering this address was once the seat of St. Patrick's authority as bishop of Ireland, and it "is now home of the North-South Ministerial Council and the Centre for Cross-Border Studies," a place where "the new culture of consensus and good neighborliness is being incubated each day and rolled out across the island." By making this geographic connection to St. Patrick's ministry, she lends credibility and gravity to Irish reconciliation.

Besides connecting current reconciliation efforts with Patrick's ancient example, McAleese also draws liberally from modern Irish literature. She quotes from three different poems by Seamus Heaney—the greatest Irish poet of her time—and ends with a verse by William McClure that features the shamrock as the symbol of Irish communion. From beginning to end, President McAleese eloquently presents Irish reconciliation as a project that is rooted in Irish culture and must therefore surely succeed.

Inaugural St. Patrick's Day Lecture at Armagh[7]

Armagh, Ireland
March 19, 2010

[Greeting the audience in Irish] *Dia dhíbh a chairde tráthnóna. Tá gliondar orm bheith anseo libh ar an ócáid speisialta seo agus ba mhaith liom mo bhuíochas a chur in iúl díbh as an chaoin-chuireadh agus an fháilte.*

Where better to be in this week of St. Patrick than in the ecclesiastical capital of Ireland? I thank Councillor Thomas O'Hanlon, the Mayor of Armagh City and District Council, for the kind invitation to give the inaugural "St. Patrick's Day Lecture at Armagh."

In divided communities, particularly where the divisions are bitter and where memories are often invoked only to sharpen the division, the calling to mind of a shared heritage, a shared memory, can be an important bridge to reconciliation and to recognition of one another as brothers and sisters rather than strangers. Gathering here as we do in the name of St. Patrick, across borders of history and of hearts and minds, we acknowledge that whatever our politics or perspective, we are each one a child of St. Patrick; his story is our story, his legacy our legacy. Patrick created for us a platform of shared inheritance strong enough to help us to share more, to share better with one another in the days and years ahead.

It is always going to be difficult to interrogate thoroughly a life lived over a millennium and a half ago. Patrick's life has gathered legends and contradictions in the generations between his day and ours, but there is neither mystery nor legend about the fact that he came among us as a stranger, that he was a passionate ambassador for the Christian faith and that the message he espoused left an enduring impact and indeed an enduring challenge on this island that he came to love so much and to be identified with in every corner of the known world.

The man who came as an immigrant slave to these shores became by sheer force of principle and personality, a powerful catalyst for change. He was a victim of violence, a child kidnapped, held captive and abused. He was one of the downtrodden, the overlooked, the disregarded. He knew the cruelty of loss and loneliness for he was taken away from those he loved and who loved him. He knew well the inhumanity of which his fellow human beings were capable, for they visited enough of it directly on him to leave him in no doubt that almost all the unnecessary suffering in the world is inflicted by human beings on one another. Seamus Heaney's poem "The Cure at Troy" says tersely, "Human beings suffer, They torture one another, They get hurt and get hard."[8] And there is truth in those words, as this country has cause to know. But not everyone gets hard. There are some who refuse to become hardened and bitter, who do not, through their acts, add more to the pile of human misery but instead commit their lives to softening, to reducing the mountain of hurt, to ending the cycle of misery. Patrick was one of those rare human beings; a man whose righteous frustration and indignation, his anger and his pain, distilled not into more hatred but into a loving forgiveness that stopped the toxin of hate dead in its tracks.

Sometimes we remember only Patrick the bishop, striding through Ireland powerful, persuasive and compelling, but there is another Patrick more pertinent to these times. He is the slave boy, herding sheep on Slemish, frozen to the bone, realizing the sheep were regarded more highly than he was and wondering was there ever to be a life for him—would he ever know freedom to live life on his own terms.

In this city and country and around Northern Ireland, there are men, women and children who feel that they too have been left out and left behind. They have been demoralized and drained by the conflict, they feel their youth and potential was robbed by forces beyond them and though peace is gathering momentum, consolidating day by day, the benefits of this great historic shift are not yet evenly distributed. That will take time. It will also take the same kind of courage, focus and commitment that was demanded of Patrick. The seemingly wasted years of his youth distilled into a passion that would make his name resound a millennium and a half later. Instead of letting victimhood and vengeance consume the rest of his life, he used the present not to dwell on the past or in the past but to fix what he thought needed to be fixed so that the future would be a place of hope—a place where all could safely belong. There are more and more people trying to do just that here in Northern Ireland. They are trying to build a reconciled society and at the same time trying to address the underlying tensions and problems which helped fuel the conflict. They are searching for ways to deal effectively and sensitively with the many deep traumas of the past. The fresh new momentum they have gathered into this phenomenon we call the Peace Process has offered such a new vista that more and more people have become peacemakers, including many who once sought to advance their cause through violence. The transformation in their thinking and their lives is the very thing that gives us such hope that real change is possible, that love can indeed transcend hatred and help heal hurt. The conversion to peace is not unlike the conversion of Ireland to the vision of St. Patrick, for he too knew the wonder and the miracle of persuading sceptics and enemies to give up their old ways of thinking and join his mission. Patrick also knew what it was like to make hard choices, to put the common good before his own safety and wellbeing, to put his life in the service of others. He had escaped from captivity after six miserable years. He had gone home. He was safe. He was free, but a voice called him back to Ireland and he surrendered to that voice very reluctantly; as he said in his *Confessio*,[9] "I did not proceed to Ireland on my own accord until I was almost giving up."[10]

Had he given up, there would be much more than a big vacant hole in the March calendar. In every generation, whatever its circumstances, there has been a part of St. Patrick's story to inspire, to comfort and to engender hope. In this once deeply fractured Ireland, which is on the journey to healing, there is his capacity for forgiveness of those who hurt him and his great love of this island. His status as an emigrant lodged deep in the hearts of the many millions of Irish who left their homeland driven out by poverty and politics. His arrival as a nonentity of a stranger who was to leave a massive imprint on the country of his adoption, reminds those of us who live in post-Plantation Ireland and who live in multicultural Ireland that the stranger is a repository of new energies, ambitions and perspectives that can make a rich contribution to our society. So Patrick teaches the stranger to have faith in the contribution he or she can make and he teaches the native to see inward migration as an opportunity.

A key element of Patrick's success was that he respected and worked alongside the old pagan culture so that his form of Christianity was absorbed easily and fluently into Irish life, growing side by side with the old pagan culture, with no anxiety to obliterate it. As a result, Ireland was transformed into something new, a place with a distinctive psychological identity, capable of seamless yet radical change.

When we speak of radical change, it is easy to miss the import of the cumulative changes we ourselves have lived through. Perhaps we are as yet too close to these events to see their true magnitude. But who could ever have imagined that an Irish Government would purchase the site of the Battle of the Boyne and develop there a heritage site for all the people of the island of Ireland? Who could have imagined a government in Northern Ireland with Sinn Féin Ministers working side by side with Democratic Unionist colleagues? It is only when we pause and take a step back to look at the bigger picture, over a longer perspective of time, that we truly appreciate how momentous this process of change really is and how much closer it brings us to Patrick's vision for the people of this island.

We are no longer the one-time island of saints and scholars that illumined all of Europe with scholarship, erudition, literacy and the great commandment to love one another. But that Ireland is still embedded in our DNA, just as the memory of those wandering monks is still to be found in the street names all over the European mainland. Centuries later, the children who had grown up on those European streets and who had slaughtered each other in their millions in two devastating World Wars would, out of the craven wreckage of those times, create the European Union, a most unlikely partnership of old enemies. They put war behind them and a future of friendship in front of them, and it was our membership of that Union, along with the United Kingdom, that set the scene for the development of one of the most crucial dynamics in our Peace Process. Shared membership of the Union allowed the relationship between Ireland and Britain to metamorphose rapidly from lukewarm and distrustful to fulsome and warm. A new collegiality opened up the space for a joint endeavor to bring peace to Northern Ireland and to put all the fraught relationships of history on a fresh and healthy footing.

This city was to become associated with the recalibration of those relationships in a very special way, for appropriately, the city where Patrick established his See is now home of the North-South Ministerial Council and the Centre for Cross-Border Studies. Here the new culture of consensus and good neighborliness is being incubated each day and rolled out across the island. North-South cooperation has replaced the wasteful days of living with "back turned to back." So much potential, for everything from simple friendship, safety and commerce, leached away into the sands of time because of the embedded culture of conflict. We are the first generation to know the joy of a future to look forward to, one that is humanly decent and uplifting. The politics that deliver this new horizon are not always pretty or straightforward but they have a visible forward momentum and importantly they result from democratic dialogue, plain speaking and compromise.

Now we have Ministers from the Irish Government and the Northern Ireland Executive cooperating regularly across a range of issues of common importance. We share North-South bodies like InterTradeIreland and Tourism Ireland. We harmonize our plans for building roads together. We share our precious natural resources and provide cancer and GP services on a cross-border basis. These things show what happens when our energy and initiative are liberated to be a positive force that makes a real difference to the lives of people on both sides of the border. There is no better place to observe that force at work than here in Armagh.

Last month, with the agreement reached on the devolution of policing and justice powers, we witnessed a moment when the Peace Process transitioned from potential to reality. It was a lumpy, awkward and difficult business. All of us on this island know that politics is at times a painstaking business, but in the end something inspirational did occur; the two traditions began to look more and more like one community and they spoke more and more convincingly with one voice. The politicians answered the call of the people for leadership just as St. Patrick answered the voice that called him to leadership in Ireland.

He wrote in his *Confessio*, "I am the sinner Patrick. I am the most unsophisticated of people, the least of Christians."[11] He was an ordinary man who found in himself the capacity for extraordinary, heroic things. Every community needs such people—the simple and the sincere who don't follow the giddy crowd, but who give remarkable leadership in their families, streets, communities, workplaces, clubs and country. They are the men and women who stop the toxin of hatred by refusing to laugh at the sectarian or racist joke. They are the men and women who make friends across the fractures of history's making. They are the men and women who teach their children to respect all others and to expect difference as well as to respect it. They are the backbone of the Peace Process and they have always been true to Patrick's call to love one another, forgive one another and to see each other as brothers and sisters.

We have rounded the cusp of change and now need to gather the momentum which will build, grow and consolidate this new emerging culture of good neighborliness. That momentum is being quietly gathered in so many corners of this island by the persistent but largely unsung transformational work that is being done by individuals and all sorts of voluntary groups. They are unobtrusively fixing things that are or were wrong; they are filling in the "centuries' arrears."

The Peace Process went through many a wobble—some of them of seismic proportions—but today its robustness is a cause of real hope. The economy is going through a considerable wobble and history teaches us that we will find a way out of it—and this time we have on our side the resource of a peace, a resource denied to so many other generations over the centuries.

In his great poem "From the Canton of Expectation," Seamus Heaney described the grim psychological hinterland inhabited by the generations before us: "We lived deep in a land of optative moods, under high, banked clouds of resignation."[12] Not anymore we don't. Today there is a lovely stanza from "Station Island" that describes this moment better:

> As little flowers that were all bowed and shut
> By the night chills rise on their stems and open
> As soon as they have felt the touch of sunlight,
> So I revived my own wilting powers
> And my heart flushed, like somebody set free.[13]

There is the touch of sunlight in this hard-won peace. And in this week we think of the littlest flower of them all, the shamrock, so beloved as a teaching tool by St. Patrick.

In his poem "The Shamrock and Laurel," the Rev. William McClure points the way to our coming future:

> As the Lily was the glory
> Of the olden flag of France;
> As the Rose illumes the story
> Of Albion's advance—
> In the Shamrock is communion
> Of all Irish faith, and love.[14]

Notes

1. For a brief history of the Troubles as well as an examination of three Irish religious communities' efforts to promote reconciliation during that period, see Ronald A. Wells, *People behind the Peace: Community and Reconciliation in Northern Ireland* (Grand Rapids, MI: William B. Eerdmans, 1999). See also Jeff Wallenfeldt, "The Troubles," *Encyclopaedia Britannica*, https://www.britannica.com/event/The-Troubles-Northern-Ireland-history.
2. Wells, 34.

3. See John O'Farrell, "Apartheid," *New Statesman*, November 28, 2005, 14–17, Academic Search Complete.
4. For more on McAleese's life, see Patsy McGarry, *First Citizen: Mary McAleese and the Irish Presidency* (Dublin: The O'Brien Press, 2008).
5. See Seamus Heaney, "Foreword," in President Mary McAleese, *Building Bridges: Selected Speeches and Statements* (Dublin: The History Press Ireland, 2011), 11–15.
6. For her own account of this spirituality of love and the life experiences that shaped it amid Northern Ireland's sectarian conflict, see Mary McAleese, *Love in Chaos: Spiritual Growth and the Search for Peace in Northern Ireland* (New York: Continuum Press, 1999).
7. This speech was previously printed in McAleese, *Building Bridges*, 267–73. It is reprinted here with permission from the publisher.
8. Seamus Heaney, *The Cure at Troy: A Version of Sophocles' Philoctetes* (New York: Farrar, Straus, and Giroux, 1991), 77.
9. *Confessio* is Latin for *confession*.
10. St. Patrick, *The Confession of St. Patrick*, trans. Ludwig Bieler (Grand Rapids, MI: Christian Classics Ethereal Library), 12. Available online: https://www.orthodoxroad.com/wp-content/uploads/2014/03/confession-of-st-patrick.pdf.
11. Here, McAleese is either quoting from a different translation of *The Confession of St. Patrick* or, more likely, adapting it for the purposes of her speech. In the version cited above, the statement is found on page 16.
12. Seamus Heaney, "From the Canton of Expectation," in *The Haw Lantern* (London: Faber & Faber, 1995), 46–47.
13. Seamus Heaney, "Station Island," in *Station Island* (New York: Farrar, Straus, and Giroux, 1985), 76.
14. The full poem is available at http://www.from-ireland.net/song/the-shamrock-and-laurel/.

CHAPTER NINE

Bridging America's Racial Divide: Barack Obama

In 2004, the Democratic National Convention keynote address was delivered by a little-known Illinois state senator and U.S. Senate candidate named Barack Obama. This speech electrified the nation with its inspiring oratory. According to Robert C. Rowland and John M. Jones, the key to its appeal was Obama's romantic recasting of liberal/progressive values within the narrative of the American Dream, joining an emphasis on community responsibility with a celebration of personal responsibility and hard work.[1] I would add that the keynote address evinced a comic view of the nation as fundamentally united beneath its ideological differences. Similarly, David A. Frank argued that the speech embodied a rhetoric of *consilience*, "in which disparate members of a composite audience are invited to 'jump together' out of their separate experiences in favor of a common set of values or aspirations."[2] As such, Frank suggested that the speech offered a way forward toward racial reconciliation. On the other hand, Mark Lawrence McPhail noted that it failed to acknowledge the nation's real and present racial disparities and injustices, with the result that its romanticized picture of America undermined its potential to promote genuine reconciliation.[3] In any case, on the strength of this address, Obama quickly rose in the national spotlight as a black/biracial politician who could appeal to a wide swath of Americans.

In 2007, Obama officially announced his candidacy for U.S. president. Speaking in Springfield, Illinois, "where Lincoln once called on a house divided to stand together," Obama cast himself in the mold of that leader, who sought to realize the promise of the nation's founding ideals and fought to preserve the Union rooted in those ideals.[4] From Lincoln's example, Obama drew the lesson that "beneath all the differences of race and region, faith and station, we are one people." As the primaries unfolded, Obama quickly joined Sen. Hillary Clinton as a front-runner.

However, Obama's viability as a presidential candidate came under serious question when the media began repeatedly airing YouTube clips of his pastor, the Reverend Jeremiah Wright, apparently "damning" America for the de facto racism of its criminal justice system. He was also heard claiming that 9/11 was "America's chickens ... coming home to roost" from its policies of violent militarism around the world.[5] As it turned out, Wright had taken his assessment of 9/11 from a white U.S. ambassador being interviewed on Fox News;[6] moreover, Frank argues that Wright's comments, when taken in their original context, actually fall within the Biblical prophetic tradition.[7] Nonetheless, most Americans heard his comments as hateful and unpatriotic. When Obama's brief statements denouncing the controversial sermon statements failed to quell the media firestorm, he crafted and delivered his important and much-studied speech about race in America, "A More Perfect Union."

Besides effectively quieting Obama's critics and salvaging his presidential campaign, "A More Perfect Union" arguably spoke to the racial divide more clearly and effectively than any president or president-to-be had ever done. It certainly addressed race better than Obama's DNC keynote. Numerous pundits and rhetoricians highly praised the speech, although a few commentators sharply criticized Obama's handling of the Wright controversy.[8] Frank demonstrates that much of the speech's significance and power lies in its connections to the prophetic tradition of Martin Luther King Jr., the black church, and the larger Jewish and Christian faith traditions, as well as Obama's capacity to bring into open conversation the angry racial perspectives normally voiced only in blacks' and whites' separate "hush harbors."[9] Robert E. Terrill argues that the speech offers a "stereoscopic gaze" at race through the eyes both of blacks and whites.[10] Susanna Dilliplane demonstrates that the speech successfully met the political challenges inherent in responding to Wright's comments by using two themes of Obama's campaign—"toward a more perfect union" and "out of many, we are one"—to reframe both Wright and Obama.[11]

In this speech, Obama offers a relatively well-rounded perspective on racial division and reconciliation by applying the complete tetrad of frames to the exigence of Wright's controversial remarks and the broader challenge of American race relations. While judiciously incorporating the tragic language of sin and condemnation, he more strongly emphasizes the comic discourse of colorful diversity, family connectedness, forgivable misunderstandings, common ground, and common cause. At the same time, Obama realistically faces the past and present facts of racial oppression and division while holding on to a romantic, hopeful vision of perfecting the nation's union. In the process of reframing the Wright controversy and America's racial division, Obama draws inspiration not only from the U.S. Constitution and the nation's heritage of democratic progress but also from religion, including his experience of the black church (with its strong sense of community and its compelling appropriation of Bible stories to meet life's present challenges), as well as the ethic of the Golden Rule, found in Scripture and in "all the world's great religions."

Peeling back the curtain on both black and white anger, Obama dispassionately exposes the factual, historical roots of these feelings. While he affirms both races' resentments as understandable, he also points out how racial anger has been channeled counter-productively at times. Having provided a realistic picture of racial division, Obama recommends a way to "move beyond some of our old racial wounds," a "path to a more perfect union." What he suggests is less a path than an orientation—a tragicomic reframing of race relations. For black Americans, he says, the path to a more perfect union involves not only pursuing "a full measure of justice in every aspect of American life," but also "binding our particular grievances, for better health care and better schools and better jobs, to the larger aspirations of all Americans," including whites who struggle—thus recognizing Americans' common ground and interdependence. For white Americans, Obama similarly commends a tragicomic approach: acknowledging and addressing racial injustice faced by black people, while recognizing that such race-specific efforts actually promote the common good—"that your dreams do not have to come at the expense of my dreams, that investing in the health, welfare, and education of black and brown and white children will ultimately help all of America prosper." In addition, as an antidote to despair over persistent racial inequities, Obama offers black Americans a healthy dose of romantic framing, encouraging them to maintain audacious hope, engage in self-help, believe in America's capacity to change, and teach their children to "believe that they can write their own destiny."

As he nears his conclusion, Obama challenges Americans to turn their attention from petty divisions to their common needs. He ends the address with an anecdote that illustrates how Americans can work toward a more perfect union: by recognizing the humanity, vulnerability, and aspirations they share across their real differences. In sum, "A More Perfect Union" reaffirms the rhetoric of consilience introduced in Obama's 2004 DNC keynote address, while speaking much more fully to America's racial divisions and injustices and proposing an approach to healing these wounds. As such, despite imperfections in Obama's handling of the Wright controversy, this speech offers a more robust vision of racial reconciliation than his DNC keynote. Indeed, what Obama says about the nation's union near the end of this speech could well be said of reconciliation: it "may never be perfect, but ... it can always be perfected."

"A More Perfect Union"

Philadelphia, Pennsylvania
March 18, 2008

"We the people, in order to form a more perfect union." Two hundred and twenty-one years ago, in a hall that still stands across the street, a group of men gathered and, with these simple words, launched America's improbable experiment in democracy. Farmers and scholars, statesmen and patriots who had traveled across the ocean to escape tyranny and persecution finally made real their Declaration of Independence at a Philadelphia convention that lasted through the spring of 1787.

The document they produced was eventually signed, but ultimately unfinished. It was stained by this nation's original sin of slavery, a question that divided the colonies and brought the convention to a stalemate until the founders chose to allow the slave trade to continue for at least 20 more years, and to leave any final resolution to future generations. Of course, the answer to the slavery question was already embedded within our Constitution—a Constitution that had at its very core the ideal of equal citizenship under the law; a Constitution that promised its people liberty and justice, and a union that could be and should be perfected over time.

And yet words on a parchment would not be enough to deliver slaves from bondage, or provide men and women of every color and creed their full rights and obligations as citizens of the United States. What would be needed were Americans in successive generations who were willing to do their part—through protests and struggles, on the streets and in the courts, through a civil war and civil disobedience, and always at great risk—to narrow that gap between the promise of our ideals and the reality of their time.

This was one of the tasks we set forth at the beginning of this presidential campaign: to continue the long march of those who came before us, a march for a more just, more equal, more free, more caring, and more prosperous America. I chose to run for President at this moment in history because I believe deeply that we cannot solve the challenges of our time unless we solve them together, unless we perfect our union by understanding that we may have different stories, but we hold common hopes; that we may not look the same and may not have come from the same place, but we all want to move in the same direction: towards a better future for our children and our grandchildren. And this belief comes from my unyielding faith in the decency and generosity of the American people. But it also comes from my own story.

I'm the son of a black man from Kenya and a white woman from Kansas. I was raised with the help of a white grandfather who survived a Depression to serve in Patton's army during World War II, and a white grandmother who worked on a bomber assembly line at Fort Leavenworth while he was overseas. I've gone to some of the best schools in America and I've lived in one of the world's poorest nations. I am married to a black American who carries within her the blood of slaves and slave owners, an inheritance we pass on to our two precious daughters. I have brothers, sisters, nieces, nephews, uncles, and cousins of every race and every hue scattered across three continents, and for as long as I live, I will never forget that in no other country on earth is my story even possible. It's a story that hasn't made me the most conventional of candidates. But it is a story that has seared into my genetic makeup the idea that this nation is more than the sum of its parts—that out of many, we are truly one.

Now throughout the first year of this campaign, against all predictions to the contrary, we saw how hungry the American people were for this message of unity. Despite the temptation to view my candidacy through a purely racial lens, we won commanding victories in states with some of the whitest populations in the country. In South Carolina, where the Confederate flag still flies, we built a powerful coalition of African Americans and white Americans. This is not to say that race has not been an issue in this campaign. At various stages in the campaign, some commentators have deemed me either "too black" or "not black enough." We saw racial tensions bubble to the surface during the week before the South Carolina primary. The press has scoured every single exit poll for the latest evidence of racial polarization, not just in terms of white and black, but black and brown as well.

And yet, it's only been in the last couple of weeks that the discussion of race in this campaign has taken a particularly divisive turn. On one end of the spectrum, we've heard the implication that my candidacy is somehow an exercise in affirmative action; that it's based solely on the desire of wild and wide-eyed liberals to purchase racial reconciliation on the cheap. On the other end, we've heard my former pastor, Jeremiah Wright, use incendiary language to express views that have the potential not only to widen the racial divide, but views that denigrate both the greatness and the goodness of our nation and that rightly offend white and black alike.

Now I've already condemned, in unequivocal terms, the statements of Reverend Wright that have caused such controversy, and in some cases, pain. For some, nagging questions remain: Did I know him to be an occasionally fierce critic of American domestic and foreign policy? Of course. Did I ever hear him make remarks that could be considered controversial while I sat in the church? Yes. Did I strongly disagree with many of his political views? Absolutely, just as I'm sure many of you have heard remarks from your pastors, priests, or rabbis with which you strongly disagree.

But the remarks that have caused this recent firestorm weren't simply controversial. They weren't simply a religious leader's efforts to speak out against perceived injustice. Instead, they expressed a profoundly distorted view of this country, a view that sees white racism as endemic and that elevates what is wrong with America above all that we know is right with America; a view that sees the conflicts in the Middle East as rooted primarily in the actions of stalwart allies like Israel instead of emanating from the perverse and hateful ideologies of radical Islam.

As such, Reverend Wright's comments were not only wrong but divisive, divisive at a time when we need unity; racially charged at a time when we need to come together to solve a set of monumental problems: two wars, a terrorist threat, a falling economy, a chronic health care crisis, and potentially devastating climate change—problems that are neither black nor white or Latino or Asian, but rather problems that confront us all.

Given my background, my politics, and my professed values and ideals, there will no doubt be those for whom my statements of condemnation are not enough. Why associate myself with Reverend Wright in the first place, they may ask? Why not join another church? And I confess that if all that I knew of Reverend Wright were the snippets of those sermons that have run in an endless loop on the television sets and YouTube, if Trinity United Church of Christ conformed to the caricatures being peddled by some commentators, there is no doubt that I would react in much the same way.

But the truth is, that isn't all that I know of the man. The man I met more than 20 years ago is a man who helped introduce me to my Christian faith, a man who spoke to me about our obligations to love one another, to care for the sick and lift up the poor. He is a man who served his country as a United States Marine, and who has studied and lectured at some of the finest universities and seminaries in the country, and who over 30 years has led a church that serves the community by doing God's work here on Earth—by housing the homeless, ministering to the needy, providing day care services and scholarships and prison ministries, and reaching out to those suffering from HIV/AIDS.

In my first book, *Dreams from My Father*, I described the experience of my first service at Trinity, and it goes as follows:

> People began to shout, to rise from their seats and clap and cry out, a forceful wind carrying the reverend's voice up into the rafters....
>
> And in that single note—hope!—I heard something else; at the foot of that cross, inside the thousands of churches across the city, I imagined the stories of ordinary black people merging with the stories of David and Goliath, Moses and Pharaoh, the Christians in the lion's den, Ezekiel's field of dry bones. Those stories—of survival, and freedom, and hope—became our stories, my story; the blood that spilled was our blood, the tears our tears; until this black church, on this bright day, seemed once more a vessel carrying the story of a people into future generations and into a larger world. Our trials and triumphs became at once unique and universal, black and more than black; in chronicling our journey, the stories and songs gave us a meaning[12] to reclaim memories that we didn't need to feel shame about ... memories that all people might study and cherish—and with which we could start to rebuild.[13]

That has been my experience at Trinity. Like other predominantly black churches across the country, Trinity embodies the black community in its entirety—the doctor and the welfare mom, the model student and the former gang-banger. Like other black churches, Trinity's services are full of raucous laughter and sometimes bawdy humor. They are full of dancing and clapping and screaming and shouting that may seem jarring to the untrained ear. The church contains in full the kindness and cruelty, the fierce intelligence and the shocking ignorance, the struggles and successes, the love and, yes, the bitterness and biases that make up the black experience in America.

And this helps explain, perhaps, my relationship with Reverend Wright. As imperfect as he may be, he has been like family to me. He strengthens my faith, officiated my wedding, and baptized my children. Not once in my conversations with him have I heard him talk about any ethnic group in derogatory terms or treat whites with whom he interacted with anything but courtesy and respect. He contains within him the contradictions—the good and the bad—of the community that he has served diligently for so many years.

I can no more disown him than I can disown the black community. I can no more disown him than I can disown my white grandmother, a woman who helped raise me, a woman who sacrificed again and again for me, a woman who loves me as much as she loves anything in this world, but a woman who once confessed her fear of black men who passed her by on the street, and who on more than one occasion has uttered racial or ethnic stereotypes that made me cringe.

These people are part of me. And they are part of America, this country that I love.

Now, some will see this as an attempt to justify or excuse comments that are simply inexcusable. I can assure you it is not. And I suppose the politically safe thing to do would be to move on from this episode and just hope that it fades into the woodwork. We can dismiss Reverend Wright as a crank or a demagogue, just as some have dismissed Geraldine Ferraro, in the aftermath of her recent statements, as harboring some deep-seated bias.

But race is an issue that I believe this nation cannot afford to ignore right now. We would be making the same mistake that Reverend Wright made in his offending sermons about America: to simplify and stereotype and amplify the negative to the point that it distorts reality. The fact is that the comments that have been made and the issues that have surfaced over the last few weeks reflect the complexities of race in this country that we've never really worked through, a part of our union that we have not yet made perfect. And if we walk away now, if we simply retreat into our respective corners, we will never be able to come together and solve challenges like health care or education or the need to find good jobs for every American.

Understanding this reality requires a reminder of how we arrived at this point. As William Faulkner once wrote, "The past isn't dead and buried. In fact, it isn't even past." We do not need to recite here the history of racial injustice in this country. But we do need to remind ourselves that so many of the disparities that exist between the African-American community and the larger American community today can be traced directly to inequalities passed on from an earlier generation that suffered under the brutal legacy of slavery and Jim Crow. Segregated schools were, and are, inferior schools. We still haven't fixed them, 50 years after Brown versus Board of Education. And the inferior education they provided, then and now, helps explain the pervasive achievement gap between today's black and white students.

Legalized discrimination—where blacks were prevented, often through violence, from owning property, or loans were not granted to African-American business owners, or black homeowners could not access FHA mortgages, or blacks were excluded from unions, or the police force, or the fire department—meant that black families could not amass any meaningful wealth to bequeath to future generations. That history helps explain the wealth and income gap between blacks and whites and the concentrated pockets of poverty that persist in so many of today's urban and rural communities. A lack of economic opportunity among black men and the shame and frustration that came from not being able to provide for one's family contributed to the erosion of black families, a problem that welfare policies for many years may have worsened. And the lack of basic services in so many urban black neighborhoods—parks for kids to play in, police walking the beat, regular garbage pick-up, building code enforcement—all helped create a cycle of violence, blight, and neglect that continues to haunt us.

This is the reality in which Reverend Wright and other African Americans of his generation grew up. They came of age in the late '50s and early '60s, a time when segregation was still the law of the land and opportunity was systematically constricted. What's remarkable is not how many failed in the face of discrimination, but how many men and women overcame the odds, how many were able to make a way out of no way for those like me who would come after them.

But for all those who scratched and clawed their way to get a piece of the American Dream, there were many who didn't make it—those who were ultimately defeated, in one way or another, by discrimination. That legacy of defeat was passed on to future generations—those young men and increasingly young women who we see standing on street corners or languishing in our prisons, without hope or prospects for the future. Even for those blacks who did make it, questions of race, and racism, continue to define their worldview in fundamental ways. For the men and women of Reverend Wright's generation, the memories of humiliation and doubt and fear have not gone away, nor has the anger and the bitterness of those years.

That anger may not get expressed in public, in front of white co-workers or white friends, but it does find voice in the barbershop or the beauty shop or around the kitchen table. At times, that anger is exploited by politicians to gin up votes along racial lines or to make up for a politician's own failings. And occasionally it finds voice in the church on Sunday morning, in the pulpit and in the pews. The fact that so many people are surprised to hear that anger in some of Reverend Wright's sermons simply reminds us of that old truism that the most segregated hour of American life occurs on Sunday morning.

That anger is not always productive. Indeed, all too often it distracts attention from solving real problems. It keeps us from squarely facing our own complicity within the African-American community in our own condition. It prevents the African-American community from forging the alliances it needs to bring about real change. But the anger is real; it is powerful, and to simply wish it away, to condemn it without understanding its roots only serves to widen the chasm of misunderstanding that exists between the races.

In fact, a similar anger exists within segments of the white community. Most working- and middle-class white Americans don't feel that they've been particularly privileged by their race. Their experience is the immigrant experience. As far as they're concerned, no one handed them anything; they built it from scratch. They've worked hard all their lives, many times only to see their jobs shipped overseas or their pensions dumped after a lifetime of labor. They are anxious about their futures, and they feel their dreams slipping away. And in an era of stagnant wages and global competition, opportunity comes to be seen as a zero-sum game, in which your dreams come at my expense. So when they are told to bus their children to a school across town, when they hear that an African American is getting an advantage in landing a good job or a spot in a good college because of an injustice that they themselves never committed, when they're told that their fears about crime in urban neighborhoods are somehow prejudice, resentment builds over time.

Like the anger within the black community, these resentments aren't always expressed in polite company. But they have helped shape the political landscape for at least a generation. Anger over welfare and affirmative action helped forge the Reagan coalition. Politicians routinely exploited fears of crime for their own electoral ends. Talk show hosts and conservative commentators built entire careers unmasking bogus claims of racism while dismissing legitimate discussions of racial injustice and inequality as mere political correctness or reverse racism. And just as black anger often proved counterproductive, so have these white resentments distracted attention from the real culprits of the middle-class squeeze: a corporate culture rife with inside dealing, questionable accounting practices, and short-term greed; a Washington dominated by lobbyists and special interests; economic policies that favor the few over the many. And yet, to wish away the resentments of white Americans, to label them as misguided or even racist without recognizing they are grounded in legitimate concerns—this, too, widens the racial divide and blocks the path to understanding.

This is where we are right now.

It's a racial stalemate we've been stuck in for years. And contrary to the claims of some of my critics, black and white, I have never been so naïve as to believe that we can get beyond our racial divisions in a single election cycle or with a single candidate—particularly a candidacy as imperfect as my own. But I have asserted a firm conviction, a conviction rooted in my faith in God and my faith in the American people, that, working together, we can move beyond some of our old racial wounds and that, in fact, we have no choice—we have no choice if we are to continue on the path of a more perfect union.

For the African-American community, that path means embracing the burdens of our past without becoming victims of our past. It means continuing to insist on a full measure of justice in every aspect of American life. But it also means binding our particular grievances, for better health care and better schools and better jobs, to the larger aspirations of all Americans—the white woman struggling to break the glass ceiling, the white man who's been laid off, the immigrant trying to feed his family. And it means also taking full responsibility for our own lives—by demanding more from our fathers, and spending more time with our children, and reading to them, and teaching them that while they may face challenges and discrimination in their own lives, they must never succumb to despair or cynicism. They must always believe that they can write their own destiny.

Ironically, this quintessentially American—and, yes, conservative—notion of self-help found frequent expression in Reverend Wright's sermons. But what my former pastor too often failed to understand is that embarking on a program of self-help also requires a belief that society can change. The profound mistake of Reverend Wright's sermons is not that he spoke about racism in our society. It's that he spoke as if our society was static, as if no progress had been made, as if this country—a country that has made it possible for one of his own members to run for the highest office in the land and build a coalition of white and black, Latino, Asian, rich, poor, young, and old—is still irrevocably bound to a tragic past. What we know, what we have seen, is that America can change. That is the true genius of this nation. What we have already achieved gives us hope—the audacity to hope—for what we can and must achieve tomorrow.

Now, in the white community, the path to a more perfect union means acknowledging that what ails the African-American community does not just exist in the minds of black people; that the legacy of discrimination, and current incidents of discrimination, while less overt than in the past—that these things are real and must be addressed. Not just with words, but with deeds—by investing in our schools and our communities; by enforcing our civil rights laws and ensuring fairness in our criminal justice system; by providing this generation with ladders of opportunity that were unavailable for previous generations. It requires all Americans to realize that your dreams do not have to come at the expense of my dreams, that investing in the health, welfare, and education of black and brown and white children will ultimately help all of America prosper.

In the end, then, what is called for is nothing more and nothing less than what all the world's great religions demand: that we do unto others as we would have them do unto us. Let us be our brother's keeper, Scripture tells us. Let us be our sister's keeper. Let us find that common stake we all have in one another, and let our politics reflect that spirit as well.

For we have a choice in this country. We can accept a politics that breeds division and conflict and cynicism. We can tackle race only as spectacle, as we did in the O.J. trial; or in the wake of tragedy, as we did in the aftermath of Katrina; or as fodder for the nightly news. We can play Reverend Wright's sermons on every channel every day and talk about them from now until the election, and make the only question in this campaign whether or not the American people think that I somehow believe or sympathize with his most offensive words. We can pounce on some gaffe by a Hillary supporter as evidence that she's playing the race card; or we can speculate on whether white men will all flock to John McCain in the general election regardless of his policies. We can do that. But if we do, I can tell you that in the next election, we'll be talking about some other distraction, and then another one, and then another one. And nothing will change.

That is one option.

Or, at this moment, in this election, we can come together and say, "Not this time." This time we want to talk about the crumbling schools that are stealing the future of black children and white children and Asian children and Hispanic children and Native American children. This time we want to reject the cynicism that tells us that these kids can't learn; that those kids who don't look like us are somebody else's problem. The children of America are not "those kids"—they are our kids, and we will not let them fall behind in a 21st-century economy. Not this time. This time we want to talk about how the lines in the emergency room are filled with whites and blacks and Hispanics who do not have health care, who don't have the power on their own to overcome the special interests in Washington, but who can take them on if we do it together.

This time we want to talk about the shuttered mills that once provided a decent life for men and women of every race, and the homes for sale that once belonged to Americans from every religion, every region, every walk of life. This time we want to talk about the fact that the real problem is not that someone who doesn't look like you might take your job; it's that the corporation you work for will ship it overseas for nothing more than a profit. This time we want to talk about the men and women of every color and creed who serve together, and fight together, and bleed together under the same proud flag. We want to talk about how to bring them home from a war that should've never been authorized and should've never been waged.[14] And we want to talk about how we'll show our patriotism by caring for them, and their families, and giving them the benefits that they have earned.

I would not be running for President if I didn't believe with all my heart that this is what the vast majority of Americans want for this country. This union may never be perfect, but generation after generation has shown that it can always be perfected. And today, whenever I find myself feeling doubtful or cynical about this possibility, what gives me the most hope is the next generation—the young people whose attitudes and beliefs and openness to change have already made history in this election.

There's one story in particular that I'd like to leave you with today, a story I told when I had the great honor of speaking on Dr. King's birthday at his home church, Ebenezer Baptist, in Atlanta. There's a young, 23-year-old woman, a white woman named Ashley Baia, who organized for our campaign in Florence, South Carolina. She'd been working to organize a mostly African-American community since the beginning of this campaign, and one day she was at a roundtable discussion where everyone went around telling their story and why they were there. And Ashley said that when she was nine years old, her mother got cancer. And because she had to miss days of work, she was let go and lost her health care. They had to file for bankruptcy, and that's when Ashley decided that she had to do something to help her mom.

She knew that food was one of their most expensive costs, and so Ashley convinced her mother that what she really liked and really wanted to eat more than anything else was mustard and relish sandwiches—because that was the cheapest way to eat. That's the mind of a nine-year-old. She did this for a year until her mom got better. And so Ashley told everyone at the roundtable that the reason she had joined our campaign was so that she could help the millions of other children in the country who want and need to help their parents, too.

Now, Ashley might have made a different choice. Perhaps somebody told her along the way that the source of her mother's problems were blacks who were on welfare and too lazy to work, or Hispanics who were coming into the country illegally. But she didn't. She sought out allies in her fight against injustice.

Anyway, Ashley finishes her story and then goes around the room and asks everyone else why they're supporting the campaign. They all have different stories and different reasons. Many bring up a specific issue. And finally they come to this elderly black man who's been sitting there quietly the entire time. And Ashley asks him why he's there. And he doesn't bring up a specific issue. He does not say health care or the economy. He does not say education or the war. He does not say that he was there because of Barack Obama. He simply says to everyone in the room, "I am here because of Ashley." "I'm here because of Ashley."

Now, by itself, that single moment of recognition between that young white girl and that old black man is not enough. It is not enough to give health care to the sick, or jobs to the jobless, or education to our children. But it is where we start. It is where our union grows stronger. And as so many generations have come to realize over the course of the 221 years since a band of patriots signed that document right here in Philadelphia, that is where perfection begins.

Notes

1. Robert C. Rowland and John M. Jones, "Recasting the American Dream and American Politics: Barack Obama's Keynote Address to the 2004 Democratic National Convention," *Quarterly Journal of Speech* 93, no. 4 (2007): 425–48, doi:10.1080/00335630701593675.
2. David A. Frank and Mark L. McPhail, "Barack Obama's Address to the 2004 Democratic National Convention: Trauma, Compromise, Consilience, and the (Im)possibility of Racial Reconciliation," *Rhetoric & Public Affairs* 8, no. 4 (2005): 572, doi:10.1353/rap.2006.0006.
3. Ibid., 572, 582–83.
4. Barack Obama, "Official Announcement of Candidacy for President of the United States," delivered February 10, 2007, Springfield, Illinois, available at *American Rhetoric*, http://www.americanrhetoric.com/speeches/barackobamacandidacyforpresident.htm.

5. Brian Ross and Rehab El-Buri, "Obama's Pastor: God Damn America, U.S. to Blame for 9/11," *ABC News*, March 13, 2008, https://abcnews.go.com/Blotter/DemocraticDebate/story?id=4443788&page=1.
6. See Joshua Gunn and Mark Lawrence McPhail, "Coming Home to Roost: Jeremiah Wright, Barack Obama, and the (Re)Signing of (Post) Racial Rhetoric," *Rhetoric Society Quarterly* 45, no. 1 (2015), 9, doi:10.1080/02773945.2014.973612.
7. David A. Frank, "The Prophetic Voice and the Face of the Other in Barack Obama's 'A More Perfect Union' Address, March 18, 2008," *Rhetoric & Public Affairs* 12, no. 2 (2009): 167–94, doi:10.1353/rap.0.0101.
8. For an overview of positive and negative assessments, see Ibid., 168–70.
9. Ibid., 181.
10. Robert E. Terrill, "Unity and Duality in Barack Obama's 'A More Perfect Union,'" *Quarterly Journal of Speech* 95, no. 4 (2009), 364, doi: 10.1080/00335630903296192. As Terrill acknowledges, this term is borrowed from Robert L. Ivie, "Finessing the Demonology of War: Toward a Practical Aesthetic of Humanising Dissent," *Javnost—The Public* 14, no. 4 (2007): 37–50, doi:10.1080/13183222.2007.11008951.
11. Susanna Dilliplane, "Race, Rhetoric, and Running for President: Unpacking the Significance of Barack Obama's 'A More Perfect Union' Speech," *Rhetoric & Public Affairs* 15, no. 1 (2012): 127–152, doi:10.1353/rap.2012.0002.
12. Here, Obama misquotes "means."
13. Ellipses indicate where the speaker omitted sentences or phrases from the book. Barack Obama, *Dreams from My Father: A Story of Race and Inheritance*, rev. ed. (New York: Three Rivers Press, 2004), 294.
14. This is a reference to the second Iraq War.

CHAPTER TEN

Bridging a Divide between Civilizations: Barack Obama

When Barack Obama took office as president in 2009, relations between the United States and the Islamic world stood at a low point. Ever since the 1973 oil crisis (when oil-producing Arab nations launched an embargo against selling oil to the United States and other supporters of Israel) and the Iran hostage crisis (when 52 Americans were held hostage for more than a year following Iran's 1979 Islamic revolution), sentiments toward Arabs and Muslims had been negative among many Americans. Likewise, many Muslims resented the United States for its strong support of the state of Israel and its exertion of military and economic power in the Middle East and the larger Muslim world. Then came the horrific 9/11 attacks by al-Qaeda terrorists, stirring up American fear and animosity toward Muslims and precipitating the "War on Terror," which included the invasion and occupation of Afghanistan and Iraq under the administration of George W. Bush. When Obama took office, the world situation seemed to confirm Samuel P. Huntington's thesis that after the end of the Cold War, international conflicts would re-emerge along ancient cultural/religious fault-lines between civilizations.[1]

Believing that such a "clash of civilizations" was neither inevitable nor beneficial, Barack Obama addressed the tensions between the United States and the Islamic world and sought to put their relations on a new, more positive footing. To this end, in the first year of his presidency, he gave an important address at Egypt's Cairo University on the theme of "A New Beginning." Watched by millions around the world, the speech received mixed reviews, with some Americans criticizing it as too apologetic for previous U.S. foreign policy, while some Muslim leaders argued that it did not display a strong enough commitment to change that policy.[2] Other observers responded quite favorably, however. Public theologian Miroslav Volf, whom we encountered earlier in this book, characterized Obama's speech as "brilliant" and potentially "historic," writing that its "wise words, beautifully crafted and compellingly delivered, have the potential of becoming seeds from which a new future will sprout and flourish."[3] As a theorist and advocate of reconciliation, Volf praised Obama for his truthfulness in recognizing both *differences* and *commonalities* between the U.S. and the Muslim world. He also commended Obama for lifting up the Golden Rule in the conclusion of his speech, since truth cannot bridge the divide between estranged parties unless they also care for one another's well-being.

Whatever one's estimation of Obama's foreign policy in the Muslim world, his Cairo speech certainly constitutes a ground-breaking attempt to reconcile U.S. Americans and the world's Muslims through rhetoric. Noteworthy features of this speech include Obama's use of Arabic expressions and the Qur'an (Muslims' holy book) to build bridges of identification with his audience; commitment to speaking the truth in dialogue; reference to his own cultural roots that bridge Christianity and Islam; acknowledgment of Western civilization's debt to Islamic culture and learning (as well as the West's negative impact on Islamic nations through colonialism and the Cold War); mention of positive relations with Muslims early in U.S. history; emphasis on common ground amid the admitted differences between the two broad cultures; a focus on humans' global interdependence; countering stereotypes on both sides; and squarely facing areas of tension between them in detail, explaining why and how they should be overcome. Obama seals his call to common ground and cooperation with verses from the holy writings of the three Abrahamic faiths—Islam, Judaism, and Christianity—each calling the faithful to the way of peace. In this way, his speech foreshadows one given by King Abdullah II of Jordan a decade later (also included in this book), which emphasized that these faiths share a core principle: loving God and loving one's neighbor.

Of the values in the tetrad, the two repeatedly mentioned in this speech are *truth* (seven times) and *peace* (29 times). At the outset, Obama expresses a determination to speak truth, and as he proceeds, he challenges his listeners to face various truths. For instance, regarding the murderous actions and character of al-Qaeda, he asserts, "These are not opinions to be debated; these are facts to be dealt with." Although a sober realism pervades the speech, its master frame is a *restorative truth*—a truth that serves as a basis for reconciliation. As stated in Obama's introduction, this is "the truth that America and Islam are not exclusive and need not be in competition. Instead, they overlap and share common principles." Circling back to this theme in his conclusion, Obama highlights a common principle "at the heart of every religion—that we do unto others as we would have them do unto us. This truth transcends nations and peoples."

Restorative truth represents ontological ground for peace. Conversely, when one views the world through a frame of peace, one tends to notice and emphasize such truths. The moral good of peace pervades Obama's address, coloring his truth-telling. If reconciliation is tragicomic, this speech clearly favors the comic side of the coin, emphasizing that "the interests we share as human beings are far more powerful than the forces that drive us apart" and viewing the tensions between the two civilizations as a misrecognition of their true and overlapping character. In an insightful scholarly analysis of this speech, Kundai Chirindo and Ryan Neville-Shephard characterize Obama's foreign policy vision as "comic exceptionalism," in that it holds up America's democratic ideals while "present[ing] Americans and citizens of the Muslim world as co-members in a society of flawed but improving human beings."[4] This stands in sharp contrast with the previous administration's post-9/11 rhetoric, which had liberally applied the tragic language of "evil" to hostile forces in the Muslim world.[5] While Obama does condemn the acts of al-Qaeda terrorists, he distinguishes them from mainstream Islam and emphasizes America's common ground with the latter. He also disparages the Bush administration's use of torture (to get information from suspected terrorists) as a violation of American principles. By making this assessment, he places Americans and Muslims on a common plane of human fallibility and moral accountability. Significantly, Obama frames this particular use of torture not as a manifestation of evil, but rather a misguided expression of "understandable" fear and anger in the wake of 9/11, an error of moral judgment that his administration will correct. On the whole, then, Obama's framing of American-Muslim relations is thoroughly comic.

Because the speech is very long and addresses numerous issues of foreign and domestic policy, it has been substantially abridged here, omitting some of those policy discussions.

"A New Beginning"[6]

Cairo University, Egypt
June 4, 2009

Good afternoon. I am honored to be in the timeless city of Cairo, and to be hosted by two remarkable institutions. For over a thousand years, Al-Azhar has stood as a beacon of Islamic learning; and for over a century, Cairo University has been a source of Egypt's advancement. And together, you represent the harmony between tradition and progress. I'm grateful for your hospitality, and the hospitality of the people of Egypt. And I'm also proud to carry with me the goodwill of the American people, and a greeting of peace from Muslim communities in my country: *Assalaamu alaykum.*

We meet at a time of great tension between the United States and Muslims around the world—tension rooted in historical forces that go beyond any current policy debate. The relationship between Islam and the West includes centuries of coexistence and cooperation, but also conflict and religious wars. More recently, tension has been fed by colonialism that denied rights and opportunities to many Muslims, and a Cold War in which Muslim-majority countries were too often treated as proxies without regard to their own aspirations. Moreover, the sweeping change brought by modernity and globalization led many Muslims to view the West as hostile to the traditions of Islam.

Violent extremists have exploited these tensions in a small but potent minority of Muslims. The attacks of September 11, 2001 and the continued efforts of these extremists to engage in violence against civilians has led some in my country to view Islam as inevitably hostile not only to America and Western countries, but also to human rights. All this has bred more fear and more mistrust.

So long as our relationship is defined by our differences, we will empower those who sow hatred rather than peace, those who promote conflict rather than the cooperation that can help all of our people achieve justice and prosperity. And this cycle of suspicion and discord must end.

I've come here to Cairo to seek a new beginning between the United States and Muslims around the world, one based on mutual interest and mutual respect, and one based upon the truth that America and Islam are not exclusive and need not be in competition. Instead, they overlap and share common principles—principles of justice and progress, tolerance and the dignity of all human beings.

I do so recognizing that change cannot happen overnight. I know there's been a lot of publicity about this speech, but no single speech can eradicate years of mistrust, nor can I answer in the time that I have this afternoon all the complex questions that brought us to this point. But I am convinced that in order to move forward, we must say openly to each other the things we hold in our hearts and that too often are said only behind closed doors. There must be a sustained effort to listen to each other; to learn from each other; to respect one another; and to seek common ground. As the Holy Qur'an tells us, "Be conscious of God and speak always the truth." That is what I will try to do today—to speak the truth as best

I can, humbled by the task before us, and firm in my belief that the interests we share as human beings are far more powerful than the forces that drive us apart.

Now part of this conviction is rooted in my own experience. I'm a Christian, but my father came from a Kenyan family that includes generations of Muslims. As a boy, I spent several years in Indonesia and heard the call of the *azaan* at the break of dawn and at the fall of dusk.[7] As a young man, I worked in Chicago communities where many found dignity and peace in their Muslim faith.

As a student of history, I also know civilization's debt to Islam. It was Islam—at places like Al-Azhar—that carried the light of learning through so many centuries, paving the way for Europe's Renaissance and Enlightenment. It was innovation in Muslim communities that developed the order of algebra; our magnetic compass and tools of navigation; our mastery of pens and printing; our understanding of how disease spreads and how it can be healed. Islamic culture has given us majestic arches and soaring spires; timeless poetry and cherished music; elegant calligraphy and places of peaceful contemplation. And throughout history, Islam has demonstrated through words and deeds the possibilities of religious tolerance and racial equality.

I also know that Islam has always been a part of America's story. The first nation to recognize my country was Morocco. In signing the Treaty of Tripoli in 1796, our second President, John Adams, wrote, "The United States has in itself no character of enmity against the laws, religion, or tranquility of Muslims." And since our founding, American Muslims have enriched the United States. They have fought in our wars; they have served in our government; they have stood for civil rights; they have started businesses; they have taught at our universities; they've excelled in our sports arenas; they've won Nobel Prizes, built our tallest building, and lit the Olympic Torch. And when the first Muslim American was recently elected to Congress, he took the oath to defend our Constitution using the same Holy Qur'an that one of our Founding Fathers—Thomas Jefferson— kept in his personal library.

So I have known Islam on three continents before coming to the region where it was first revealed. That experience guides my conviction that partnership between America and Islam must be based on what Islam is, not what it isn't. And I consider it part of my responsibility as President of the United States to fight against negative stereotypes of Islam wherever they appear.

But, that same principle must apply to Muslim perceptions of America. Just as Muslims do not fit a crude stereotype, America is not the crude stereotype of a self-interested empire. The United States has been one of the greatest sources of progress that the world has ever known. We were born out of revolution against an empire. We were founded upon the ideal that all are created equal; and we have shed blood and struggled for centuries to give meaning to those words—within our borders, and around the world. We are shaped by every culture, drawn from every end of the Earth, and dedicated to a simple concept: *E pluribus unum*—"Out of many, one."

Now much has been made of the fact that an African American with the name Barack Hussein Obama could be elected President. But my personal story is not so unique. The dream of opportunity for all people has not come true for everyone in America, but its promise exists for all who come to our shores—and that includes nearly seven million American Muslims in our country today who, by the way, enjoy incomes and educational levels that are higher than the American average.

Moreover, freedom in America is indivisible from the freedom to practice one's religion. That is why there is a mosque in every state in our union, and over 1200 mosques within our borders. That's why the United States government has gone to court to protect the right of women and girls to wear the hijab, and to punish those who would deny it.

So let there be no doubt: Islam is a part of America. And I believe that America holds within her the truth that regardless of race, religion, or station in life, all of us share common aspirations—to live in peace and security; to get an education and to work with dignity; to love our families, our communities, and our God. These things we share. This is the hope of all humanity.

Of course, recognizing our common humanity is only the beginning of our task. Words alone cannot meet the needs of our people. These needs will be met only if we act boldly in the years ahead, and if we understand that the challenges we face are shared and our failure to meet them will hurt us all.

For we have learned from recent experience that when a financial system weakens in one country, prosperity is hurt everywhere. When a new flu infects one human being, all are at risk. When one nation pursues a nuclear weapon, the risk of nuclear attack rises for all nations. When violent extremists operate in one stretch of mountains, people are endangered across an ocean. When innocents in Bosnia and Darfur are slaughtered, that is a stain on our collective conscience. That is what it means to share this world in the 21st century. That is the responsibility we have to one another as human beings.

And this is a difficult responsibility to embrace. For human history has often been a record of nations and tribes—and, yes, religions—subjugating one another in pursuit of their own interests. Yet in this new age, such attitudes are self-defeating. Given our interdependence, any world order that elevates one nation or group of people over another will inevitably fail. So whatever we think of the past, we must not be prisoners to it. Our problems must be dealt with through partnership; our progress must be shared.

Now, that does not mean we should ignore sources of tension. Indeed, it suggests the opposite: We must face these tensions squarely. And so in that spirit, let me speak as clearly and as plainly as I can about some specific issues that I believe we must finally confront together.

The first issue that we have to confront is violent extremism in all of its forms.

In Ankara,[8] I made clear that America is not—and never will be—at war with Islam. We will, however, relentlessly confront violent extremists who pose a grave threat to our security—because we reject the same thing that people of all faiths reject: the killing of innocent men, women, and children. And it is my first duty as President to protect the American people.

The situation in Afghanistan demonstrates America's goals, and our need to work together. Over seven years ago, the United States pursued al-Qaeda and the Taliban with broad international support. We did not go by choice; we went because of necessity. I'm aware that there's still some who would question or even justify the events of 9/11. But let us be clear: al-Qaeda killed nearly 3,000 people on that day. The victims were innocent men, women and children from America and many other nations who had done nothing to harm anybody. And yet al-Qaeda chose to ruthlessly murder these people, claimed credit for the attack, and even now states their determination to kill on a massive scale. They have affiliates in many countries and are trying to expand their reach. These are not opinions to be debated; these are facts to be dealt with.

…. Indeed,[9] none of us should tolerate these extremists. They have killed in many countries. They have killed people of different faiths—but more than any other, they have killed Muslims. Their actions are irreconcilable with the rights of human beings, the progress of nations, and with Islam. The Holy Qur'an teaches that whoever kills an innocent—it is as if he has killed all mankind. And the Holy Qur'an also says whoever saves a person, it is as if he has saved all mankind. The enduring faith of over a billion people is so much bigger than the narrow hatred of a few. Islam is not part of the problem in combating violent extremism—it is an important part of promoting peace….[10]

And finally, just as America can never tolerate violence by extremists, we must never alter or forget our principles. Nine-eleven was an enormous trauma to our country. The fear and anger that it provoked was understandable, but in some cases, it led us to act contrary to our traditions and our ideals. We are taking concrete actions to change course. I have unequivocally prohibited the use of torture by the United States, and I have ordered the prison at Guantanamo Bay closed by early next year.

So America will defend itself, respectful of the sovereignty of nations and the rule of law. And we will do so in partnership with Muslim communities which are also threatened. The sooner the extremists are isolated and unwelcome in Muslim communities, the sooner we will all be safer.

[***Remarks omitted on Israeli-Arab relations, nuclear weapons, and democracy***]

The fifth issue that we must address together is religious freedom.

Islam has a proud tradition of tolerance. We see it in the history of Andalusia and Cordoba during the Inquisition. I saw it firsthand as a child in Indonesia, where devout Christians worshiped freely in an overwhelmingly Muslim country. That is the spirit we need today. People in every country should be free to choose and live their faith based upon the persuasion of the mind and the heart and the soul. This tolerance is essential for religion to thrive, but it's being challenged in many different ways.

Among some Muslims, there's a disturbing tendency to measure one's own faith by the rejection of somebody else's faith. The richness of religious diversity must be upheld—whether it is for Maronites in Lebanon or the Copts in Egypt. And if we are being honest, fault lines must be closed among Muslims, as well, as the divisions between Sunni and Shia have led to tragic violence, particularly in Iraq.

Freedom of religion is central to the ability of peoples to live together. We must always examine the ways in which we protect it. For instance, in the United States, rules on charitable giving have made it harder for Muslims to fulfill their religious obligation. That's why I'm committed to working with American Muslims to ensure that they can fulfill zakat.

Likewise, it is important for Western countries to avoid impeding Muslim citizens from practicing religion as they see fit—for instance, by dictating what clothes a Muslim woman should wear. We can't disguise hostility towards any religion behind the pretense of liberalism.

In fact, faith should bring us together. And that's why we're forging service projects in America to bring together Christians, Muslims, and Jews. That's why we welcome efforts like Saudi Arabian King Abdullah's interfaith dialogue and Turkey's leadership in the Alliance of Civilizations. Around the world, we can turn dialogue into interfaith service, so bridges between peoples lead to action—whether it is combating malaria in Africa, or providing relief after a natural disaster.

[***Remarks omitted on women's rights and economic development***]

The issues that I have described will not be easy to address. But we have a responsibility to join together on behalf of the world that we seek—a world where extremists no longer threaten our people, and American troops have come home;

a world where Israelis and Palestinians are each secure in a state of their own, and nuclear energy is used for peaceful purposes; a world where governments serve their citizens, and the rights of all God's children are respected. Those are mutual interests. That is the world we seek. But we can only achieve it together.

I know there are many—Muslim and non-Muslim—who question whether we can forge this new beginning. Some are eager to stoke the flames of division, and to stand in the way of progress. Some suggest that it isn't worth the effort—that we are fated to disagree, and civilizations are doomed to clash. Many more are simply skeptical that real change can occur. There's so much fear, so much mistrust that has built up over the years. But if we choose to be bound by the past, we will never move forward. And I want to particularly say this to young people of every faith, in every country: You, more than anyone, have the ability to reimagine the world, to remake this world.

All of us share this world for but a brief moment in time. The question is whether we spend that time focused on what pushes us apart, or whether we commit ourselves to an effort—a sustained effort—to find common ground, to focus on the future we seek for our children, and to respect the dignity of all human beings.

It's easier to start wars than to end them. It's easier to blame others than to look inward. It's easier to see what is different about someone than to find the things we share. But we should choose the right path, not just the easy path. There's one rule that lies at the heart of every religion—that we do unto others as we would have them do unto us. This truth transcends nations and peoples—a belief that isn't new; that isn't black or white or brown; that isn't Christian or Muslim or Jew. It's a belief that pulsed in the cradle of civilization, and that still beats in the hearts of billions around the world. It's a faith in other people, and it's what brought me here today.

We have the power to make the world we seek, but only if we have the courage to make a new beginning, keeping in mind what has been written.

The Holy Qur'an tells us: "O mankind! We have created you male and a female; and we have made you into nations and tribes so that you may know one another."

The Talmud tells us: "The whole of the Torah is for the purpose of promoting peace."

The Holy Bible tells us: "Blessed are the peacemakers, for they shall be called sons of God."

The people of the world can live together in peace. We know that is God's vision. Now that must be our work here on Earth.

Thank you. And may God's peace be upon you.

Notes

1. Samuel P. Huntington, *The Clash of Civilizations and the Remaking of the World Order* (New York: Simon & Schuster, 1996).
2. For examples of both negative and positive reactions, see Brian Fung, "Responses to Obama in Cairo: The Best of the Talking Heads," *FP*, June 4, 2009, https://foreignpolicy.com/2009/06/04/responses-to-obama-in-cairo-the-best-of-the-talking-heads/; Deborah Amos, "Mixed Reaction in Cairo to Obama Speech," *NPR*, June 4, 2009, https://www.npr.org/templates/story/story.php?storyId=104967625; Martyn Indyk, "Reactions to President Obama's Speech to the Muslim World," *Brookings*, June 4, 2009, https://www.brookings.edu/opinions/reactions-to-president-obamas-speech-to-the-muslim-world/; Daniel Nasaw, "American Right Blasts Obama's Cairo Speech," *The Guardian*, June 4, 2009, https://www.theguardian.com/world/2009/jun/04/barack-obama-cairo-speech-republicans.
3. Miroslav Volf, "Obama Speech not Historic, but Could Become So," *Reuters*, June 4, 2009, http://blogs.reuters.com/faithworld/2009/06/04/guestview-obama-speech-not-historic-but-could-become-so/.
4. Kundai Chirindo and Ryan Neville-Shephard, "Obama's 'New Beginning': US Foreign Policy and Comic Exceptionalism," *Argumentation and Advocacy* 51, no. 4 (2015): 215–30, https://doi.org/10.1080/00028533.2015.11821851 (quoted from html version available through Gale General Onefile).
5. See Joshua Gunn, "The Rhetoric of Exorcism: George W. Bush and the Return of Political Demonology," *Western Journal of Communication* 68, no. 1 (2004): 1–23, doi:10.1080/10570310409374786.
6. The complete transcript of this speech is available from the Obama White House archives: https://obamawhitehouse.archives.gov/the-press-office/remarks-president-cairo-university-6-04-09.
7. *Azaan* refers to the Islamic call to prayer.
8. The capital of Turkey.
9. At the start of this paragraph, Obama clarifies the limited scope and sole purpose of U.S. military intervention in Afghanistan, which is to deal with dangerous extremists.
10. Here, I have omitted three paragraphs on Obama's commitment to provide economic support and relief in Afghanistan and Pakistan, his assessment of the U.S. mission in Iraq, and his commitment to start removing troops from that country.

CHAPTER ELEVEN

Bridging Religious Divides: King Abdullah II of Jordan

The final speech in Part I was delivered by a Muslim political leader: His Majesty King Abdullah II of Jordan. The Hashemite Kingdom of Jordan serves as a significant bridge between Christians and Muslims in the Middle East, in that Jordan has assumed responsibility for protecting and maintaining both faiths' holy sites in Jerusalem, including the Al-Aqsa Mosque and the Church of the Holy Sepulchre. Moreover, King Abdullah II has been a vocal advocate of Muslim-Christian dialogue and mutual respect, most notably by spearheading "A Common Word between Us and You," an open letter from many Muslim religious leaders to Christian leaders around the world.

The exigency that led to the drafting of the letter was a controversial lecture given by Pope Benedict XVI the previous year (2006), in which he had quoted a 14th-century Byzantine emperor's harsh criticism of the teachings of Muhammad. Taken out of context by many who heard about it, the Pope's use of this quotation provoked mass protests in cities around the Muslim world and bombings of Christian churches in some places. In effect, Benedict had unintentionally sparked ancient resentment rooted in the Crusades, when popes had repeatedly sent armies to Muslim-held lands in the Middle East in order to wrest Christian holy sites from Muslim control and establish Christian dominion in the Holy Land.

In sharp contrast to the angry protests and violent reactions against Pope Benedict's lecture, "A Common Word" constituted a conciliatory response from

Muslim religious scholars and leaders—a gesture toward reconciliation, as it were, after a long history of animosity between Christians and Muslims. The open letter's fundamental premise is that while "Islam and Christianity are obviously different religions—and whilst there is no minimising some of their formal differences—it is clear that the Two Greatest Commandments are an area of common ground and a link between the Qur'an, the Torah and the New Testament."[1] The letter's introduction emphasizes the importance of affirming this common ground:

> Muslims and Christians together make up well over half of the world's population. Without peace and justice between these two religious communities, there can be no meaningful peace in the world.
>
> The basis for this peace and understanding already exists. It is part of the very foundational principles of both faiths: love of the One God, and love of the neighbour. These principles are found over and over again in the sacred texts of Islam and Christianity.[2]

Originally signed by 138 prominent Muslim religious leaders worldwide,[3] "A Common Word" prompted affirming responses from hundreds of Christian leaders, scholars, and organizations.[4]

In 2018, the John Templeton Foundation awarded King Abdullah II the prestigious Templeton Prize for having "done more to seek religious harmony within Islam and between Islam and other religions than any other living political leader."[5] The award was presented to him in a ceremony at the National Cathedral in Washington D.C., where he was introduced at length by Islamic scholar Shaykh Hamza Yusuf and Christian theologian Miroslav Volf (whose 2001 speech at the U.N. is included in this book).[6] His Majesty then delivered an acceptance speech that can be characterized as predominantly comic and romantic in orientation, emphasizing common ground among the world's three great monotheistic faiths and believers' responsibility to work for self-betterment and "for a world of peace, harmony, and love."

King Abdullah II begins by highlighting his country's tradition of peaceful coexistence and mutual respect among the three great monotheistic faiths. This heritage is rooted in Jordan's ancient history of having been visited by all five of the "prophets of great resolve," as Muslims call them: Noah, Abraham, Moses, Jesus, and Mohammad. Although Jews, Christians, and Muslims differ on the relative status of these religious figures, Abdullah II establishes common ground by honoring all of them and claiming that each one modeled "the *jihad* within each of us, to be the best person we can be." While many people associate jihad with the hate-driven violence perpetrated by some fundamentalist Islamic groups, King Abdullah II argues that such Muslims are not practicing true jihad. The "greater *jihad*," he says, is the inner struggle to develop one's moral character to the fullest extent, which contributes to unity rather than division. Abdullah II believes that genuine jihad derives from two principles that Judaism, Christianity, and Islam share in common: "the great commandments to love God and love one's neighbor." The struggle to look beyond oneself and fulfill these commands, he says, provides "the source and hope of all coexistence." Much as he began by heralding Jordan's multi-religious heritage, so near the end of the speech King Abdullah II emphasizes the importance of safe-guarding Jerusalem as a unifying city of peace for all three faiths. He concludes with a direct challenge to "do all we can to maximize the good in our world," beginning with our own personal struggle for excellent character.

Templeton Prize Acceptance Speech[7]

National Cathedral, Washington, DC
November 13, 2018

Bismillahir Rahmanir Rahim—In the name of God, the compassionate, the merciful....[8] Today I am truly humbled to be recognized by all of you. But let me say, everything you honor me for simply carries onward what Jordanians have always done, and how Jordanians have always lived—in mutual kindness, harmony and brotherhood. And so I accept this extraordinary prize not on my own behalf, but on behalf of all Jordanians.

My friends, our country has long upheld religious mutual respect. The five prophets of great resolve, as they are called in the Qur'an—the prophets of Judaism, Christianity, and Islam, peace be upon them all—have blessed our land with their presence. Noah has a tomb in Karak; Abraham came through from the land of what is now Iraq on his way to Hebron; Moses died in Jordan on Mount Nebo. Jesus Christ, the Messiah, was baptized in Jordan, on the East Bank of the River Jordan, by John the Baptist. My country preserves this special site and others, with great care, welcoming Christian pilgrims and other visitors from around the world. The prophet Mohammad, may peace and blessings be upon him, came to Jordan twice: once with his uncle as a boy—when he was witnessed by a Byzantine priest as a future prophet—and then later as a young merchant. It was that first encounter—under a tree which is still present in the Jordanian desert—that set the tone for Muslim-Christian coexistence and harmony in Jordan.

My friends, these prophets of great resolve were on a journey, an internal journey of the self to fulfill God's commands. And the first step of any such journey begins with the struggle, the *jihad* within each of us, to be the best person we can be. The greater *jihad*, the greater *jihad* of the great prophets, bore illumination to all of us. So here at this cathedral, as a Muslim, I'd like to say a word about *jihad*—and I'm sure that's not something you hear too often within these walls! But nothing is more important to understand.

The greater *jihad* has nothing to do with the hate-filled fiction promoted by the *khawarij*; the outlaws of Islam, such as Daesh and the like;[9] or the Islamophobes,[10] who also distort our religion. It is instead the personal internal struggle to defeat the ego, and the struggle we all share for a world of peace, harmony, and love. As has been said, in Islam, to love God and love one's neighbor are core commandments. As Shaykh Hamza noted, the prophet Mohammad—peace and blessings be upon him—said, "None of you has faith until you love for your neighbor what you love for yourself." *This* is the Islam I learned in Jordan: the Islam of kindness and mercy, not of madness and cruelty; traditional orthodox Islam, not modern fundamentalist Islam; the Islam of "forgive and let live," not of "attack and nit-pick"; the Islam of fundamental principles—or *usul* in Arabic—not of fundamentalist details; the Islam of the holistic vision of the Qur'an and the *Sunnah*, and not the cherry-picking of verses to suit a political agenda. This is the traditional orthodox Islam that is the faith of the vast majority of Muslims around the world—1.8 billion good neighbors and good citizens who are helping build the future in Jordan and the Middle East, in the U.S. and Asia, and Europe and beyond. And we are working on every continent to defend Islam against the malignant sub-minority who abuse our religion. And we do this not to please our friends, not to please the world, but to please God. And as long as there is life in our bodies and faith in our hearts, we will continue to do so—God willing, *In sha Allah*.

And we are not alone. The great commandments to love God and love one's neighbor, as has been said this evening, are found again and again in Judaism, Christianity, and Islam, and other faiths around the world. It is a profound message, calling every one of us to struggle, to look beyond ourselves—and this outward insight is the source and hope of all coexistence. And when we talk about hope and coexistence, no issue is more important than Jerusalem. More than half of the world's people belong to religions that hold Jerusalem as a holy city: Islam, Christianity, and Judaism. For Muslims, Jerusalem stands, along with Mecca and Medina, as one of Islam's three holiest places. And a special duty binds me and all Jordanians as Hashemite Custodian of Jerusalem's Islamic and Christian holy sites. With its long multi-faith heritage, Jerusalem must be protected as a unifying city of peace. And I am tremendously grateful to the Templeton Prize for making it possible to further this work. A portion of the Templeton Prize will help renovate and restore religious sites in Jerusalem, including the Church of the Holy Sepulchre. And the entire remaining sum is also being donated to humanitarian interfaith and intra-faith initiatives in Jordan and around the world.

My friends, God says in the Qur'an, "For those who say 'Our Lord is God' and then follow the straight path, there is no fear, nor shall they grieve." And the prophet Mohammad, peace and blessings be upon him, said, "Whoever believes in God and the last day, let him behave with excellence and virtue—*ihsan*—towards his neighbor." It is time to do all we can to maximize the good in our world and bring people together in understanding. But it begins with the struggle, the *jihad* within ourselves, to be the best we can be. And it's been said that all it takes for evil to prevail is for good people to do nothing. But together, God willing, we can achieve something important: we can create the future of coexistence that humanity so desperately needs. Let us keep up the struggle. Thank you.

Notes

1. "A Common Word between Us and You," *A Common Word*, https://www.acommonword.com/the-acw-document/.
2. Ibid.
3. "Signatories," *A Common Word*, October 13, 2007, https://www.acommonword.com/signatories/.
4. See "Christian Responses," *A Common Word*, https://www.acommonword.com/christian-responses/.
5. "King Abdullah II of Jordan Awarded 2018 Templeton Prize," *PR Newswire*, June 27, 2018, https://www.prnewswire.com/news-releases/king-abdullah-ii-of-jordan-awarded-2018-templeton-prize-300671672.html.
6. See "The King and the Cathedral," *John Templeton Foundation*, November 20, 2018, https://www.templeton.org/news/the-king-and-the-cathedral.
7. This speech is published with permission from The Royal Hashemite Court of Jordan.
8. Here, I have omitted the king's informal opening remarks thanking individuals on the platform and expressing concern about recent natural disasters. The unabridged text of the speech is found at https://kingabdullah.jo/en/speeches/2018-templeton-prize-ceremony.
9. *Daesh* refers to the terrorist group ISIS. *Khawarij* alludes to a 7th-century Islamic cult; Abdullah II uses it here to characterize Muslim extremists as false/apostate believers.
10. I.e., people who fear/hate Muslims.

PART II

PURSUING RECONCILIATION THROUGH APOLOGY, FORGIVENESS, AND REPARATION

Introduction to Part II

The speech texts in Part I represented rhetorical efforts to commend and explain reconciliation for particular audiences and contexts. With varying emphases, they framed reconciliation as a project of realigning and rejoining divided groups through a process that reconstitutes an ethical unity of truth, agency, justice, and peace in the relationship between parties. The speeches drew upon different aspects of the Jewish, Christian, Islamic, and Buddhist traditions to warrant their claims and give specific shape to their visions of reconciliation. For the most part, however, they did not act to accomplish reconciliation directly; they oriented their audiences to that work but did not speak forth gestures of reconciliation from one party to another.

Part II presents *direct speech-acts* of reconciliation (with one exception). This part includes several public apologies by spokespersons for nations and religious institutions, as well as one request for an apology and one formal response to an apology. One address in Part II commends recent speech-acts of forgiveness and the power of grace to bring about repentance. Readers will also encounter two examples of reconciliation as a dialogic rhetorical process. The first of these, discussed further down in this introduction, is a public interpersonal exchange including an apology, rejection of the apology, and eventual forgiveness, occurring within the context of a structured national reconciliation process. The second is a set of three related speech-acts: a public apology, a formal response to the apology two years later, and a follow-up apology 10 years after that. To understand, appreciate, and evaluate these rhetorical acts of reconciliation, we must consider the dialogic nature of reconciliation and the kinds of rhetorical acts that make up this dialogic process.

Reconciling Perceptual Frames through Dialogue with the Other Party

Because violating the rights of another party entails distortion and division in ethical perspectives, lasting reconciliation requires that the distortions be corrected and the divided perspectives be brought together. The parties' perspectives will always be somewhat different because of their different experiences, but in the process of genuine reconciliation they come together like two eyes or a pair of glasses, creating depth-perception as the parties act to repair the relational damage from the past. If the divided parties' perspectives do not sufficiently realign, injustice and tension will persist.

The only way this realignment can occur is if both parties work at being Other-oriented—seeing their actions and the structure of their relationship through the other party's eyes. This entails more than just trying to imagine how the Other sees the situation, because our imaginations are rather limited by our own life experiences. When we try to put ourselves in someone else's shoes—especially someone of another race or culture—we really can only "dip our toes" in the social reality that surrounds them like deep waters. Speaking from such a limited perspective, we can make matters worse if we presume to have grasped what the other party is thinking and feeling. Thus, we must engage in dialogue, wherein the other party voices their experience and we listen to better understand and appreciate where they are coming from.

This is something that both parties must be willing to do. Each of us is responsible for our own perspective and addressing its limitations by considering the perspectives of others. At the same time, if one party has substantially acted as the oppressor and the other has substantially been the victim of that oppression, the first party has the greater weight of responsibility to consider the other's perspective. Violating the rights of a people entails seeing them as less human or less worthy and devaluing their perspectives and feelings, in order to justify the oppressor's actions. Over time, wearing these blinders becomes an ingrained habit that is not easily unlearned, even after active oppression has ceased. Meanwhile, during the period of oppression, the oppressed (often a minority) had to learn how to identify with the oppressors (often the majority) for their own survival—to imagine what they are thinking, learn their ways, anticipate their desires and reactions. As a result, members of an oppressed minority tend to be more attuned to the majority's perspectives than vice versa (although this is not the case for every individual, of course). This means that the members of the group that perpetrated oppression should be prepared to work harder to bridge the gap.

Speech-Acts of Reconciliation

While reconciliation is dialogic, emerging organically through interaction among parties, it is also *rhetorical*, in the sense of utilizing/adapting established forms and genres of communication to accomplish particular persuasive or relational goals. In the case of reconciliation, these genres include making an *apology*, conveying *forgiveness* (or at least acknowledging/accepting the apology), and making some form of *reparation*, which may be primarily symbolic or material but generally involves material cost to the party that caused harm.

Apology

When one party has wronged another, that party has different communicative work to do than the wronged party, including greater responsibility to rebalance the scales of justice in the victim's favor. I refer to the offending party's work of inward reflection/re-orientation and outward confession/correction as *repentance*.[1] The communicative expression of repentance is most fully captured in an *apology*.[2] This is quite different from the traditional rhetorical notion of *apologia*—the act of verbal self-defense against public criticism or accusation.[3] (In contemporary rhetorical studies, this idea has been broadened into the umbrella term "image repair," which can incorporate various strategies to make oneself look better in the eyes of the audience after one's image has suffered damage.)[4] A related term in religious discourse is *apologetics*—the practice of making a reasoned defense of one's faith to unbelievers. While all of these terms share the notion that one is responding publicly to criticism or distrust, what sets apart our modern, everyday use of the word "apology" from *apologia* and "apologetics" is the nature of the response: not defending, but rather admitting fault or deficiency, taking responsibility for it, and expressing regret or remorse—that is, *apologizing*.[5]

When someone attempts to apologize, we are likely to find their words unsatisfactory if they weave *apologia* into their apology—rationalizing their offense, minimizing its negative impact, avoiding full responsibility for it, and so forth. In other words, we are unimpressed if their apology is more about self-defense or self-repair than empathizing with the recipient and repairing the damage suffered by that person. Especially when the offense is serious, the ethics of the situation require that the apology be other-centered, whole-hearted, and holistic, "rounding the bases" of the reconciliation tetrad.[6] As such, we can identify four key moves that make up a satisfactory apology:

1. Thoroughly acknowledge one's offending acts and their consequences (TRUTH orientation/*realistic* frame)
2. Condemn these acts as violations of moral order and the victim's rights (JUSTICE orientation/*tragic* frame)
3. Identify and empathize with the victim as a fellow human, expressing appropriate regret and remorse for the violence done to the victim and the relationship (PEACE orientation/*comic* frame)
4. Express a commitment to make a better future by rectifying the injustice and collaborating with the victim as equal/active partner in the work of healing (AGENCY orientation/*romantic* frame)[7]

Clearly, a good apology requires careful self-examination and the hard work of humbling oneself and taking multiple perspectives. When an apology for serious wrongdoing incorporates all four of these elements, it is more likely to make a positive and significant contribution to reconciliation. In some cases, the apology itself may not contain all of them, but they may emerge in the process of dialogue toward reconciliation.

Forgiveness

The victim's counterpart to an apology is to accept the apology (if it is satisfactory) and possibly to express forgiveness (if the victim is ready and willing to do so). If the apology is not satisfactory, the offended party has the right to explain how it falls short and ask for more from the offender.[8] Indeed, from the perspective of justice between parties, victims have a moral right to withhold forgiveness, because forgiving by definition is an expression of grace in response to injustice, and as such it must be an act of freewill. On the other hand, because forgiveness can be understood as an act of self-liberation from the offense and its emotional effects—thus transforming oneself from victim to survivor—a victim may express forgiveness, or a willingness to work toward forgiveness, even before the offender comes to the point of repentance and apology. (This corresponds with Volf's "will to embrace," which is not dependent on justice being done.) In fact, the grace of forgiveness from the offended party may be the thing that liberates the offender from a defensive posture of denial. Nonetheless, it is normal and right for the apology to come first because an apology is owed to the victim as a moral *debt*, while forgiveness is by nature a *gift*, not an obligation.[9]

In either case, forgiveness, like apologizing, involves "rounding the bases" of the reconciliation tetrad. Victims of terrible abuse or oppression typically find themselves in a tragic frame of mind, gripped by anger or bitterness at their mistreatment and wishing for the weight of justice to come down on the offender. According to Robert Enright, the father of forgiveness studies in the field of psychology, forgiveness involves moving beyond this resentment through a process of psychologically reframing the hurt and the offender. The first three phases of this process are

1. honestly facing the effects of the offense and critically examining one's various psychological reactions to it (i.e., facing truth);
2. making a free choice and commitment to forgive (i.e., exercising agency, which transcends the circumstances); and
3. working to see the offender in a new light, empathizing with them as a fellow human being who is flawed and vulnerable like oneself (finding common ground as a basis for peace with them).[10]

In other words, besides the tragic frame (the natural starting point for one who has been wronged), one tries to see the situation through each of the other three frames: realistic, then romantic, then comic.

While substantial examples of formal, public apologizing are not hard to find, public statements of forgiveness are rare and usually very brief. This is for three reasons: (1) an apology involves repayment of a moral debt, which requires an effort to say all the words that are owed to the victim, whereas the victim does not owe the offender anything; (2) forgiveness is a costly gift (a free choice, but also a sacrifice), and the victim may not be instantly ready to give that gift upon hearing the apology; (3) most of the work of forgiveness is internal and personal: finding a way to let go of resentment. Thus, it tends not to be as open and public as an apology.

An award-winning documentary on the South African TRC, *Long Night's Journey into Day*,[11] includes a rare recorded example of forgiveness being conveyed in a rhetorical manner—that is, a victim making an argument for her decision to forgive, in a somewhat public context—as part of a larger interpersonal exchange that includes the offender's apology. Since this expression of forgiveness is not, strictly speaking, an example of public address, it did not qualify as a separate entry for this anthology, but it merits attention here. The encounter occurred when a black security officer named Thapelo Mbelo was applying for amnesty from the TRC for his participation in a government death-squad operation that had slaughtered seven young anti-apartheid activists (ages 16 to 23) in the township of Gugulethu under the pretext of stopping a "terrorist" attack. In reality, it was a case of entrapment: the white supremacist security force had paid black officers, including Mbelo, to go undercover and infiltrate the group of youths, giving them weapons and enticing them to plan an attack on a police bus. Since these officers reported everything to their superiors, the security force was prepared, and on the planned day of the attack, 25 heavily armed police ambushed the youths, killing all of them; only one even had a chance to shoot back. During his amnesty hearing, Mbelo requested an opportunity to meet with the mothers of the "Gugulethu Seven" to express his remorse and ask their forgiveness, to which the mothers reluctantly agreed. Their encounter with Mbelo, captured in the documentary, illustrates the role of victims' voices in reconciliation and the importance of respecting their agency to choose how to respond to an apology, whether with forgiveness or unforgiveness.

In his apology, Mbelo does not demand forgiveness from the mothers; rather, he expresses shame before them, empathizes with their pain, and humbly requests their forgiveness, while acknowledging that they might not find it in their hearts to forgive him. In response, the mothers do not go easy on Mbelo; rather, they express their grief and anger, talk about their suffering, challenge his conscience, and fault his character for selling out his own people. As the conversation proceeds, one of the mothers concludes, "I have no forgiveness for you." Cynthia Ngewu, however, finally decides to forgive Mbelo, and she conveys her rationale for doing so:

> Just a minute, my son. Doesn't the name Thapelo mean "prayer"? I see what your name means, and I don't know whether you follow it or not. Speaking as Christopher's mother, I forgive you, my child. Because you and Christopher are the same age. I forgive you my child, and the reason I say I forgive you is that my child will never wake up again. And it's pointless for me to hold this wound against you. God will be the judge. We must forgive those who sin against us, even as we wish to be forgiven. So I forgive you, Thapelo. I want you to go home knowing the mothers are forgiving the evil you have done, and we feel compassion for you. There is no place for throwing stones at you, even though you did those things. So Jesus told us when he was on the cross, forgive those who sin against you. Because we want to get rid of this burden we are carrying inside, so that we too can feel at peace. So for my part, I forgive you, my child. Yes, I forgive you. Go well my child.[12]

In this example, the forgiving party chooses to focus on a similarity between her son and the offender as a basis for identification and compassion. She also chooses to focus on what she has agency over (her attitude) rather than what she has no capacity to change (her son's death), leave the burden of justice and judgment with God, and participate in the grace of divine forgiveness in order to experience inner peace. In forgiving, she believes that she gains a measure of freedom for herself as well as the one she forgives. While we might admire Ngewu's response to a man who was instrumental in the murder of her son, it is crucial to recognize that this forgiveness was not forced or rushed; Ngewu and the other mothers were allowed by the TRC to voice their anger and hurt, challenge the offender, and even refuse to forgive him. This was fitting, for forgiveness must be a free choice, without compulsion.

Reparation

While apology and forgiveness employ words to heal relational and psychological wounds, the offenses addressed in this book involve grave material harms as well—loss of liberty, physical well-being, land, livelihood, and/or life itself. For public repentance to be meaningful in such cases—for reconciliation to be *just*—there must be good-faith effort to make reparation or restitution of some kind. When former perpetrators or their descendants make no effort to compensate for the losses suffered by the victims and their descendants, words of apology carry little weight—especially when the former are enjoying benefits accrued from past oppression, such as political dominance, cultural privilege, land ownership, natural resources, and/or financial capital.

Reparation can take a number of different forms, one of which is direct payment to the victims of wrongdoing. For instance, when President Ronald Reagan made an apology on behalf of the U.S. government to Japanese-Americans (mostly American citizens) who had been wrongfully removed from their homes and businesses and interred in concentration camps during World War II, each living survivor was given reparations of $20,000 by the federal government. Since the 1950s, the German government has paid out billions of dollars to Holocaust survivors, including reimbursements to the state of Israel for the costs of resettling many survivors there.

Another form of reparations is land, such as the 40 acres of farmland originally promised to liberated African-American slaves. Since they never received any compensation after the Civil War, and they and their descendants suffered continual discrimination and oppression for another century after that (resulting in a legacy of disproportionate and entrenched poverty), a credible case can still be made for reparations to black slave descendants. In *The Debt*, Randall Robinson makes such an argument:

As Germany and other interests that profited *owed* reparations to Jews following the holocaust of Nazi persecution, America and other interests that profited *owe* reparations to blacks following the holocaust of African slavery which has carried forward from slavery's inception for 350-odd years to the end of U.S. government-embraced racial discrimination—an end that arrived, it would seem, only just yesterday.[13]

More recently, journalist and *Black Panther* comics author Ta-Nehisi Coates has argued the case for black reparations, both in writing and in hearings before the U.S. Congress.[14] Jennifer Warren, a white scholar who studies religion and race, argues that white American Christian churches should lead the way in offering reparations to African Americans.[15] She suggests that the dominant frame through which these churches have viewed race relations in recent decades—"reconciliation"—has skewed their attention away from the Biblical and moral obligation of justice and allowed them to focus solely on racial unity and togetherness. In terms of the tetrad, one could say that they have conflated reconciliation with the comic frame, to the neglect of the other frames (especially the tragic). While affirming the goal of racial reconciliation, Warren calls on churches to adopt a reparations frame to bring justice into focus, and with this corrected vision, to redress the long history of white Christians using and abusing black people.[16]

If one accepts the moral argument for present-day reparations to African Americans, this raises the question of what form they should take—a matter of considerable debate. Legal scholar Roy L. Brooks argues that *compensatory reparations*—that is, direct payments from the government to individuals—would not be appropriate so long after the end of slavery and Jim Crow. Rather, he advocates *rehabilitative reparations*, aimed not toward strict justice (as in a lawsuit seeking damages) but rather toward restorative justice and reconciliation, working to restore the health and strength of the community that has suffered harm.[17] As such, Brooks calls for reparations in the form of a government trust fund for black slave descendants, to be used only for economic self-development in furthering one's education or starting/building a business[18]—much as Thaddeus Stevens called for land to be held in trust for ex-slaves so they could earn a living and gain a measure of economic security. Brooks also recommends the creation of a national slavery museum—a substantial material investment in remembering and redressing a national atrocity. Brooks's approach emphasizes moral rectification over financial compensation: "Redressing slavery should be about honor, not alms. It should be about black pride and dignity, and, last but not least, it should be about commemorating and memorializing the slaves."[19]

Whatever form they take, reparations can never truly replace what has been lost or destroyed; they can only ameliorate the lingering consequences of the offense and pave the way toward a more just future. As they make a material difference in the lives of victims, they also work symbolically and rhetorically, potentially lending credibility to expressions of repentance, reasonability to forgiveness, and emotional relief from feelings of resentment and bitterness.

Negotiating Apology, Forgiveness, and Reparative Action

The rhetoric of reconciliation is *dialogic*, not only in the sense that it brings together former perpetrators and victims in the complementary speech-acts of apology and forgiveness, but also that these acts in themselves, together with reparation, are negotiated in public dialogue. For instance, Jane W. Yamazaki's studies of Japanese apologies for war crimes against South Korean victims revealed that making a collective apology can be a process of "interaction, negotiation, and even co-creation," as victims reject a weak apology, demand a better apology, and communicate what that would require.[20] Likewise, Vincent R. Waldron and Douglas L. Kelley's research on interpersonal forgiveness found that offending and offended parties engage in dialogue about the offense and negotiate the moral terms under which the latter may forgive; to account for this communicative process, Waldron and Kelley developed a theoretical framework called Negotiated Morality Theory.[21]

Reparation, too, calls for rhetorical dialogue. According to David W. Augsburger, it is a process of "reestablishing … mutual justice" and a "creative, responsive work."[22] As Derek R. Brookes notes, this collaborative effort should result in "a fair and mutually acceptable form of restitution and/or compensation."[23] While victims of collective wrongdoing might seek reparation through legal ruling in a civil court, Roy Brooks argues that restorative justice is better served through a process of dialogue and deliberation in a legislative body, especially when confronting such a complex matter as redress for slavery in the U.S. Compared with involuntary reparation through court order, voluntary reparation negotiated among representatives of the parties can more readily work hand-in-glove with apology, encourage forgiveness, and promote reconciliation for the common good.

The speech transcripts assembled in Part II exemplify the public discourse of apology, forgiveness, and reparation. The significance of these exemplars lies not only in their construction as distinct rhetorical acts but also in the larger public conversations of which they were a part.

Overview of Part II Speeches

Part II begins with an unusual address from Jewish writer and Holocaust survivor Elie Wiesel, recipient of the 1986 Nobel Peace Prize. In January 2000, the

German Parliament dedicated a new Holocaust memorial in the heart of Berlin called the Memorial to the Murdered Jews of Europe, and Wiesel was invited to speak at this ceremony. Drawing on historical facts, personal stories, and the Jewish rabbinic tradition, Wiesel not only bore witness to the horrific and painful truths of Nazi Germany's genocide and spoke for the victims/survivors, but also urged the German government to directly ask forgiveness from the Jewish people. This address demonstrates how the victim's desire to hear an apology and possibly forgive can precede the victimizer's act of asking forgiveness. (Indeed, less than a month later, the president of Germany stood before Israel's national legislature and humbly asked forgiveness "for what Germans have done, for myself, my generation, for the sake of our children and grandchildren, whose future I would like to see alongside the children of Israel."[24])

Following Wiesel's speech are two addresses on slavery delivered by American politicians around the start of the 21st century in the region of West Africa (a major hub of the European and American slave trade in the 18th and 19th centuries). The first of these addresses has been characterized as "the most important speech on slavery since Abraham Lincoln."[25] At Goree Island in the Republic of Senegal, President George W. Bush recounted and confessed the sin of slavery, offered a providential perspective on liberation, and implicitly offered a kind of restitution to African nations in the form of economic and political partnerships. Following Bush's speech is an address by U.S. Rep. Tony Hall making an apology to African Americans for the American institution of slavery that held their ancestors in bondage under the laws of the land. Hall offered this apology at a reconciliation conference in the Republic of Benin, West Africa. Although he could not formally speak on behalf of the U.S. Congress, he explained why he had introduced an apology resolution into Congress, how dismayed he was by the negative reaction to his proposal, and why he still believed such an apology was necessary and valid.

The next speech deals with the legacy of slavery in the form of present-day racial hatred that was displayed in a white supremacist's mass shooting of black parishioners at Emanuel AME Church in 2015. President Barack Obama's eulogy for Rev. Clementa Pinckney and the other victims of the shooting (arguably his greatest speech) highlights the power of divine grace—humanly expressed in the forms of transcendent goodness, forgiveness, and repentance—to overcome the sins of the past and present and promote progress in race relations.

Part II ends with a set of speech-acts exemplifying reconciliation as a dialogic rhetorical process between perpetrators and victims. This speech set consists of formal public statements between representatives of the United Church of Canada denomination (UCC) and its First Nations peoples (the equivalent of Native American nations in the United States). In 1986, at the request of indigenous leaders within the UCC, the Church's white leader apologized on behalf of the denomination for devaluing the culture and spirituality of the First Nations. Two years later, a representative of First Nations peoples acknowledged the apology and spoke of the further work of reconciliation to be done. A decade later, another leader in the UCC made a public apology to the First Nations specifically for the Church's involvement in the Indian Residential School system (which had taken First Nations children away from their parents, forced them to assimilate into white culture, and exposed many of them to acts of physical, sexual, and psychological abuse by school staff). This set of speeches illustrates how reconciliation, as an Other-centered dialogic process, requires the voice and initiative of victims and takes more than just a "one-and-done" apology.

Notes

1. John B. Hatch, *Race and Reconciliation: Redressing Wounds of Injustice* (Lanham, MD: Lexington, 2008), 180–83.
2. Ibid., 187–92.
3. See B. L. Ware and Wil A. Linkugel, "They Spoke in Defense of Themselves: On the Generic Criticism of Apologia," *Quarterly Journal of Speech* 59, no. 3 (October 1973): 273–83, doi:10.1080/00335637309383176.
4. See William L. Benoit, *Accounts, Excuses, and Apologies: A Theory of Image Restoration Strategies*, SUNY Series in Speech Communication (Albany: State University of New York Press, 1995); William L. Benoit, "Queen Elizabeth's Image Repair Discourse: Insensitive Royal or Compassionate Queen?" *Public Relations Review* 25, no. 2 (Summer 1999): 145–66, doi:10.1016/S0363-8111(99)80159-3.
5. See John B. Hatch, "Beyond *Apologia*: Racial Reconciliation and Apologies for Slavery," *Western Journal of Communication* 70, no. 3 (July 2006): 186–211, doi:10.1080/10570310600843496.
6. See John B. Hatch, "Rounding (out) the Bases of Racial Reconciliation: (Dia)logology and Virginia's Apology for Slavery," in *Transcendence by Perspective: Meditations on and with Kenneth Burke*, ed. Bryan Crable (Anderson, SC: Parlor Press, 2014), 87–113; John B. Hatch, "Resolutions of Regret: The Other in the Evolution of a State Apology for Slavery," in *The Philosophy of Communication Ethics: Alterity and the Other*, ed. Ronald C. Arnett and Pat Arneson (Madison, NJ: Fairleigh Dickinson University Press), 153–81.
7. See Hatch, *Race and Reconciliation*, 180.
8. See ibid., 185 and 192–95.
9. For further discussion of these issues, see ibid., 168–73.
10. See Robert D. Enright, *Forgiveness is a Choice*, Washington, DC: American Psychological Association, 2001. See also Hatch, *Race and Reconciliation*, 173–80.
11. *Long Night's Journey into Day: South Africa's Search for Truth & Reconciliation*, DVD, directed by Deborah Hoffman (San Francisco: Iris Films, 2000). The film received the Grand Prize for Best Documentary from the Sundance Film Festival; see http://newsreel.org/video/LONG-NIGHTS-JOURNEY-INTO-DAY.

12. Quoted with permission. For the entire recorded exchange between Mbelo and the mothers of the Guguletu Seven, view *Long Night's Journey into Day* from 1:20:40 to 1:27:28, or read that portion of the transcript, available online at http://newsreel.org/transcripts/longnight.htm.
13. Randall Robinson, *The Debt: What America Owes to Blacks* (New York: Plume, 2001), 9.
14. See Ta-Nehisi Coates, "The Case for Reparations," *The Atlantic* May 21, 2014: 54–71, https://www.theatlantic.com/magazine/archive/2014/06/the-case-for-reparations/361631/; Olivia Paschal and Madeleine Carlisle, "Read Ta-Nehisi Coates's Testimony on Reparations," *The Atlantic* June 19, 2019, https://www.theatlantic.com/politics/archive/2019/06/ta-nehisi-coates-testimony-house-reparations-hr-40/592042/.
15. Jennifer Harvey, *Dear White Christians: For Those Still Longing for Racial Reconciliation* (Grand Rapids, MI: William. B. Eerdmans, 2014).
16. For a succinct contextualization of Harvey's argument, see her speech at the 2018 A.C.T. to End Racism rally: https://www.youtube.com/watch?v=6t7v4v5ouH8.
17. Roy L. Brooks, *Atonement and Forgiveness: A New Model for Black Reparations* (Berkeley: University of California Press, 2004), 157.
18. Ibid., 159–62.
19. Ibid., 142.
20. Jane W. Yamazaki, "Crafting the Apology: Japanese Apologies to South Korea in 1990," *Asian Journal of Communication* 14, no. 2 (September 2004), 156, doi:10.1080/0129298042000256776.
21. Vincent R. Waldron and Douglas L. Kelley, *Communicating Forgiveness* (Thousand Oaks, CA: SAGE, 2007).
22. David W. Augsburger, *Conflict Mediation across Cultures: Pathways and Patterns* (Louisville, KY: Westminster, 1992), 281.
23. Derek R. Brookes, "Evaluating Restorative Justice Programs," *Humanity and Society* 22 (1998), 23, https://doi.org/10.1177/016059769802200103.
24. Associated Press, "German President Asks for Israel's Forgiveness," *Deseret News*, February 16, 2000, https://www.deseretnews.com/article/744059/German-president-asks-for-Israels-forgiveness.html.
25. Martin J. Medhurst, "George W. Bush at Goree Island: American Slavery and the Rhetoric of Redemption," *Quarterly Journal of Speech* 96, no. 3 (August 2010), 258, doi:10.1080/00335630.2010.499107.

CHAPTER TWELVE

Remembering and Redressing Incomprehensible Evil: Elie Wiesel

A professor, activist, and writer who authored more than 50 books and received many awards (including the Nobel Peace Prize), Elie Wiesel was born to Jewish parents in Romania and endured the horrors of the Nazi concentration camps at Auschwitz and Buchenwald as a teenager. Although his parents died in the Holocaust, he survived to become one of its most esteemed chroniclers and interpreters,[1] as well as an advocate for oppressed groups around the world. For this reason, at the start of the new millennium, the German Bundestag (Parliament) invited Wiesel to speak at the dedication of a site in Berlin where a massive memorial to the Jewish victims of the Holocaust was to be built. This case serves to highlight the importance both of historical monuments and victims' voices to the work of reconciliation.

At their best, monuments and memorials to crimes against humanity (1) preserve history, keeping alive the memory of these wrongs so we might never repeat them; (2) honor the victims (while condemning the acts of brutality through which they were dishonored and dehumanized); (3) promote healing and harmony, building on a foundation of interdependence and restorative justice; and (4) inspire ongoing effort to protect and promote human rights. Thus, they work rhetorically, promoting truth, justice, peace, and human agency for the common good. Much as a tombstone, inscribed with an *epitaph*, enables visitors both to remember and honor the dead, so memorials such as the one in Berlin enable visitors to remember and honor the murdered victims of collective wrongdoing (whose bodies were never properly buried); and it is fitting that a surviving victim should have the honor of giving voice to their humanity and sufferings—offering, in effect, an *epitaphios* or funeral address for the dead. In ancient Greece, the *epitaphios* honored soldiers who died for their country, challenging the living to emulate their virtue.[2] In the case of genocide, such as the Holocaust, it is not so much the virtuous character of the dead as the intrinsic value of their humanity that must be honored, challenging a society to atone for the sins of its past and protect and honor all human life going forward.

Wiesel's *epitaphios* exemplifies some of the burdens borne by victims of heinous acts when they engage in the work of reconciliation. These include (1) speaking the truth about their unspeakable suffering to members of the group that caused the suffering; (2) striving to do so without bitterness or hatred; (3) trying to comprehend the evil that caused such suffering; (4) speaking as a representative of one's group, when different members of that group have different perspectives on, and assessments of, the reconciliation efforts; (5) apportioning blame and guilt justly—recognizing a group's collective responsibility for wrongdoing without impugning every individual member (or descendant) of that group—and (6) asking the responsible party to do more to promote healing for the victims.

Given this burden, Wiesel feels it necessary to begin by reciting a brief Jewish prayer. He regards himself as a witness, sworn to tell the truth no matter how difficult it may be, and tells stories as a way to highlight the humanity of those destroyed by the Holocaust. Wiesel frames the body of his speech through the collective wisdom of the Jewish people by beginning with a story from a famous rabbi and ending with a saying from another rabbi. Thus, although he is just one witness, Wiesel draws strength and credibility from the ancient religious/cultural tradition of his people in order to speak on behalf of six million Jewish Holocaust victims.

Wiesel's address to the German Parliament includes a number of distinctive features. Notice how he is sensitive to his audience even though they are descendants of a nation that tried to wipe his people off the face of the earth: "Will my words hurt you? That is not my intention. But please understand, when I entered this Chamber, I did not leave my memories behind." Wiesel also takes care not to over-generalize blame and guilt: "I know, there were Germans who did not comply. And we must remember them, you and I …. Only, sadly, they were few." Wiesel asserts very strongly that he does not believe in collective or inherited guilt, and he empathizes with the present generation of Germans, who have to live with the fact that "Auschwitz will remain a part of your history."

Another distinctive feature of Wiesel's speech is his repeated effort to grapple with the incomprehensible evil of the crime committed against his people:

I still don't understand it. I go on trying and trying.... How is one to comprehend the cult of hatred and death that flourished in this country?... did it really make these killers feel strong and heroic to murder defenseless children?... Were the killers still human?

Widening his perspective beyond Germany, Wiesel laments the Allies' lack of assistance to Jews who were trying to escape the Nazis' grasp. Raising his sights, he observes: "Not even God, the God of Israel, seemed to care. More than anyone else's, his silence was a mystery that continues to puzzle and distress many of us to this day."

Wiesel not only decries the inhumanity that destroyed so many of his people, he also honors the victims, who were of irreducible value despite being dehumanized by the Nazis. While the stories of six million murders may seem to blend together, he notes that "each episode is unique, for every human being, created in God's image, is unique." To reinforce this claim, he shares the story of one nameless family—a mother, father, and their two children—murdered by the Nazis. Extrapolating from this example, he laments: "A million and a half Jewish children perished, Ladies and Gentlemen. If I were to begin reciting their names, the Moischeles, the Jankeles, the Sodeles, here and now, I would have to stand here for months and years." Cognizant of humanity's interdependence, Wiesel goes on to lament these children's deaths as the world's loss—so much talent and virtue snuffed out before it had the chance to benefit humanity.

Perhaps the most distinctive aspect of this address is found in Wiesel's assessment of efforts to repair the damage caused by the Holocaust. Noting that Germany had failed to express clear moral contrition for its crimes in the early years after World War II, he expresses appreciation for their more recent efforts to atone. These include consistent support for the nation of Israel, financial reparations to victims of the Holocaust, the Chancellor's plans to fund increased education about the Holocaust, and the Parliament's creation of an annual National Holocaust Remembrance Day. Wiesel acknowledges that some people will dismiss the act of devoting just one day a year to remembrance as "too easy ... a mockery," but Wiesel disagrees with them, affirming the good intent behind it.

Most important, Wiesel challenges the German president to do something further "that would have world-wide repercussions." Noting that President Rau had recently "met a group of Auschwitz survivors" and "asked for forgiveness for what the German people had done to them," he asks, "Why shouldn't you do it here?" Wiesel's challenge did not go entirely unanswered: less than a month later, President Rau visited Israel and spoke before its legislature (the Knesset), humbly apologizing for the Holocaust and begging Israel's forgiveness on behalf of the German people.

Wiesel's address to the German Parliament serves as a powerful reminder that reconciliation is a dialogic process. The party that perpetrated the wrong cannot unilaterally redeem themselves or unilaterally reconcile with the victimized party. The victims, who once were deprived of agency, must now be allowed to speak for themselves, exerting full agency and influence on the process of reconciliation. It is their prerogative to accept an apology or not, and no representative of theirs can presume to forgive on behalf of the whole group. Indeed, although Wiesel said that a German apology to the Jewish people would be very significant, some members of Israel's Knesset boycotted Rau's speech; and while those who were present applauded politely, they did not appear to be moved by his emotional address[3]—a reminder that forgiveness is a difficult and highly personal matter.

Address to the German Parliament at the Dedication of the Memorial to the Murdered Jews of Europe[4]

Berlin, Germany
January 27, 2000

President Rau, President of the Bundestag, President of the Bundesrat, My dear Chancellor Schröder, Members of the cabinet, Distinguished Members of the Bundestag, Excellencies, Friends:

Allow me to tell you a story. But, first, I hope you understand that I speak to you as a witness. When a witness speaks, he or she must take a vow to tell the truth. The Jew that I am feels that he ought to make a prayer. Fifty-five years ago the Russians came a bit too late for me and those who are close to me. Do not look at me and see the man that I am now. Please try and see in me the person I was 55 years ago. Today, I am here with my wife, Marion, and two very close friends, Inga and Ira, and so I will say a prayer. The prayer is from the Book of Baruch: "Blessed be the Lord for enabling me to be here at this day."

And now a story.

Once upon a time in a faraway land, there lived a benevolent king. One day, he was told by his astrologists that the next harvest would be cursed and that whosoever would eat from it would go mad. And so he ordered an enormous granary built and stored there all that remained from the previous year's crop. He then entrusted the granary's key to his closest friend and this is what he told him:

> When my subjects and their king will have been struck with madness, you and you alone will have the right to enter the storehouse and eat uncontaminated food. Thus you will escape the malediction. But in exchange, my poor friend, you will be duty-bound to fulfill a vital and impossible task. Your mission will be to crisscross the earth,

going from country to country, from town to town, from marketplace to marketplace, from person to person, shouting with all your might: "Good people, do not forget that you are mad! Men and women, do not forget, do not forget that you are mad!"

This tale, told by the very great Rabbi Nahman of Bratzlav, who was a forerunner of Franz Kafka, surely applies to this century which has just ended, a century in which madness erupted in history and turned it often into a nightmare. And so the witnesses that we are, some of us, we, too, go around the world simply to say: "Don't forget that you were mad, don't forget that history has carried madness in it." And so the man you so kindly invited to take part in this solemn and moving session devoted to the memory of the victims of what we so inadequately call Shoah or Holocaust—there are no words for it—is a son of an ancient people whose mission over the centuries has been to teach the oneness of God and the sacredness of human life. Some sixty years ago, in this very metropolis, in this city, this man that I am and his community, were condemned to isolation, distress, despair and death. And yet, I hope you believe me, I am a witness and I speak to you today with neither bitterness nor hate. All my adult life I have tried to use language to fight hate, to denounce it, to disarm it, not to spread it.

Will my words hurt you? That is not my intention. But please understand, when I entered this Chamber, I did not leave my memories behind. In fact, here, because of you, they are more vivid than ever. All I wish to do in this short time is to evoke in a few words an unprecedented event which will, for generations to come, continue to weigh on the destiny of my people and yours.

And this event, I still don't understand it. I go on trying and trying. Since my liberation, on April 11, 1945, I have read everything I could lay my hands on that deals with its implications. Historical essays, psychological analyses, testimonies and testaments, poems and prayers, assassins' diaries and victims' meditations, even children's letters to God. But though I managed to assimilate the facts, the numbers and the technical aspects of the "Aktionen", the implacable significance which transcends them continues to elude me. The Nuremberg Laws, the anti-Jewish decrees, the Kristallnacht, the public humiliation of proud Jewish citizens, including brave World War I veterans, the first concentration camps, the euthanasia of German citizens, the Wannsee conference, where the highest officials of the land simply met to discuss the validity, the legality and the ways of killing an entire people. And then of course Dachau, Auschwitz, Majdanek, Sobibor—the capitals of this century. Yes, these names … flags, black flags, reminding a world that will come, of a world that has been. What made them possible? How is one to comprehend the cult of hatred and death that flourished in this country? How could bright young men, many superbly educated, from fine families, with diplomas from Germany's best universities, which then were the best in the world, how could they allow themselves to be seduced by Evil to the point of devoting their genius, the genius of Evil, to the torture and the killing of Jewish men, women and children whom they had never seen? They didn't do it because these Jews were rich or poor, believers or non-believers, political adversaries, patriots or universalists, but simply because they had been born Jewish. Their birth certificate had become a de facto death sentence. But did it really make these killers feel strong and heroic to murder defenseless children? Could they really have been so afraid of old and sick people, of small children as to make them their priority targets? What was it about them that was frightening? Their weakness, their innocence perhaps? Were the killers still human? That is the question which is my obsession. At what point does humanity end? Is there a limit beyond which humanity doesn't deserve its name anymore?

While preparing myself for today's encounter with you—an encounter of course which is symbolic on more than one level, as you put it very well, President of the Bundestag—I reread certain chronicles by survivors and witnesses, both living and dead. And I was struck again by how similar the scenes of cruelty were. It is as though one German, always the same, tortured and killed one Jew, forever the same, six million times. Yet each episode is unique, for every human being, created in God's image, is unique.

Since I am not a historian, rather than discuss history I tell stories. And here is one, just one: it takes place in September 1941 in Babi-Yar, in Kiev, as reported by an eyewitness, a certain B.A. Liebmann.

He tells of a Jewish family which has spent several days hiding in a cave. The mother decides to seek help in a nearby village with her two small children. They are intercepted by a group of drunken Germans who, in front of the mother, behead one child, then the second. As the distraught mother clutches the bodies of her dead children, the Germans, obviously delighted with the spectacle, kill the mother as well. And when the father appears on the scene, they murder him too. I don't understand.

One could tell you more stories, six million more. Of all the crimes committed against my people, the Jewish people, the murder of its children is the worst. They were always the first to be taken and sent off to death. A million and a half Jewish children perished, Ladies and Gentlemen. If I were to begin reciting their names, the Moischeles, the Jankeles, the Sodeles, here and now, I would have to stand here for months and years.

Haven't the peoples of the world lost so much, too, not only my own, through what was done? How many benefactors of humanity perished when they were a month old, or a year? There could have been among them scientists who would have discovered a remedy for AIDS, a cure for cancer. They could have written great poems to inspire everybody, to renounce violence and war, a few words perhaps or a song to bring people together at last.

There is a picture that shows laughing soldiers surrounding a Jewish boy in a ghetto, I think probably in the Warsaw ghetto. I look at it often. What was it about that sad and frightened Jewish child with his hands up in the air that amused the German soldiers so? Why was tormenting him so funny? Were these soldiers, who likely were good husbands and fathers, not conscious of what they were doing? Weren't they thinking of their own children and grandchildren, who one day would have to carry the burden of their crimes although, as I shall say later, they are innocent? Ivan Karamazov believed that "cruel people are sometimes very fond of children." Yes, but not of Jewish children.

Of course, for us Jews in occupied Europe, it soon became clear that the free world was aware of and therefore responsible, though to a much different degree, for what was happening to us. The Allies seemed not to care very much; they did not open their borders to us when there was still time. And so Berlin became convinced that our fate was of no real concern to anyone. Not even God, the God of Israel, seemed to care. More than anyone else's, his silence was a mystery that continues to puzzle and distress many of us to this day. But that is another matter, one we debate mostly when we are among ourselves. Today, we shall speak only of Jews and Germans, then and now. My people has had innumerable enemies since it appeared on the world stage. We remember them all. But none had wounded us as deeply as Hitler's Germany. Over time, we endured discrimination, persecution, many forms of isolation, we survived the Crusades, the Inquisition, the pogroms, the various results of ingrained antisemitism. But the Holocaust went much farther indeed. I say it with pain: no nation, no ideology, no system has ever inflicted brutality, suffering and humiliation on such a scale on any people as yours has on mine in such a short period.

The sentence the Third Reich imposed upon us was deadly and irrevocable. The Final Solution, precisely outlined, was eschatological in nature; its goal was to annihilate every Jew, down to the last one on the surface of the earth. That was actually a kind of principal objective; the deportation of Hungarian Jews, and I am one of them as you know, had priority over the military convoys taking much-needed soldiers to the front.

I know, there were Germans who did not comply. And we must remember them, you and I. Those who had the courage to oppose the official racist ideology. Those who resisted the Nazi totalitarian regime. Those who tried to topple it and paid with their lives. And you are right in honoring their bravery. Only, sadly, they were few. And those who rescued Jewish friends and neighbors even fewer.

Now, many in Germany and elsewhere choose to put all the blame on the Nazis. "The Nazis did this or that," is the accepted formula. The Nazis, not the Germans.

Does it mean that there were two parallel histories of Germany, a Nazi history and a German history? Of course, all Germans were not Nazis. But I can tell you again as a witness, I remember in those times that the word German inspired fears; we were afraid when we heard that the Germans were coming.

Here, in this very place, the new leaders of the German people are so valiantly and honorably trying to build a new destiny, a more human philosophy of living. And we are here to tell you that we appreciate this. In those times, the decision to kill the Jews was taken at the highest level of government but was implemented down below. And for the victims, everything was German: the Zyklon gas was German, those who built the crematoriums were German, those who built the gas chambers were German, the orders given were German. As Paul Celan put it: "Der Tod ist ein Meister aus Deutschland" ["Death is a master from Germany"[5]]. And Celan committed suicide because he felt probably that his words could not communicate this essential truth of his or our experience. Until the end of times, Ladies and Gentleman, Auschwitz will remain a part of your history, just as it will continue to be a part of mine.

I know, it is difficult and painful for you to think in these terms. Yours is a new generation, none of you have had to swear allegiance to Hitler. Of course, none of you have committed any crime or any sin. But I am sure that, in moments of anguish, you wonder where your parents were then, where did they stand then?

I feel compelled to tell you what I repeat everywhere I go, not only here: I do not believe in collective guilt; only the guilty and their accomplices are guilty, but surely not those who were not yet born, surely not their children. The children of killers are not killers, but children. And your children, many of them are so good. I know some of them; a few have been my students. They are so marvelous, so highly motivated, and at the same time tormented, understandably so. They somehow feel guilty, although they should not feel guilty at all. And what they are doing to somehow redeem your country, your people, is extraordinary. Whatever touches the spirit is of concern to them. They go to Israel to build, and they help any cause that deals with violation of human rights because they feel, your children feel that it is important not to forget this dark period.

So what is what we call the Holocaust? Was it the consequence of history, an aberration of history? This is not the time, nor the place to speak about that. There are other times, in school, when education is important. The Chancellor and I yesterday participated in a meeting in Stockholm about education on the Holocaust. And your words were very highly appreciated there. I am not sure that

I have the answer to the Holocaust, but surely education is a major component of that answer. So emphasize education, increase the budget, do whatever you can so that the children, your children, who want to know, are able to know.

I am here, and I remember 55 years ago. I remember, and if I were to tell you what I remember, you would, like me, tremble. So, let us speak rather of what has to be done. I as a Jew, of course, speak of the Jewish victims, my people. Their tragedy was unique, but I do not forget other victims. When, as a Jew, I evoke the Jewish victims, I honor the others as well. As I like to put it: not all victims were Jewish but all Jews were victims.

And it is to remember them, Mr. President, Mr. Chancellor, President of the Bundestag, that this Parliament is marking the 27th of January as a day for commemorating the victims of the Nazi regime or, as I would call it, National Holocaust Remembrance Day. And this decision does you honor. And my presence here is meant, of course, to highlight your willingness to open the gates of memory and to declare together our conviction and resolution that it is high time for Cain to stop murdering his brother Abel.

Surely, there will be those who will say that it is too easy for you to devote one day a year just to pay a kind of homage and then go back to your normal business. Some will say it is a mockery. I don't agree. I take your move very seriously. I don't believe that it is to forget Auschwitz that you wish to remember its liberation. On the contrary, I believe that you wish to recall its liberation so as to condemn what preceded it, and to know more about it. I also believe that you will not listen to the indecent voices here in this land urging you to "turn the page" because you allegedly are "fed up with those stories". Those who want to turn the page have done so already. Not only have they turned the page, they have ripped it out of their consciousness. But by conspiring to obliterate the victims' memory, those who want to turn the page are killing them a second time, and that will be their burden.

After the war, some of us expected a defeated and humiliated Germany to deliver a more powerful message of remorse and contrition, one that would be linked to morality; instead, in those years it was related more to politics. But, since Chancellor Konrad Adenauer's time, you have become a democracy, worthy of taking its place in the family of nations. You have consistently supported Israel, and your record of financial reparations to the victims, mainly to the Jewish victims, but also to all slave laborers, as the law you are introducing in Parliament stipulates, is positive. But I believe that perhaps the time has come for you to make a gesture that would have world-wide repercussions.

President Rau, you met a group of Auschwitz survivors few weeks ago. And one of them told me that you expressed something very moving. You asked for forgiveness for what the German people had done to them. Why shouldn't you do it here? In the spirit of this solemn occasion. Why shouldn't the Bundestag simply let this be known to Germany and its allies and its friends, and especially to young people? Have you asked the Jewish people to forgive Germany for what the Third Reich did in Germany's name to so many of us? Do it, and it will have extraordinary repercussions in the world. Do it, and the significance of this day will acquire a higher dimension. Do it, and the world will know that its faith in this Germany is justified. For, beyond national, ethnic or religious considerations, it was mankind itself that was threatened then, in those darkest of days. And in some ways, it still is. Whatever this new century holds in store, and we desperately want to have hope for the new century and its new generation, Auschwitz will continue to force men to explore the deepest recesses of his and her being so as to confront their fragile truth.

I told you before that I prefer stories. I would like to conclude with the story of a little Jewish girl who died with her mother the night they arrived in Birkenau in May 1944. She was eight years old, and believe me, she had done nothing to hurt or harm your people—why did she have to die such an atrocious death?[6] If her brother lives to be as old as the world itself, he will never understand. And so, he will simply quote another great Hasidic Master: Rabbi Moshe Leib of Sassov. He was known for his great compassion and he said: "My friends, do you wish to find the spark? Look for it in the ashes."

Notes

1. Wiesel's most famous book records his experience of the Holocaust and his struggle with the reality of human evil: Elie Wiesel, *Night*, trans. Marion Wiesel, commemorative ed. (New York: Hill and Wang, 2017).
2. See Andreea D. Ritivoi, *Paul Ricoeur: Tradition and Innovation in Rhetorical Theory* (SUNY Press, 2006), 100.
3. "German President Asks for Israel's Forgiveness, *Deseret News*, February 16, 2000, https://www.deseretnews.com/article/744059/German-president-asks-for-Israels-forgiveness.html.
4. Printed here by permission of Georges Borchardt, Inc., on behalf of Elirion Associates, Inc.
5. This line is taken from Celan's famous "Deathfugue." See John Felstiner, *Paul Celan: Poet, Survivor, Jew* (New Haven, CT: Yale University Press, 2001), 31–32.
6. Here, Wiesel appears to be speaking of his younger sister, Tzipora.

CHAPTER THIRTEEN

Acknowledging a Heinous Historical Crime: George W. Bush

In July of 2003, President George W. Bush made a five-day tour of African nations. During his visit to the Republic of Senegal, Bush went to Goree Island, famous for its museum and memorials about the horrors of the transatlantic slave trade in West Africa. There, Bush delivered an address that distinguished rhetoric scholar Martin J. Medhurst regards as "the most important speech on slavery since Abraham Lincoln."[1] Medhurst explains:

> Bush, in his speech at Goree Island, succeeds in putting American slavery into historical, political, and theological perspective in such a way as simultaneously to confess our national sin and to begin to make restitution for it by offering economic and political partnerships to states in Africa, partnerships that will help to restore what America had previously taken.[2]

Crafted primarily by Bush speechwriter Michael Gerson, this address adopts what Medhurst refers to as "a Providential or God-centered perspective on time, history, and knowledge."[3] In this respect, it harks back to Lincoln's Second Inaugural Address, which had taken a providential view of America's Civil War as a moral consequence of slavery—a paradoxical punishment in the sense that divine judgment came through human warfare. As Medhurst notes, Bush's Goree Island address suggests a providential paradox: "it was not white Americans that freed the black slaves; it was the slaves that freed white America."[4] Medhurst identifies another paradox toward the end of the speech, where "[t]he evil trade of slavery is rhetorically transformed into the empowering trade of international commerce" as African nations become adopted as "'full partners in the trade and prosperity of the world.'"[5] Glaringly absent from this picture, Medhurst notes, is attention to the present-day needs and concerns of the African-American descendants of slaves.[6]

In terms of the reconciliation tetrad, Bush's Goree Island speech first works through the truths of slavery, and then weighs white people's oppression of black people on the scales of justice. While it condemns the evil of white-perpetrated slavery, it also heralds the agency of African Americans who challenged America to live up to its ideals, the agency of African nations to write a new page in their history, and the U.S. government's agency to support their development. The speech's moral vision of reconciliation and redress would have been more complete and coherent if it had recognized the U.S. government's responsibility to further redress the racialized legacy of slavery within its own borders—a responsibility that U.S. Rep. Tony Hall conveyed in his 1999 address in West Africa (see next speech) and his advocacy for a Congressional apology to African Americans.

Remarks on Goree Island

Republic of Senegal, West Africa
July 8, 2003

Mr. President and Madam First Lady, distinguished guests and residents of Goree Island, citizens of Senegal, I'm honored to begin my visit to Africa in your beautiful country.

For hundreds of years on this island peoples of different continents met in fear and cruelty. Today we gather in respect and friendship, mindful of past wrongs and dedicated to the advance of human liberty.

At this place, liberty and life were stolen and sold. Human beings were delivered and sorted, and weighed, and branded with the marks of commercial enterprises, and loaded as cargo on a voyage without return. One of the largest migrations of history was also one of the greatest crimes of history.

Below the decks, the middle passage was a hot, narrow, sunless nightmare; weeks and months of confinement and abuse and confusion on a strange and lonely sea. Some refused to eat, preferring death to any future their captors might prepare for them. Some who were sick were thrown over the side. Some rose up in violent rebellion, delivering the closest thing to justice on a slave ship. Many acts of defiance and bravery are recorded. Countless others, we will never know.

Those who lived to see land again were displayed, examined, and sold at auctions across nations in the Western Hemisphere. They entered societies indifferent to their anguish and made prosperous by their unpaid labor. There was a time in my country's history when one in every seven human beings was the property of another. In law, they were regarded only as articles of commerce, having no right to travel, or to marry, or to own possessions. Because families were often separated, many were denied even the comfort of suffering together.

For 250 years the captives endured an assault on their culture and their dignity. The spirit of Africans in America did not break. Yet the spirit of their captors was corrupted. Small men took on the powers and airs of tyrants and masters. Years of unpunished brutality and bullying and rape produced a dullness and hardness of conscience. Christian men and women became blind to the clearest commands of their faith and added hypocrisy to injustice. A republic founded on equality for all became a prison for millions. And yet in the words of the African proverb, "no fist is big enough to hide the sky." All the generations of oppression under the laws of man could not crush the hope of freedom and defeat the purposes of God.

In America, enslaved Africans learned the story of the exodus from Egypt and set their own hearts on a promised land of freedom. Enslaved Africans discovered a suffering Savior and found he was more like themselves than their masters. Enslaved Africans heard the ringing promises of the Declaration of Independence and asked the self-evident question, then why not me?

In the year of America's founding, a man named Olaudah Equiano was taken in bondage to the New World. He witnessed all of slavery's cruelties, the ruthless and the petty. He also saw beyond the slave-holding piety of the time to a higher standard of humanity. "God tells us," wrote Equiano, "that the oppressor and the oppressed are both in His hands. And if these are not the poor, the broken-hearted, the blind, the captive, the bruised which our Savior speaks of, who are they?"

Down through the years, African Americans have upheld the ideals of America by exposing laws and habits contradicting those ideals. The rights of African Americans were not the gift of those in authority. Those rights were granted by the Author of Life, and regained by the persistence and courage of African Americans themselves.

Among those Americans was Phyllis Wheatley, who was dragged from her home here in West Africa in 1761, at the age of seven. In my country, she became a poet, and the first noted black author in our nation's history. Phyllis Wheatley said, "In every human breast, God has implanted a principle which we call love of freedom. It is impatient of oppression and pants for deliverance."

That deliverance was demanded by escaped slaves named Frederick Douglas and Sojourner Truth, educators named Booker T. Washington and W.E.B. DuBois, and ministers of the Gospel named Leon Sullivan and Martin Luther King Jr. At every turn, the struggle for equality was resisted by many of the powerful. And some have said we should not judge their failures by the standards of a later time. Yet, in every time, there were men and women who clearly saw this sin and called it by name.

We can fairly judge the past by the standards of President John Adams, who called slavery "an evil of colossal magnitude." We can discern eternal standards in the deeds of William Wilberforce and John Quincy Adams, and Harriet Beecher Stowe, and Abraham Lincoln. These men and women, black and white, burned with a zeal for freedom, and they left behind a different and better nation. Their moral vision caused Americans to examine our hearts, to correct our Constitution, and to teach our children the dignity and equality of every person of every race. By a plan known only to Providence, the stolen sons and daughters of Africa helped to awaken the conscience of America. The very people traded into slavery helped to set America free.

My nation's journey toward justice has not been easy and it is not over. The racial bigotry fed by slavery did not end with slavery or with segregation. And many of the issues that still trouble America have roots in the bitter experience of other times. But however long the journey, our destination is set: liberty and justice for all.

In the struggle of the centuries, America learned that freedom is not the possession of one race. We know with equal certainty that freedom is not the possession of one nation. This belief in the natural rights of man, this conviction that justice should reach wherever the sun passes, leads America into the world.

With the power and resources given to us, the United States seeks to bring peace where there is conflict, hope where there is suffering, and liberty where there is tyranny. And these commitments bring me and other distinguished leaders of my government across the Atlantic to Africa.

African peoples are now writing your own story of liberty. Africans have overcome the arrogance of colonial powers, overturned the cruelties of apartheid, and made it clear that dictatorship is not the future of any nation on this continent. In the process, Africa has produced heroes of liberation—leaders like Mandela, Senghor, Nkrumah, Kenyatta, Selassie and Sadat. And many visionary African leaders, such as my friend, have grasped the power of economic and political freedom to lift whole nations and put forth bold plans for Africa's development.

Because Africans and Americans share a belief in the values of liberty and dignity, we must share in the labor of advancing those values. In a time of growing commerce across the globe, we will ensure that the nations of Africa are full partners in the trade and prosperity of the world. Against the waste and violence of civil war, we will stand together for peace. Against the merciless terrorists who threaten every nation, we will wage an unrelenting campaign of justice. Confronted with desperate hunger, we will answer with human compassion and the tools of human technology. In the face of spreading disease, we will join with you in turning the tide against AIDS in Africa.

We know that these challenges can be overcome, because history moves in the direction of justice. The evils of slavery were accepted and unchanged for centuries. Yet, eventually, the human heart would not abide them. There is a voice of conscience and hope in every man and woman that will not be silenced—what Martin Luther King called a certain kind of fire that no water could put out. That flame could not be extinguished at the Birmingham jail. It could not be stamped out at Robben Island Prison. It was seen in the darkness here at Goree Island, where no chain could bind the soul. This untamed fire of justice continues to burn in the affairs of man, and it lights the way before us.

May God bless you all.

Notes

1. Martin J. Medhurst, "George W. Bush at Goree Island: American Slavery and the Rhetoric of Redemption," *Quarterly Journal of Speech* 96, no. 3 (August 2010), 258, doi:10.1080/00335630.2010.499107, 258.
2. Ibid.
3. Ibid.
4. Ibid., 258–59.
5. Ibid., 259.
6. Ibid., 269–72.

CHAPTER FOURTEEN

Explaining and Offering a Historical Apology: U.S. Rep. Tony Hall

A career-long public servant, long-time advocate for the world's poor and hungry, and three-time Nobel Peace Prize nominee, Tony P. Hall served as a U.S. Congressman for over 20 years, until he was appointed United States Ambassador to the U.N. Agencies for Food and Agriculture in 2002.[1] In 1997, Hall proposed that the U.S. Congress issue a simple, formal apology to African Americans for the institution of slavery that had been propagated under its laws, for which it had never apologized. However, critics from both major political parties, both white and black, dismissed the idea. To Republicans, it was too backward-looking; to black Democrats, it was an empty (if well-meaning) response to the material legacy of the past.[2]

Two years later, the West African nation of Benin hosted a reconciliation conference aimed at addressing the legacy of the slave trade in that country and beyond. From the 17th to 19th centuries a large number of slaves were shipped from Benin's coast to the Americas, and several of the African peoples living in that region had actively participated in this vile trade by capturing Africans from enemy groups and selling them to the European slave traders. The purpose of the 1999 conference was for representatives of all the parties whose ancestors had been perpetrators or victims of the slave trade to meet together and address the painful legacy of this historic crime against humanity, so that they could turn over a new leaf as the new millennium began. At the invitation of Benin's president, Mathieu

Kérékou, political and economic leaders representing white Americans, white Europeans, and West African peoples came together with African-American leaders to face the heinous crimes of the slave trade, make apologies, and seek forgiveness from the latter, whose ancestors had been enslaved. In this way, Kérékou hoped to lay a foundation of ethnic and racial healing for all of the parties and positive economic development for West Africa.[3]

Tony Hall was one of the leaders invited to speak at the 1999 conference. His involvement in this event inspired him to reintroduce his apology resolution into Congress the following year. Although his effort was again unsuccessful, the idea eventually gained traction after Hall was no longer in Congress, and in 2008, the House of Representatives finally passed a resolution apologizing for slavery and segregation, with the Senate following suit in 2009.[4] It was Hall's advocacy that had led the way a decade earlier, and his 1999 Benin address most openly drew on religious discourse to warrant the idea. Because Kérékou had explicitly framed the conference as a spiritual response to the legacy of the slave trade, Hall was unusually free (for a politician) to speak of his religious identity and draw on his faith in this address. Although he could not officially apologize on behalf of the U.S. government, he could offer his own apology and present his rationale—personal, historical, and spiritual—for Congress to do so.[5]

Readers will notice that Hall's address excels at Other-centeredness—the key quality that makes for a satisfactory apology. He focuses on the concerns and feelings of African Americans, who have suffered under centuries of slavery, segregation, and persistent racial inequality. As he empathizes with them, he does not presume to understand all that they are thinking and feeling nor the realities they deal with; he presents himself as a learner and partner in a task much bigger than himself. He regards his apology to be a necessary yet insufficient recompense for the gravity of the wrongs they have suffered.

In addition to being Other-centered, Hall's speech is ethically well-rounded, as it views reconciliation from each angle of the tetrad. His portrayal of race relations is realistic, facing the facts of African Americans' past mistreatment and present disadvantages. Amid the emotion and controversy over apologizing for slavery, Hall offers straightforward historical precedent for doing so, as he runs through examples of governmental apologies and reparations from the U.S. and other nations for wrongs they had committed against minorities and oppressed groups.

In the process, Hall also views America's race problem through a tragic lens, recognizing slavery as a "terrible act" and a "'grave and revolting wrong'" that has left behind a legacy of injustice. He validates the anger that many black people feel at their mistreatment in history and even refers to his own "sin" as a white man complicit in the racialization of American society. In this tragic frame, Hall recognizes that words of apology are not weighty or substantial enough to rectify the offense of racial oppression. An apology is a foundation or "necessary first step," but "more will be necessary." (It became clear that Hall was alluding to reparation here when he reintroduced his slavery apology resolution in Congress the next year: "I personally believe that ... there ought to be some kind of restoration, some kind of restitution, whether it be scholarships, alleviation of poverty, a slave museum, acceleration of civil rights cases...."[6])

This tragic framing is counterbalanced by Hall's assertion that humans are one family—that differences in race and gender, social status and political party are insignificant compared with their underlying unity as God's children and the call to reconcile through divine love, grace, and mercy. In other words, he also applies the comic frame, taking human differences more lightly in view of a deeper and often overlooked oneness.

Finally, Hall casts a hopeful, romantic light on the troubled history of race relations when he commends humans' God-given capacity to turn from past wrongs and "surrender to forgiveness in order to start afresh." He cites the Biblical account of Joseph and the teachings of Jesus and St. Paul as a warrant for courageous acts of vulnerability in pursuit of reconciliation. He commends black people who transcended slavery and racism by choosing grace over bitterness, forgiveness over retaliation. He insists that words of apology, though small (like a rudder), can begin to turn the ship of race relations in a new direction, toward greater justice and peace. Above all, Hall looks to the grace of God to infuse and enable human efforts toward reconciliation.

Apology to African Americans for Slavery[7]

Cotonou, Republic of Benin, West Africa
December 2, 1999
President Kérékou and President Rawlings; Distinguished Ministers and Guests; My friends from Dayton, Ohio, The Home of Peace, the Dayton Peace Accords; Senator Inhofe and my friend, Congressman Frank Wolf; Brothers and Sisters:

.... I want to read to you the text of the resolution that I introduced into the Congress of the United States two years ago to apologize for slavery.[8] This is all it says:

> Resolved by the House of Representatives (the Senate concurring) that the Congress apologizes to African Americans, whose ancestors suffered as slaves, under the Constitution and the laws of the United States until 1865.

That's all it said. It has not passed yet. It hasn't been taken up for debate. I don't know if it will pass while I'm a member of Congress, but someday it will. Someday our government, our Congress, will apologize for this terrible, terrible act.

These 30 words, they don't seem like much, but I want to share with all of you a few thoughts on why I think we're here, and why I introduced the apology. Those of us who have come here to the Republic of Benin, we carry a special burden. Our hearts are heavy with the need for repentance and reconciliation. Our minds understand the many problems related to slavery. Our souls are in tune with the will of God and that God's children should not be divided. We are all here, as President Kérékou has stated, "to surrender to forgiveness in order to start afresh." And we want the coming millennium to be one of love and reconciliation, not hatred and division. And we pray that God will look upon us today and this week and what we do in the next few days with grace and mercy.

A few years ago, I saw a television program where a black minister and a white minister were on television together, and it was on Martin Luther King holiday in the United States. And they were talking about that the United States government has never apologized for slavery.

I had never heard that before. I couldn't believe it, so I asked the Library of Congress if they would research this and find out if it's true. Did the Congress or did the President, any of our presidents, ever apologize for slavery to African Americans? And they couldn't find anything. And I still found it hard to believe, and I myself personally went to the Library of Congress and I asked for as many books as I could find. I did as much research as I could on my own to find out have we ever apologized for slavery. And I found out that we had not.

So without worrying about political consequences, I set out to correct this glaring omission in history. So, in June of 1997, I introduced this very simple resolution. What happened next was a complete surprise to me. It exploded on the political scene at about the same time President Clinton was conducting his "National Dialogue on Race." And both conservatives and liberals, black and white dismissed it as "a meaningless gesture" or "an avoidance of trying to solve the problem."

I received hundreds of letters and phone calls about the apology. Most of the people I heard from opposed the idea; some were blatantly racist and hateful; very few people stood by my side and defended the idea or the necessity for it. At times, I felt very alone in this struggle.

I know that my resolution will not fix the lingering injustice resulting from slavery. But reconciliation does begin with an apology. Most of my time and energy in Congress, outside of trying to take care of my district, I'm involved mostly with hunger and famine and drought and working with the poor and human rights.

And I've traveled throughout my country and the world trying to learn about the problems of hunger and some of the solutions. I'm not an expert on the issue of race. In fact, I know very little about all the dimensions of the issue. I only see the racial division in my country. And I know about the poverty that infests the black community in the U.S. I know about the plight of Africa and her starving children. But I do not claim to know a great deal about slavery and its legacy of racism.

My faith in Jesus leads me to have a clear purpose in my life. I hope that I can be a man that loves God with all his heart, soul, mind and strength, and loves others as we love ourselves. I hope I can be that person. I know that I would not want my children sold as slaves. I know that it would tear me apart if my wife was taken from me. I know that I would be angry if I was beaten or whipped simply because of the color of my skin.

We have tried to fix the problem before, but in the wrong ways. We have started new programs, given money away, or written useless reports. But that is not enough.

Many of the opponents to the apology argued that slavery had been abolished over a century ago and no one alive in the United States today had been a slave or a slave owner. But that ignores the fact that slavery's effects are still with us. Just one of the many examples of slavery's legacy is in terms of assets.

Slaves, of course, were not able to earn any money or pass on an inheritance to their children. When African-Americans were freed after the Civil War, they started at a distinct disadvantage. Then they were shackled with Jim Crow laws and segregation that prevented them from truly entering into society. It has only been in the last two generations that descendants of slaves have been legally able to join American society, not to mention all of the discrimination that still exists today. Not only is it not a level playing field, the whole rules of the game were stacked against people of color.

On the eve of the 21st century in the richest nation in the world, blacks control only 1.3% of the nation's financial assets, while they are around 12% of the population. Whites possess a staggering 95%. Almost two-thirds of black households have no net financial assets. Blacks and whites with equal incomes possess very unequal shares of wealth.[9]

There are numerous reasons why we should apologize, on the personal, historical, and Biblical levels. The first is simply that it's the right thing to do. If you offend your spouse or your friend, if you get in a fight with your best friend or your wife, if you don't say, "I'm sorry," it's never going to be resolved. And it lingers and it lingers. An apology is a necessary first step in repairing what has been broken. "I am sorry" is the first step of any person in trying to right a wrong. The words are a foundation, a part of the price for restoring lost trust.

One woman wrote me when I had introduced this bill, and she said:

An apology would show that my government and the president believe the enslavement of Africans for national gain was a grave and revolting wrong. It will document in stone for years to come the country's repentance for a tremendous crime. It is the right thing to do." And another wrote that, "The fact that you want to apologize says to me personally that you recognize and accept my pain, the pain of my ancestors, and that you care about it. On the national level, in my lifetime, no one has ever done that."

The apology will not solve all the problems, and more will be necessary, but it will begin the process for something long overdue.

The second main reason to apologize is in historical precedent. There have been numerous examples in the United States and elsewhere of public apologies in recent years, both political and religious. Congress itself apologized in 1988 to Japanese Americans for imprisoning them in concentration camps during World War II. We even paid each survivor or their descendants something like $20,000 in reparations. In 1993, Congress offered a formal apology to native Hawaiians for the role the Unites States and U.S. citizens played in the overthrow of the Kingdom of Hawaii 100 years earlier. A couple of years ago, President Clinton apologized to a number of groups of African Americans who had been wronged by the government having to do with, I believe, some health experiments or research.

Other countries have done the same. British Prime Minister Tony Blair apologized to the Irish for his country's failure to respond to the one million people who died during the potato famine. The East German legislature issued an apology for the atrocities committed against the Jews during the Holocaust, after 40 years of denying the need.

The third set of reasons to apologize are Biblical. One of my favorite stories in the Bible is about Joseph. In the book of Genesis, Joseph is sold into slavery by his own brothers. What was intended for evil, God means for good. Joseph used his power to save his family from starvation. But his brothers needed to ask him for forgiveness before true reconciliation could occur.

And Jesus of Nazareth emphasized the need for reconciliation, forgiveness and love throughout his ministry. In the Sermon on the Mount he commanded his followers to turn the other cheek, to love your enemies and pray for those who persecute you, and to be perfect as our heavenly Father is perfect.

The Bible is a mandate for reconciliation, and Paul says in his letter to Galatians, "There is no longer Jew or Greek, there is no longer slave or free, there is no longer male or female, for all are one in Christ Jesus." Then Peter came to the same conclusion in the book of Acts and said, "I truly understand that God shows no partiality, but in any nation anyone who fears him and does what is right is acceptable to him."

Every Wednesday morning in Washington, I convene a prayer group that meets. We meet at 7:00 in the Martin Luther King Library. We pray for our leaders in the City of Washington. We pray for the president, the vice president. We pray for Republicans and Democrats. We don't do it because they're better. We do it because God says to pray for our leaders. He says to pray for our leaders so that the people, which is us and you, "can live peaceful and tranquil lives in all godliness and dignity."

You have a great saying in Africa. I've heard it many times. It says that when the elephants fight, the grass dies. It's very interesting. When the leaders fight, the people perish. So we come together and we pray. We pray for the leaders that they can reconcile and be together.

I believe that if I would have experienced slavery and racial discrimination, I would be a lot more angry than most of my black friends. I am amazed at the depth of faith and forgiveness that I have witnessed among African Americans. Two close friends of mine, the late Reverends Tom Skinner and Sam Hines, taught me a great deal about reconciliation. And they accepted God's calling to be reconcilers, despite the discrimination they faced from whites and hostility they faced from blacks.

As I said, I'm not an expert on these matters. I am here to listen and to learn. I am excited to unite with all of you in healing the wounds of slavery through repentance and reconciliation. No one can do this alone …[10]

So in conclusion, I can't pass a law. I don't have the authority without my colleagues in the Congress to apologize to African Americans. But as a person and a citizen of my country, and a U.S. Congressman, I can apologize. I can say to you that I feel very inadequate to stand up here and say that. I don't have the words. I haven't experienced the suffering. I feel it in my bones that it's right. I'm very sorry for what's happened. I hope that you'll forgive me because it's easy to pray, "Well, it's those other people that did it." No, I'm part of it, too. Forgive me. Forgive me for my sins. Forgive me for my ancestors. This is just a start. It's not the end. It's the beginning. And maybe God, hopefully God, will take this conference, take these apologies and start to heal, start to close this wound that's there. Amen.

Notes

1. "Ambassador Tony P. Hall." *NCNK: The National Committee on North Korea.* https://www.ncnk.org/member-directory/ambassador-tony-p-hall.
2. For an extensive discussion of the responses, see John B. Hatch, *Race and Reconciliation: Redressing Wounds of Injustice* (Lanham, MD: Lexington, 2008), 221–27.
3. For an in-depth study of the conference, see ibid., 228–310.

4. Apologizing for the enslavement and racial segregation of African-Americans, H.Res. 194, 110th Cong. (2008), https://www.govtrack.us/congress/bills/110/hres194; A concurrent resolution apologizing for the enslavement and racial segregation of African-Americans, S.Con.Res. 26, 111th Cong. (2009), https://www.govtrack.us/congress/bills/111/sconres26.
5. A thorough rhetorical analysis of this speech is found in John B. Hatch, "Beyond *Apologia*: Racial Reconciliation and Apologies for Slavery," *Western Journal of Communication* 70, no. 3 (July 2006): 186–211, doi:10.1080/10570310600843496.
6. "U.S. Representative Tony Hall (D-TX) [sic] Holds News Conference on Having the Congress Apologize for Slavery," *Washington Transcript Service*, June 19, 2000, http://www.elibrary.com.
7. This speech was transcribed from an original recording provided by the government of Benin. The unabridged text is available from the author.
8. Hall's humorous impromptu opening remarks have been omitted.
9. Due to a gap in the recording provided by Benin's government, the previous four paragraphs are taken directly from Hall's speech manuscript (also provided to the author by Benin).
10. Hall begins his conclusion with selections from *Conversations with God: Two Centuries of Prayers by African Americans*; these have been omitted for copyright reasons.

CHAPTER FIFTEEN

Commending the Grace of Forgiveness and Repentance: Barack Obama

On Wednesday evening, June 17, 2015, a young white supremacist named Dylann Roof walked into Emanuel African Methodist Episcopal Church in Charleston, South Carolina. The oldest black congregation south of Baltimore, "Mother Emanuel" has a storied heritage of anti-slavery and civil rights activism. Knowing this legacy, Roof intended to slaughter parishioners at that evening's Bible study, including senior pastor and state senator Clementa C. Pinckney. But first, he attended the Bible study, to which they welcomed him. While they were praying at the end, Roof pulled a .45-caliber Glock handgun from his fanny pack and opened fire, killing nine of the 12 attendees, including Rev. Pinckney. During interrogation by police, he reportedly confessed that he wanted to start a race war. Later, authorities discovered that Roof had posted a photo of himself with a handgun and a Confederate battle flag on his website.

On June 19, during Roof's bond hearing, relatives of some of the nine who were slain spoke surprising words of forgiveness. For instance, the daughter of one victim told Roof, "You took something very precious away from me. I will never get to talk to her ever again. I will never be able to hold her again, but I forgive you, and have mercy on your soul." The granddaughter of another victim said, "Although my grandfather and the other victims died at the hands of hate, this is proof, everyone's plea for your soul, is proof that they lived in love and their legacies will live in love. So hate won't win." Another clarified, "I forgive him and my family forgives him. But we would like him to take this opportunity to repent. Repent."[1] On June 22, in what might be characterized as a collective act of repentance, South Carolina governor Nikki Haley, together with elected officials from both parties, called for the Confederate flag to be permanently removed from the grounds of the state capitol.

On June 26, President Barack Obama delivered the eulogy at Rev. Pinckney's funeral, which was held in the basketball arena of the nearby College of Charleston. With a mostly African-American audience in attendance, Obama was able to depart somewhat from the norms of presidential address and enter into the spirit and cadences of black preaching. In a move unprecedented for a nationally televised presidential address, he even sang the chorus of "Amazing Grace" as he reached his conclusion. Grace was the theme of the speech—inspired by the life of Rev. Pinckney, the forgiveness demonstrated by members of Emanuel AME, and Obama's conviction that receiving grace and living it out as a nation are essential to overcoming the curse of racism. The speech was widely acclaimed; former presidential speechwriter James Fallows went so far as to call it Obama's "most fully successful performance as an orator."[2] Fallows praised Obama's use of grace as a unifying theme ("a stroke of genius"), his "shifting registers" between "'black' versus 'white' modes of speech," and the "start-to-end framing of his remarks as religious, and explicitly Christian, and often African American Christian, which allowed him to present political points in an unexpected way."[3]

As discussed earlier in this book, *grace* is a rich, holistic concept, centered on agency—not in isolation from other values (as pure freedom of choice), but rather in responsible relation to truth, justice, and peace. As "first among equals" in the reconciliation tetrad, grace breaks through the vicious circle of dishonesty and deflection, resentment and resistance that characterize entrenched injustice; it awakens parties locked in conflict to unforeseen freedom, offering the opportunity to start afresh through repentance, forgiveness, and restoration.

Obama begins his eulogy by recounting the grace-filled character of the slain pastor and senator, Clementa Pinckney. Obama portrays a man who evinced divine gifting from a young age, who was gracious toward others, who drew strength from his faith and congregation, and who—though realistic about life's limitations and the injustices that wrack society—operated in a romantic frame of faith and hope, working tirelessly for a better future. Obama then widens the frame to honor the other slain parishioners, and the church as a whole, as people characterized by goodness and courage and grace, committed to "liberty and justice for all."

It is within this frame of grace that Obama introduces the killer. Although Roof's act was evil, Obama presents the young man more as a comic fool than a tragic villain—a shift in perspective made possible only via the mediating and transformative power of grace. In the president's telling, Roof is "blinded by hatred," blind to the grace demonstrated by his hosts, blind to the ways in which divine providence could fetch good out of his evil act. In this comic-romantic framing, the killer's heinous act fails to achieve its intended goal (to sharpen racial divisions and amplify racial hatred); instead, it ironically becomes the means by which divine grace is magnified,[4] seen both in the family members' forgiveness and the city and state leaders' repentance, as these leaders recognized the toxic symbolism woven through the Confederate flag and called for it to be taken down.

Obama continues to reflect on the nature of grace, alluding to the famous hymn, which features the motif of being blind and receiving the gift of sight. He then applies this frame to the nation as a whole in its approach to race relations. As Roof was blind, so many of us have blind spots where race is concerned, Obama says. As the city of Charleston and the state of South Carolina took steps of "self-examination" and corrective action, so we as a nation have been given the grace to self-examine and make changes in how we view race. In Obama's summation of the Christian story, grace springs from God's freedom and calls forth our freedom to choose, to decide how we will respond. Grace not only imparts a gift, but a responsibility. We dare not take others' forgiveness for granted; rather, forgiveness challenges us to open our eyes to injustice, examine ourselves, and where needed, repent.

As rhetoric scholar Andre Johnson points out, media pundits were quick to commend expressions of forgiveness from Emanuel AME congregants but failed to acknowledge family members who did not immediately forgive. Johnson also observes that although white people usually cry for justice when victims are white, they tend to expect black victims to show grace and express forgiveness quickly, in non-threatening ways.[5] Such double standards marginalize the agency of the victims, drain forgiveness of moral weight, undermine restorative justice, and add insult to injury. While Obama does not highlight this specific problem, he does warn that remaining complacent toward injustice and violence would be "a betrayal of everything Reverend Pinckney stood for," and that settling back into the trenches of political warfare between conservative and liberal would be "a refutation of the forgiveness expressed by those families." Like so many other speakers in this book, Obama speaks to humans' interconnectedness: "justice grows out of recognition of ourselves in each other ... my liberty depends on you being free, too." In keeping with the overall romantic framing of his eulogy, Obama concludes by highlighting the goodness and grace displayed by the victims of the Charleston shooting—a legacy for the nation to carry on.

"Amazing Grace": Eulogy for the Honorable Reverend Clementa Pinckney

Charleston, South Carolina
June 26, 2015

Giving all praise and honor to God.

The Bible calls us to hope. To persevere, and have faith in things not seen. "They were still living by faith when they died," Scripture tells us. "They did not receive the things promised; they only saw them and welcomed them from a distance, admitting that they were foreigners and strangers on Earth."

We are here today to remember a man of God who lived by faith. A man who believed in things not seen. A man who believed there were better days ahead, off in the distance. A man of service who persevered, knowing full well he would not receive all those things he was promised, because he believed his efforts would deliver a better life for those who followed.

To Jennifer, his beloved wife; to Eliana and Malana, his beautiful, wonderful daughters; to the Mother Emanuel family and the people of Charleston, the people of South Carolina:

I cannot claim to have the good fortune to know Reverend Pinckney well. But I did have the pleasure of knowing him and meeting him here in South Carolina, back when we were both a little bit younger. Back when I didn't have visible grey hair. The first thing I noticed was his graciousness, his smile, his reassuring baritone, his deceptive sense of humor—all qualities that helped him wear so effortlessly a heavy burden of expectation.

Friends of his remarked this week that when Clementa Pinckney entered a room, it was like the future arrived; that even from a young age, folks knew he was special. Anointed. He was the progeny of a long line of the faithful—a family of preachers who spread God's word, a family of protesters who sowed change to expand voting rights and desegregate the South. Clem heard their instruction, and he did not forsake their teaching.

He was in the pulpit by 13, pastor by 18, public servant by 23. He did not exhibit any of the cockiness of youth, nor youth's insecurities; instead, he set an example worthy of his position, wise beyond his years, in his speech, in his conduct, in his love, faith, and purity.

As a senator, he represented a sprawling swath of the Lowcountry, a place that has long been one of the most neglected in America. A place still wracked by poverty and inadequate schools; a place where children can still go hungry and the sick can go without treatment. A place that needed somebody like Clem.

His position in the minority party meant the odds of winning more resources for his constituents were often long. His calls for greater equity were too often unheeded, the votes he cast were sometimes lonely. But he never gave up. He stayed true to his convictions. He would not grow discouraged. After a full day at the capitol, he'd climb into his car and head to the church to draw sustenance from his family, from his ministry, from the community that loved and needed him. There he would fortify his faith, and imagine what might be.

Reverend Pinckney embodied a politics that was neither mean, nor small. He conducted himself quietly, and kindly, and diligently. He encouraged progress not by pushing his ideas alone, but by seeking out your ideas, partnering with you to make things happen. He was full of empathy and fellow feeling, able to walk in somebody else's shoes and see through their eyes. No wonder one of his senate colleagues remembered Senator Pinckney as "the most gentle of the 46 of us—the best of the 46 of us."

Clem was often asked why he chose to be a pastor and a public servant. But the person who asked probably didn't know the history of the AME church. As our brothers and sisters in the AME church know, we don't make those distinctions. "Our calling," Clem once said, "is not just within the walls of the congregation, but the life and community in which our congregation resides."

He embodied the idea that our Christian faith demands deeds and not just words; that the "sweet hour of prayer" actually lasts the whole week long—that to put our faith in action is more than individual salvation, it's about our collective salvation; that to feed the hungry and clothe the naked and house the homeless is not just a call for isolated charity but the imperative of a just society.

What a good man. Sometimes I think that's the best thing to hope for when you're eulogized—after all the words and recitations and resumes are read, to just say someone was a good man.

You don't have to be of high station to be a good man. Preacher by 13. Pastor by 18. Public servant by 23. What a life Clementa Pinckney lived. What an example he set. What a model for his faith. And then to lose him at 41—slain in his sanctuary with eight wonderful members of his flock, each at different stages in life but bound together by a common commitment to God.

Cynthia Hurd. Susie Jackson. Ethel Lance. DePayne Middleton-Doctor. Tywanza Sanders. Daniel L. Simmons. Sharonda Coleman-Singleton. Myra Thompson. Good people. Decent people. God-fearing people. People so full of life and so full of kindness. People who ran the race, who persevered. People of great faith.

To the families of the fallen, the nation shares in your grief. Our pain cuts that much deeper because it happened in a church. The church is and always has been the center of African-American life—a place to call our own in a too often hostile world, a sanctuary from so many hardships.

Over the course of centuries, black churches served as "hush harbors" where slaves could worship in safety; praise houses where their free descendants could gather and shout hallelujah; rest stops for the weary along the Underground Railroad; bunkers for the foot soldiers of the Civil Rights Movement. They have been, and continue to be, community centers where we organize for jobs and justice; places of scholarship and network; places where children are loved and fed and kept out of harm's way, and told that they are beautiful and smart and taught that they matter. That's what happens in church.

That's what the black church means. Our beating heart. The place where our dignity as a people is inviolate. And there's no better example of this tradition than Mother Emanuel, a church built by blacks seeking liberty, burned to the ground because its founder sought to end slavery, only to rise up again, a phoenix from these ashes.

When there were laws banning all-black church gatherings, services happened here anyway, in defiance of unjust laws. When there was a righteous movement to dismantle Jim Crow, Dr. Martin Luther King Jr. preached from its pulpit, and marches began from its steps. A sacred place, this church. Not just for blacks, not just for Christians, but for every American who cares about the steady expansion of human rights and human dignity in this country; a foundation stone for liberty and justice for all. That's what the church meant.

We do not know whether the killer of Reverend Pinckney and eight others knew all of this history. But he surely sensed the meaning of his violent act. It was an act that drew on a long history of bombs and arson and shots fired at churches, not random, but as a means of control, a way to terrorize and oppress. An act that he imagined would incite fear and recrimination; violence and suspicion. An act that he presumed would deepen divisions that trace back to our nation's original sin.

Oh, but God works in mysterious ways. God has different ideas.

He didn't know he was being used by God. Blinded by hatred, the alleged killer could not see the grace surrounding Reverend Pinckney and that Bible study group—the light of love that shone as they opened the church doors and invited a stranger to join in their prayer circle. The alleged killer could have never anticipated the way the families of the fallen would respond when they saw him in court—in the midst of unspeakable grief, with words of forgiveness. He couldn't imagine that.

The alleged killer could not imagine how the city of Charleston, under the good and wise leadership of Mayor Riley—how the state of South Carolina, how the United States of America would respond—not merely with revulsion at his evil act, but with big-hearted generosity and, more importantly, with a thoughtful introspection and self-examination that we so rarely see in public life.

Blinded by hatred, he failed to comprehend what Reverend Pinckney so well understood—the power of God's grace.

This whole week, I've been reflecting on this idea of grace. The grace of the families who lost loved ones. The grace that Reverend Pinckney would preach about in his sermons. The grace described in one of my favorite hymnals—the one we all know: *Amazing grace, how sweet the sound that saved a wretch like me. I once was lost, but now I'm found; was blind but now I see.*

According to the Christian tradition, grace is not earned. Grace is not merited. It's not something we deserve. Rather, grace is the free and benevolent favor of God, as manifested in the salvation of sinners and the bestowal of blessings. Grace.

As a nation, out of this terrible tragedy, God has visited grace upon us, for he has allowed us to see where we've been blind. He has given us the chance, where we've been lost, to find our best selves. We may not have earned it, this grace, with our rancor and complacency, and short-sightedness and fear of each other—but we got it all the same. He gave it to us anyway. He's once more given us grace. But it is up to us now to make the most of it, to receive it with gratitude, and to prove ourselves worthy of this gift.

For too long, we were blind to the pain that the Confederate flag stirred in too many of our citizens. It's true, a flag did not cause these murders. But as people from all walks of life, Republicans and Democrats, now acknowledge—including Governor Haley, whose recent eloquence on the subject is worthy of praise—as we all have to acknowledge, the flag has always represented more than just ancestral pride. For many, black and white, that flag was a reminder of systemic oppression and racial subjugation. We see that now.

Removing the flag from this state's capitol would not be an act of political correctness; it would not be an insult to the valor of Confederate soldiers. It would simply be an acknowledgment that the cause for which they fought—the cause of slavery—was wrong; the imposition of Jim Crow after the Civil War, the resistance to civil rights for all people was wrong. It would be one step in an honest accounting of America's history; a modest but meaningful balm for so many unhealed wounds. It would be an expression of the amazing changes that have transformed this state and this country for the better, because of the work of so many people of goodwill, people of all races striving to form a more perfect union. By taking down that flag, we express God's grace.

But I don't think God wants us to stop there. For too long, we've been blind to the way past injustices continue to shape the present. Perhaps we see that now.

Perhaps this tragedy causes us to ask some tough questions about how we can permit so many of our children to languish in poverty, or attend dilapidated schools, or grow up without prospects for a job or for a career.

Perhaps it causes us to examine what we're doing to cause some of our children to hate. Perhaps it softens hearts towards those lost young men, tens and tens of thousands caught up in the criminal justice system, and leads us to make sure that that system is not infected with bias; that we embrace changes in how we train and equip our police so that the bonds of trust between law enforcement and the communities they serve make us all safer and more secure.

Maybe we now realize the way racial bias can infect us even when we don't realize it, so that we're guarding against not just racial slurs, but we're also guarding against the subtle impulse to call Johnny back for a job interview but not Jamal. So that we search our hearts when we consider laws to make it harder for some of our fellow citizens to vote. By recognizing our common humanity by treating every child as important, regardless of the color of their skin or the station into which they were born, and to do what's necessary to make opportunity real for every American—by doing that, we express God's grace....[6]

We don't earn grace. We're all sinners. We don't deserve it. But God gives it to us anyway. And we choose how to receive it. It's our decision how to honor it.

None of us can or should expect a transformation in race relations overnight. Every time something like this happens, somebody says we have to have a conversation about race. We talk a lot about race. There's no shortcut. And we don't need more talk. None of us should believe that a handful of gun safety measures will prevent every tragedy. It will not. People of goodwill will continue to debate the merits of various policies, as our democracy requires—this is a big, raucous place, America is. And there are good people on both sides of these debates. Whatever solutions we find will necessarily be incomplete.

But it would be a betrayal of everything Reverend Pinckney stood for, I believe, if we allowed ourselves to slip into a comfortable silence again. Once the eulogies have been delivered, once the TV cameras move on, to go back to business as usual—that's what we so often do to avoid uncomfortable truths about the prejudice that still infects our society. To settle for symbolic gestures without following up with the hard work of more lasting change—that's how we lose our way again.

It would be a refutation of the forgiveness expressed by those families if we merely slipped into old habits, whereby those who disagree with us are not merely wrong but bad; where we shout instead of listen; where we barricade ourselves behind preconceived notions or well-practiced cynicism.

Reverend Pinckney once said, "Across the South, we have a deep appreciation of history—we haven't always had a deep appreciation of each other's history."

What is true in the South is true for America. Clem understood that justice grows out of recognition of ourselves in each other. That my liberty depends on you being free, too. That history can't be a sword to justify injustice, or a shield against progress, but must be a manual for how to avoid repeating the mistakes of the past—how to break the cycle. A roadway toward a better world. He knew that the path of grace involves an open mind—but, more importantly, an open heart.

That's what I've felt this week—an open heart. That, more than any particular policy or analysis, is what's called upon right now, I think—what a friend of mine, the writer Marilyn Robinson, calls "that reservoir of goodness, beyond and of another kind, that we are able to do for each other in the ordinary cause of things."

That reservoir of goodness. If we can find that grace, anything is possible. If we can tap that grace, everything can change.

Amazing grace. Amazing grace. [Begins to sing.]

Amazing grace, how sweet the sound
That saved a wretch like me;
I once was lost, but now I'm found;
Was blind but now I see.

Clementa Pinckney found that grace.
Cynthia Hurd found that grace.
Susie Jackson found that grace.
Ethel Lance found that grace.
DePayne Middleton-Doctor found that grace.
Tywanza Sanders found that grace.
Daniel L. Simmons, Sr. found that grace.
Sharonda Coleman-Singleton found that grace.
Myra Thompson found that grace.

Through the example of their lives, they've now passed it on to us. May we find ourselves worthy of that precious and extraordinary gift, as long as our lives endure. May grace now lead them home. May God continue to shed His grace on the United States of America.

Notes

1. Elahe Izadi, "The Powerful Words of Forgiveness Delivered to Dylann Roof by Victims' Relatives," *Washington Post*, June 19, 2005, https://www.washingtonpost.com/news/post-nation/wp/2015/06/19/hate-wont-win-the-powerful-words-delivered-to-dylann-roof-by-victims-relatives/.

2. James Fallows, "Obama's Grace," *The Atlantic*, June 27, 2015, https://www.theatlantic.com/politics/archive/2015/06/grace/397064/.
3. Ibid.
4. Anderson focuses on Obama's use of irony (together with the African-American practice of "signifyin[g]") to reframe the event and its implications. See Scott Anderson, "Irony in Charleston: Barack Obama's Eulogy for Clementa C. Pinckney, June 26, 2015," *Communication Quarterly* 67, no. 4 (2019): 405–23, doi:10.1080/01463373.2019.1605397.
5. Andre E. Johnson and Earle J. Fisher, "'But, I Forgive You?' Mother Emanuel, Black Pain, and the Rhetoric of Forgiveness," *Journal of Communication & Religion* 42, no. 1 (2019): 5–19.
6. Due to limited space and relevance, two paragraphs on the national problem of gun violence are omitted here. The full speech transcript is available at https://obamawhitehouse.archives.gov/the-press-office/2015/06/26/remarks-president-eulogy-honorable-reverend-clementa-pinckney.

CHAPTER SIXTEEN

Reconciliation Unfolding: United Church of Canada

As the preceding addresses by Elie Wiesel and Barack Obama illustrate the importance of victims' voices in reconciliation, the next case—a series of brief public statements occurring over a span of 12 years—demonstrates how apologies and relational repair can evolve through dialogue and negotiation, with the victims of historical wrongdoing taking initiative and thus regaining a measure of agency. In this case, the victims-turned-agents were from Canada's indigenous/aboriginal peoples, referred to as "First Nations" (comparable to "Native Americans" in the United States). The party with whom they negotiated reconciliation was the United Church of Canada (UCC).

Formed in 1925 through the merger of four Canadian denominations, the UCC (not to be confused with the U.S. denomination United Church of Christ) is Canada's largest Protestant denomination. For generations, the UCC and its tributary denominations engaged in efforts to proselytize Canada's indigenous peoples. In the process, the UCC played a key role in the mainstream white society's efforts to impose Eurocentric culture on the First Nations in order to "civilize" and "develop" these so-called backward peoples. A major means of accomplishing this goal was the Indian Residential School (IRS) system, a Canadian educational policy designed to assimilate First Nations children into the dominant culture, in effect allowing their cultures to die out with the older generations. Under this policy, young indigenous children were taken from their families and villages and placed in boarding schools where they were forced to adopt European dress, manners, religion, and languages (English or French). This abuse of cultural and institutional power created the conditions for physical, emotional, and sexual abuse of vulnerable children by school staff. Under the auspices of the Canadian government, Christian churches and denominations ran these schools, including the UCC, which was involved in the program until 1969.

In 1984, a First Nations woman (and lifelong member of the UCC) named Alberta Billy attended a meeting of the denomination's leaders to represent indigenous members of the Church. Both of her parents had attended residential schools, and she had witnessed the program's legacy of trauma in First Nations families and communities. Therefore, at one point during the meeting, she stood and issued a challenge: "'The United Church owes the Native peoples of Canada an apology for what you did to them in residential school.'"[1] This challenge precipitated a season of denominational soul-searching and dialogue; however, two years passed with no decision on an apology. In his book *Ecclesial Repentance*, Jeremy M. Bergen recounts what happened next: "Two years later, Alberta Billy repeated the request for an apology at the General Council meeting in Sudbury, Ontario and then led the Aboriginal commissioners outside to a gravel parking lot to drum, dance, and wait for a response."[2] Still inside, the General Council commissioners wrestled over what they might say. After finally approving a statement, they sent their leader to deliver the apology:

> Moderator Robert Smith led a procession out to where about 300 Aboriginal members were waiting. He entered the tepee set up in the parking lot and delivered the apology to the 20 elders gathered there, and then repeated it to the much larger crowd outside.[3]

This was the beginning of a protracted reconciliation process that included a response from the First Nations representatives in 1988 and a second apology from the UCC in 1998. All three statements are reprinted below.

The 1986 apology succinctly confesses the failings of the Church in past dealings with First Nations peoples. It begins by recognizing the spiritual heritage these peoples already had before Europeans arrived. In this way, the UCC respects the agency of those to whom the apology is directed, before speaking of the ways in which Europeans disrespected and deprived them of agency. Indeed, the first sin it identifies is the denomination's past unwillingness to see any value in the indigenous Canadians' understanding of creation and God. The apology also faults the Church's misunderstanding and diminishment of the Christian gospel message it claimed to be sharing with the First Nations and its imposition of Western culture on them. Like so many of the speeches in this book, the UCC's apology recognizes the oppressors' paradoxical interdependence with the oppressed, saying that white

Christians actually made themselves poorer when they destroyed First Nations' culture and spiritual vision.

Despite the strengths of this apology, it does not identify the UCC as a culpable party, nor does it specifically speak to the issue for which Alberta Billy had asked an apology: the denomination's involvement in the Indian Residential Schools. As a result, Billy later recalled, the First Nations representatives "were not happy with it," although they "accepted [the apology] in principle."[4] Discussion within the newly-formed All Native Circle Conference of the UCC eventually led to an official statement responding to the apology, delivered by Edith Memnook two years later.

In the 1988 statement, the First Nations representatives "acknowledge" the apology without saying that they "accept" it. Accepting an apology is often seen as the end of a conflict, but the recipients of the first apology did not find it to be adequate, and the work of repairing the damage from the offense was far from complete. Therefore, the Native Circle's response treats the apology as a first gesture of goodwill, a hopeful sign that the UCC will engage in an ongoing process of reconciliation. Their statement also reaffirms the First Nations' agency in religious matters by noting that they still hold to their ancient spiritual traditions, and they ask the UCC to respect their traditions ("our Sacred Fire") as well the natural world ("Creation"), which they hold sacred. The statement calls for peaceful coexistence between their peoples and partnership in a long-term process of healing, so that the apology may be more than merely symbolic, but rather signify a holistic commitment to reconciliation.

As time went on, the UCC did demonstrate an ongoing commitment to reconciliation, in large part owing to the agency of First Nations representatives who drew on wisdom and rituals from their indigenous traditions:

> The Rev. Alf Dumont [an indigenous leader] explained that, "In the native way, apologies are not 'accepted,' they are acknowledged. [This is because] an apology must be lived out if it's to be a real apology." On the advice of Elder Art Solomon, a stone cairn was erected on the exact spot where the [initial] apology was delivered to symbolize the unfinished and ongoing requirements of the apology. Stones were to be added as signs of healing and progress in the relationship. To mark the twentieth anniversary of the apology, Moderator Peter Short repeated it in the exact same spot. Several stones were added to the still-unfinished cairn to mark concrete steps: the establishment of the All Native Circle Conference, programmes of aboriginal theological education, a Healing Fund especially for the legacy of residential schools, and an initiative to explore the relationship of Traditional and Christian spiritualities.[5]

Bergen notes another denominational measure designed to help members view the apology as a step in an ongoing process: "A sample sermon distributed to congregations to help them remember the apology acknowledged that "[f]ull reconciliation may not happen in my lifetime or yours," yet affirmed the many ways in which an apology is a gift that occasions transformation, grace, and true relationship."[6]

In 1998, this process of transformation culminated in a second apology to First Nations peoples, issued by then-Moderator Rev. Bill Phipps. This time, the apology focused on the UCC's participation in the Indian Residential School system. The 1998 statement acknowledges indigenous members' desire to hear such an apology; the church's slowness to hear their cries; the pain and abuse they suffered; the innocence of the victims; and the "evil" of the IRS policy in which the UCC had been involved. Descendants of perpetrators often object to historical apologies on the grounds that the present generation is not guilty of past wrongs. To head off that potential objection, this statement offers a broader, more positive frame: "we are the bearers of many blessings from our ancestors, and therefore, we must also bear their burdens." Similarly, it takes a long view of reconciliation as a "painful journey" and "difficult road" to travel together, and it frames the apology as a step toward further actions that demonstrate repentance. When the apology was printed for distribution among congregations, it was addressed specifically "To former students of United Church Indian Residential Schools, and to their families and communities," and an introductory paragraph was added above the apology, framing it in a way that honors their agency and traditions:

> From the deepest reaches of your memories, you have shared with us your stories of suffering from our church's involvement in the operation of Indian Residential Schools. You have shared the personal and historic pain that you still bear, and you have been vulnerable yet again. You have also shared with us your strength and wisdom born of the life-giving dignity of your communities and traditions and your stories of survival.

This evolving series of verbal and physical symbolic acts between white and indigenous leaders in the UCC not only advanced reconciliation within the denomination but also helped to pave the way for national self-examination. Ten years after the UCC's Residential School apology, Canada launched a national truth and reconciliation commission (TRC) tasked with documenting the historical and present-day impacts of the Indian Residential School system. In its final report released in 2015, the TRC concluded that the IRS policy had amounted to "cultural genocide," and it made 94 recommendations for concrete action to repair the harms to First Nations people and promote national reconciliation. The UCC issued its own formal response to these calls for action, specifying how the denomination would continue to work for justice and reconciliation with indigenous Canadians.[7]

1986 Apology to Indigenous Peoples[8]

Rev. Robert Smith, Sudbury, Ontario, August 16, 1986
Long before my people journeyed to this land your people were here, and you received from your Elders an understanding of creation and of the Mystery that surrounds us all that was deep, and rich, and to be treasured.

We did not hear you when you shared your vision. In our zeal to tell you of the good news of Jesus Christ we were closed to the value of your spirituality.

We confused Western ways and culture with the depth and breadth and length and height of the gospel of Christ.

We imposed our civilization as a condition of accepting the gospel.

We tried to make you be like us and in so doing we helped to destroy the vision that made you what you were. As a result, you, and we, are poorer and the image of the Creator in us is twisted, blurred, and we are not what we are meant by God to be.

We ask you to forgive us and to walk together with us in the Spirit of Christ so that our peoples may be blessed and God's creation healed.

1988 Response[9]

Edith Memnook,
Representative of UCC All Native Circle Conference
Victoria, British Columbia, August 17, 1988
The Apology made to the Native People of Canada by The United Church of Canada in Sudbury in August 1986 has been a very important step forward. It is heartening to see that The United Church of Canada is a forerunner in making this Apology to Native People. The All Native Circle Conference has now acknowledged your Apology. Our people have continued to affirm the teachings of the Native way of life. Our spiritual teachings and values have taught us to uphold the Sacred Fire; to be guardians of Mother Earth, and strive to maintain harmony and peaceful coexistence with all peoples.

We only ask of you to respect our Sacred Fire, the Creation, and to live in peaceful coexistence with us. We recognize the hurts and feelings will continue amongst our people, but through partnership and walking hand in hand, the Indian spirit will eventually heal. Through our love, understanding, and sincerity the brotherhood and sisterhood of unity, strength, and respect can be achieved.

The Native People of The All Native Circle Conference hope and pray that the Apology is not symbolic but that these are the words of action and sincerity. We appreciate the freedom for culture and religious expression. In the new spirit this Apology has created, let us unite our hearts and minds in the wholeness of life that the Great Spirit has given us.

1998 Apology for Indian Residential Schools[10]

Rev. Bill Phipps, October 27, 1998

As Moderator of The United Church of Canada, I wish to speak the words that many people have wanted to hear for a very long time. On behalf of The United Church of Canada, I apologize for the pain and suffering that our church's involvement in the Indian Residential School system has caused. We are aware of some of the damage that this cruel and ill-conceived system of assimilation has perpetrated on Canada's First Nations peoples. For this we are truly and most humbly sorry.

To those individuals who were physically, sexually, and mentally abused as students of the Indian Residential Schools in which The United Church of Canada was involved, I offer you our most sincere apology. You did nothing wrong. You were and are the victims of evil acts that cannot under any circumstances be justified or excused.

We know that many within our church will still not understand why each of us must bear the scar, the blame for this horrendous period in Canadian history. But the truth is, we are the bearers of many blessings from our ancestors, and therefore, we must also bear their burdens.

Our burdens include dishonoring the depths of the struggles of First Nations peoples and the richness of your gifts. We seek God's forgiveness and healing grace as we take steps toward building respectful, compassionate, and loving relationships with First Nations peoples.

We are in the midst of a long and painful journey as we reflect on the cries that we did not or would not hear, and how we have behaved as a church. As we travel this difficult road of repentance, reconciliation, and healing, we commit ourselves to work toward ensuring that we will never again use our power as a church to hurt others with attitudes of racial and spiritual superiority.

We pray that you will hear the sincerity of our words today and that you will witness the living out of our apology in our actions in the future.

Notes

1. Martha Troian, "25 Years Later: The United Church of Canada's Apology to Aboriginal Peoples," *Indian Country Today*, August 16, 2011, https://newsmaven.io/indiancountrytoday/

archive/25-years-later-the-united-church-of-canada-s-apology-to-aboriginal-peoples-A3-5m0AmGkKwie6ZS8cCjw/.
2. Jeremy M. Bergen, *Ecclesial Repentance: The Churches Confront Their Sinful Pasts* (London: T&T Clark International, 2011), 243.
3. Ibid., 244.
4. Troian.
5. Bergen, 244–45; internal quote from Russell Daye, "An Unresolved Dilemma: Canada's United Church Seeks Reconciliation with Native Peoples," *The Ecumenist* 36, no. 2 (May 1999), 12, square brackets in source.
6. Ibid., 245; internal quote from James Scott, "The Gift in Apology," Sermon for First Nations Day of Prayer, United Church of Canada (2006).
7. See "The Truth and Reconciliation Commission," *The United Church of Canada*, https://www.united-church.ca/social-action/justice-initiatives/truth-and-reconciliation-commission.
8. Reprinted with permission from the United Church of Canada.
9. From United Church of Canada 1988 Record of Proceedings, p. 79. Reprinted with permission from the UCC.
10. Reprinted with permission from the United Church of Canada.

Conclusion: The Ongoing Work of Reconciliation

This book has presented a selection of public addresses that drew on one or more religious traditions to speak to reconciliation between races, ethnic cultures, sociopolitical factions, religions, and civilizations. It also presented a critical framework for analyzing and critiquing such speeches as rhetorical acts of moral (re)framing. While the tetrad serves as an orienting device for the study and practice of reconciliation, rhetorical criticism of reconciliation discourse also requires careful attention to a speech-act's context, its textual features, and other relevant critical concepts. The introductions to the artifacts in this book provide stepping-off points for such investigation.

Each address in this anthology offered a particular perspective on historical wrongdoing, parties in conflict, the legacy of damage, and the work of repair. While some of the speeches viewed reconciliation through the lens of a historic figure or ethnic tradition, all of them drew on religious discourse in some way, reflecting both universal theological themes (such as interdependence and divine agency) and the distinctiveness of their respective traditions (e.g. Biblical narratives, Buddhist mindfulness practices, Islamic teachings, etc.). The speeches in the second part of this book richly illustrate reconciliation as a dialogic rhetorical process of rectifying wrongs and healing relationships between parties in ways that promote their common good. We have seen that victims of wrongdoing have a need and right to exercise their own cultural and personal agency, both in shining a spotlight on the legacy of oppression and challenging the oppressor to engage in the work of repentance. We have observed how forgiveness, when freely chosen on the victims' own terms and timetable, can be self-liberating and self-empowering, as well as potentially redemptive for the perpetrator and healing for the relationship. Likewise, we have witnessed how reconciliation depends on the perpetrators' continuing openness to hear and respect the voice of victims and respond with humility, contrition, and concrete acts of repair. The reconciliation between peoples of European and indigenous descent within the United Church of Canada is a rich exemplar of this ongoing process of listening, learning, responding, and collaborating with the victim-survivors, and it showcases the way in which respectfully incorporating their cultural/spiritual resources lends depth and coherence to the process.

By studying how social activists, political representatives, religious leaders, and courageous survivors have spoken to reconciliation from their faith traditions, we can more fully appreciate the challenge of redressing the wounds of societal injustice and the potential of religious discourse to promote this end. We may also find inspiration and models to pursue some form of reconciliation within our own spheres. When reconciling after relatively recent and minor offenses, open communication and social sensitivity may suffice. However, in the wake of such heinous collective crimes as the ones addressed in these speeches, meaningful and lasting reconciliation may require a power deeper than personal aspiration, collective determination, rhetorical skill, or political programming (although these are needed). The speakers in this book believed that reconciliation ultimately demands the spiritual resources of religious faith, and that it draws upon the divine.

Whatever resources it may call for in any given instance, reconciliation between groups can be said to entail a kind of weaving or braiding. That is, reconciliation brings together strands of humanity and culture, politics and spirituality, hurtful history and inspiring stories, repentance and forgiveness, grieving and healing, and symbolic and material repair, and it braids them into cords of rhetorical and spiritual coherence. In the process, society's wounds are stitched up, and divided peoples are somewhat woven together into a social fabric of interdependent wholeness.

In part, I owe this metaphor to the First Nations leaders in the United Church of Canada, who drew both on their Christian faith and their indigenous spiritual traditions as they worked to promote repentance, repair, and healing within the denomination. Twenty years after the UCC's 1998 Residential Schools Apology, they used the creation of braids to symbolize the ongoing work of reconciliation:

> At General Council 43 in Oshawa (2018), the Youth Forum learned about the history of the United Church's Apologies. They were given a teaching from one of the Indigenous Elders present, who said that the lives of colonists, newcomers, and

Indigenous peoples of this land are braided together—and that the braiding makes us stronger. In a moving worship service, the youth then asked General Council to help them create a braid to symbolize this relationship.[1]

Thereafter, the UCC encouraged all of their congregations to mark the 20th anniversary of the apology by engaging in a ritual act of braiding during a worship service. Drawing from aboriginal tradition, small groups were to weave the braid from strips of cloth in the four colors of the indigenous Medicine Wheel: red, white, black, and yellow. They were then to gather and read a Braiding Prayer aloud. That prayer serves as a fitting conclusion to this collection of religious voices speaking to reconciliation:

> God of struggle, and of reconciliation,
> Be with us as we remember what we have been a part of:
> Cruel and unjust systems,
> Efforts to say "sorry"… and to mean it.
>
> Remind us that our history as people is like a braid;
> We are wrapped together,
> And there is tension in that, and pain
> But there is also strength.
>
> Remind us of the beauty and sacredness of braids,
> The beauty and sacredness of relationships;
> Remind us to never again sever these braids
> But to honor them in everything we do.
>
> God of struggle, and of reconciliation,
> Be with us as we recognize what we must be a part of:
> Loving and just relationships,
> Saying "sorry"… and actively meaning it.
> Amen.[2]

Notes

1. "Braiding Reconciliation," *The United Church of Canada*, https://www.united-church.ca/sites/default/files/resources/braiding-reconciliation.pdf.
2. (Ellipses are in original.) "Braiding Prayer" © 2018 The United Church of Canada/L'Église Unie du Canada. Used with permission. Accessed from "Braiding Reconciliation."

Speaking of Religion

Daniel S. Brown, *Series Editor*

Speaking of Religion grows from a scholarly attentiveness to the role that religion plays in the public sphere. The decline of religious thought in public affairs is a common yet false narrative in the United States. Americans remain a devout people who are motivated to action by their faith commitments. Several contemporary, interdisciplinary scholars including Jürgen Habermas, Charles Taylor and Tariq Ramadan point us toward the privilege that religion and faith enjoys in public life. Collectively their work asserts that the world has entered a post-secular era: Secularism is dead and faith is alive. Speaking of Religion features short books, no more than 60,000 words or approximately 150 pages in length.

For additional information about this series or for the submission of manuscripts, please contact:

Erika Hendrix, Acquisitions Editor
erika.hendrix@plang.com

To order books, please contact our Customer Service Department:

peterlang@presswarehouse.com (within the U.S.)
order@peterlang.com (outside the U.S.)

Or browse online by series at www.peterlang.com